THE GREAT CORINTHIAN

THE GREAT CORINTHIAN

*A portrait of
the Prince Regent*

by

DORIS LESLIE

New York

OXFORD UNIVERSITY PRESS

1953

For

CAMPBELL

CONTENTS

ILLUSTRATIONS

ACKNOWLEDGEMENTS

I am gratefully indebted to Professor Aspinall for his permission to quote extracts from his invaluable collection of letters in the Windsor Archives; and to Messrs. Benn Ltd., and Curtis Brown Ltd., representatives of the author's executors, for allowing me to quote the letter of Burke to Fox from *Charles James Fox* by the late John Drinkwater; to Sir John Murray for his permission to quote from *The Creevey Papers*, edited by Sir Herbert Maxwell, and also from *The Letters of Princess Lieven*, edited by Peter Quennell; to Sir Shane Leslie for his permission to quote certain extracts from *The Letters of Mrs. Fitzherbert*; to Messrs. John Lane, the Bodley Head, for permission to quote from *The Diary of Lady Charlotte Bury*; to the Trustees of the National Maritime Museum, Greenwich, for placing at my disposal Nelson's letter to Lady Hamilton from the Phillipps Collection, and for the unfailing courtesy and help of the Museum staff; to Mrs. David Loch for allowing me the privilege of examining and quoting from certain of her private family letters relating to the Seymour Case; to Mr. Clifford Musgrave, Mr. Derek Rogers, and the staff of the Brighton Art Gallery and Museum for their help with the illustrations; to the late Sir Robert Witt for permission to reproduce his drawing of the Prince by John Russell; and finally, to my husband, at whose suggestion I have written this biography, and whose criticism and advice have guided me throughout.

D. L.

THE GREAT CORINTHIAN

ERRATA

Page 18, line 19, should read 'collected and kept in glass cases in her room. She supervised the House—'

Page 23, line 13, should read 'a synonym for Beelzebub. The youthful Prince must have kept his ears wide'

Page 78, line 6, should read 'received her as a sister. The King's pious brother William, on holiday'

Page 94, line 29, should read 'proceeds. Then at last was she rid of her odious guests. Next day the Prince'

Page 128, line 21, should read 'A somewhat smug and highly respectable third brother, Edward—'

Page 153, line 40, should read 'name of another—his fifth son.'

Page 174, line 24, should read 'not this time, be persuaded to take part.'

Page 203, line 30, should read 'While the industrial centres of the Midlands and the North renewed'

Page 219, line 1, should read 'Marchioness of Conyngham to seek in her receptive arms the comfort he'

Page 248, M, 3rd entry, should read 'Majocchi, Teodore, 226–7'

Page 249, S, 2nd entry, should read 'St. George's (Hanover Square), 104'

Page 250, W, 11th entry, should read 'Weld, Edward (of Lulworth), 49'

Page 251, Z, insert 'Zoffany, 20'

CHAPTER ONE

1762–1783

ON the afternoon of August 12, 1762, a number of distinguished persons among whom were the Dowager Princess of Wales, two Dukes, seven Lords, and all the Queen's Ladies-in-Waiting, had assembled in an ante-room of St. James's Palace.

In the adjoining chamber, beside the great canopied bed, hovered the prayerfully expectant Doctor Secker, Archbishop of Canterbury.

The precedent, which, since the death of James II, demanded the immediate presence of high State officials at every such Royal event, had been, for this occasion, swept aside. Thereafter, in consequence of his close proximity to certain indispensable gentlewomen, his Grace, the Archbishop, was dubbed by that irrepressible scribe, Horace Walpole, 'the Right Reverend Midwife,' a title he bore to the end of his days.

There he stood, sole male witness to and privileged spectator of the birth of an heir to Great Britain and Ireland.

As if determined to brook no delay in this, his initial appearance, George Augustus Frederick hastened into the world with astonishing ease at seven o'clock in the evening. His mother, Queen Charlotte of Mecklenburg-Strelitz, wife of King George III, had been in labour barely two hours.

The Princess, the Lords, and the Ladies, were not only amazed and delighted at Her Majesty's early deliverance, they were also immensely relieved. They had been prepared for an all night session, unrefreshed and over-heated in that airless waiting-room. Yet, so speedy had been the emergence that Dr. Hunter, the Queen's personal physician, standing by in readiness to offer his assistance, found, something to his chagrin, his advice was not required. To one Mrs. Stephen, in her equally important professional capacity, fell the honour of exhibiting to an ecstatic audience the red, wizened, gasping, squirming atom whose destiny was kingship; whose eyes unscrewed their tight closed lids to gaze unimpressed at the bowing, bobbing persons who circled him in homage.

Light from a sky of rose and gold poured through the window to spend itself in one last brightening ray on the pale damp brow of his mother, stretched exhausted but at peace on the bed of her travail; and to her with rising clamour he proclaimed his urgent need, to meet his first frustration.

Royal custom which denied him in this, the greatest moment of his life, that privacy accorded to the humblest of his father's subjects, denied him also that maternal comfort for which the most lowly of God's creatures do not ask in vain. But in eighteenth-century England the exalted estate of a Queen did not permit her to suckle her young. That unmentionable duty was the office of a hireling; in this case Mrs. Scott. She washed him, she covered his nakedness. She offered him her stranger's breast for solace. He gurgled contentment, subsided; and slept.

The moment the announcement had gone forth that the Queen was safely delivered of a Prince, the messenger despatched to the anxious young father received a gift of five hundred pounds in token of his gratitude to the bearer of such glad tidings: an impulsive gesture, which, in view of the rigid economy subsequently studied in the Household, it would seem His Majesty regretted.

Great was the general rejoicing. From every steeple joy-bells pealed. Both Houses of Parliament and the Universities offered congratulatory addresses. In Clubland the blades of St. James's drank health to their Prince all night; while Thames-side taverns, not to be outshone, did a roaring trade in Holland's gin and honest English ale. Scarce a man of them stayed sober. 'All', Mrs. Papendiek innocently tells us, 'was merriment and gladness in London.'

Undeniably his prospects were felicitous. His father's succession to the Throne two years before had met with nation-wide approval as an augury for good. The earnest young King had, however, made it known that he intended to govern his own people in his own way, with the help of the Almighty who had thus ordained him. He may have been unduly optimistic.

The immediate predecessors of George III have left behind them a palimpsest on which is inscribed a lively saga of debauchery. Three parts of the year God's Anointeds left the land of their adoption to herself while they rollicked with their mistresses in Herrenhausen. True, the dapper little George II had proved to be a gallant enough soldier when he fought in his youth under Marlborough at Oudenarde, and, in his elderly age, at Dettingen as Commander-in-Chief of his armies. But he followed in his rakish father's footsteps to the Throne, guzzled sauerkraut and sausages, drank himself under the table every night, ogled the girls, kept a harem; yet he was married to and loved by that most gracious and accomplished of German Princesses, Caroline Wilhelmina of Anspach. And when she died her husband sat and wept before her portrait, blubber-

16

QUEEN CHARLOTTE AT HER DRESSING TABLE WITH THE PRINCE OF WALES AND THE
DUKE OF YORK

From the picture by Zoffany in the Royal collection at Windsor Castle, by gracious permission of Her
Majesty the Queen (*Copyright reserved*)

ing for all his gentlemen to hear that 'not a woman alive was worthy to buckle her shoe'.

He outlived her by more than twenty years, during which time his weakling son, the Prince of Wales, succumbed in his turn to dissipation, leaving an heir in his stead. No wonder the hopes of the people of Britain were centred on that chubby fair-haired boy, their future King; the first of his dynasty born an Englishman.

And English he was, despite his German mother, to his backbone. How Britain must have longed for the time when she could crown him hers and be done with the influence of Hanover, personified in that strutting, red-faced, goggle-eyed old satyr, George II. Not to him could his subjects look for strength or guidance in those tense seven years of war which wracked the end of his reign. But, as always in British crises, there rose one to hold the citadel when its walls were tottering; one who turned the tide of French successes to ignominious defeat. In India, in Africa, in Canada and on the Rhine, Britain and her allies were guided by the vigour and sagacity of William Pitt, 'the Elder'. And at the height of victory, George II, aged seventy-seven, still seemingly healthy and strong, still pawing his women and drinking his wine, woke early one morning and went to the closet, rang for his chocolate, lapped it; lurched forward on his breakfast tray and died.

It was a happy day for England.

No scandalous youthful vicissitudes trailed young George III to the Throne. The new King was as pure and unsullied as the old King, his grandfather, was not. His pastimes were innocent and sportive; his tastes musical. He played the harpsichord; sang hymns. He hunted with the staghounds and took the keenest interest in farming. A youth of most regular habits, he rose betimes each morning for his ride from Carlton House, his widowed mother's residence, to Kensington and back.

On one of these excursions he sighted a dazzling nymph, dressed as a shepherdess, making hay in a field near Holland House.

He pulled up his horse, inquired her name: Sarah Lennox—very soon to be coupled with his. Her beauty is extolled by Horace Walpole. George was head over ears in love. But although of noble birth and the daughter of a Duke,[1] she could not possibly be countenanced as England's future Queen. Vows were exchanged, a kiss or two, a sigh—to sigh no more. The King had come into his own and his German bride was on her way to England.

Lady Sarah bore her disappointment with stoic fortitude. She appears, indeed, to have shown more concern at the death of her pet squirrel than

[1] Duke of Richmond.

17

at the loss of a lover who had just become a king. Or it may be she relied on her superlative attractions to oust his sense of duty from his country and his Throne. Surely such a dowdy, plain, frump of a girl as Charlotte of Mecklenburg-Strelitz could never steal the King's half-broken heart from Sarah Lennox? But, strange to say, she did.

If the lesser subjects of King George III were delighted to see so touching a picture of marital felicity as existed between their Sovereign and his ugly little wife, the King's courtiers were one huge snigger in their sleeves. A change indeed from the glitter and sparkle, the frolics, the jigs, the brilliant extravagant frivolities of the old King's reign—and then the ladies! Where were those delicious provocative young creatures with their high powdered 'heads' and their panniers, their promises, their giggling enticements, euphemistically styled Maids of Honour?

This Queen had brought with her a bevy of Maids as prim and as plain as herself. But the cream of them all was a side-splitting caricature of a person, stout, waddling, elderly, moustached: Frau—soon to be altered to Madame—Schwellenberg.

This lady fostered a fancy for toads—a singular hobby—which she collected and kept in glass cages in her room. She supervised the Household, engaged all the servants, and was the most favoured of Her Majesty's attendants.

The new Court, then, differed greatly from the old Court, and the beaux and belles who hankered for the gaieties and vanities, the pretty backstair intrigues, the masquerades, the fun, found little to their liking in this latest strict propriety. The entertainments, to which a select few would be invited, were of the simplest: a formal dance, a tune played by the Queen on the spinet, Handel or a hymn, a song; a sermon, read by the King to an audience half-choked with stifled yawns, and, supperless, to bed. The new Sovereign and his Consort were reputed to be miserly. Their board was frugal. The Queen indulged herself, upon occasion, in a surreptitious pinch of snuff, and the King, no gourmet, preferred above all dishes, boiled mutton with caper sauce and turnips.

Fans were raised to hide the smiles, chins stroked to hide the grins. How long, ran the question at these courtly functions, would His Majesty stay so flat a course? Would boiled mutton and his homely Charlotte satisfy his appetite, or would he soon go haymaking again?

The welcome arrival of a Prince of Wales put an end to speculation. More than ever was George captivated by his Charlotte; and she, proud of her triumph, her fine sturdy boy, arranged that everyone who wished to see him, should.

So, at twelve days old, he was on view again. Ladies flocked from all over the country for a glimpse of the Prince in his cradle, surmounted by three tall ostrich feathers, emblem of his rank, and barred from the contaminating touch of the inquisitive by a screen of Chinese lattice.

It is a moot point whether he or the Queen's caudle, her cake, and other gratuitous refreshment, drew the vast crowds, who for two hours daily, filed past George Augustus Frederick where he lay in his lace-covered crib under a canopy of crimson velvet. Certain it is that the cost of cake alone during this exhibition amounted to more than forty pounds a day, and that the consumption of wine far exceeded the maximum estimate. But the eighteen-year-old Charlotte could not cavil at expense in such a cause.

No mother was ever more doting. None of her children, and the poor lady had fifteen in rapid succession, aroused in the Queen such love as she showered on this, her first-born. Indeed, her adoration bordered on idolatry. She surrounded herself with his image in alabaster, marble, silhouette: a bust of him here, a miniature there, a model in wax in the nude. This held a permanent place on her toilet-table, reclining on a cushion under glass. She also conceived the odd notion of dressing him and his brother Frederick, Duke of York, in Roman togas.

Frederick, at the age of seven months, had been created by the King, the Right Reverend Father in God, the Bishop of Osnabrück.[1] The two little princes were still in petticoats – or togas – when the Royal physicians observed in His Majesty's demeanour certain disquieting symptoms; yet the medical reports, which pronounced him to be suffering from mild fever and a cough, were so guarded that not even Mr. Walpole, arch-scavenger of gossip, could tell his correspondents more than that: 'It is the fashion to call him very well; I wish it may be true.'

True it was, in so far as the attack appeared to be of short duration; but as a precautionary measure, which met with His Majesty's eager approval, a Regency Bill was proposed and discussed by the Cabinet, and introduced into the Lords.

Worded with careless ambiguity, it empowered 'the Queen or any other of the Royal Family, usually residing in Britain, to act as Regent'. On its second reading the Bill was revised, nominating a Regency Council that included the Queen and the sons of the late King. The name of the Princess Dowager of Wales, mother of George III, did not appear in the list.

The gossips of St. James's were enchanted. Here was spice enough to feed them for a month. Rumour had it that the ex-Premier, Lord Bute,

[1] The Bishopric of Osnabrück in Hanover was alternately occupied by a prelate of the Church and a secular Prince of the House of Brunswick-Lüneberg.

who had held office barely a year, paid visits after dusk to the house of the Dowager Princess. Every evening a sedan, closely curtained, was carried to Carlton House. A man with his collar turned up, his hat pulled down, had been seen to descend from the chair, to creep up the steps and to knock at the door, which was opened in a very stealthy manner.

It was all most exciting and mysterious; and so soon as the news-sheets had wind of the affair, every kind of noxious pamphlet and lampoon was slung at Her Royal Highness and Lord Bute. No wonder, then, that the omission of the Royal widow's name in the list of nominees for the Regency had raised a storm of malicious conjecture. And so 'The Princess Dowager', the indefatigable Mr. Walpole gleefully assures us, 'is left in the mire'.

She was not left there long.

The King, who, on belated reflection, realized he had grossly insulted his parent, turned upon his Ministers and accused them of falsifying his intention. Not for one moment would he countenance the omission of Her Royal Highness's name from the list.

So there it was: and there was she, rescued from the 'mire', reinstated, and appeased. The noise died down and the Council for the Regency Bill, the first of King George III's reign, was agreed.

Who could have guessed at its significance?

Certainly not the plump little rosy-faced boy whom Zoffany has left us in that charming trio, in which Queen Charlotte is seated at her dressing-table with the Prince of Wales in a gladiatorial plumed helmet at her side; and, supporting himself at his mother's knee, the Bishop of Osnabrück.

During the early years of his nonage, George, Prince of Wales, lived under the eyes of his parents at Buckingham House, or at the King's country palace at Kew. But when the almost perennial influx of babies filled the Royal nurseries to capacity, the Prince and his brother, the Duke of York, were removed to a house on the Green.

At the gates of Kew Gardens in those mellowed brick villas of Anne's time, dwelled an army of retainers: equerries, physicians, tutors, pages. A house in the grounds of the palace was assigned to the Royal governess, Lady Charlotte Finch, who taught all the King's children, irrespective of sex, at their lisping age. Nearby a flight of steps led to the waterside where lodged the King's Clerk of the Works, Mr. Kirby. Facing the Green, Sir John Pringle, Physician-in-Ordinary, and the King's surgeons, Caesar and Pennell Hawkins, inhabited those houses formerly occupied by the Dukes of Cumberland and Cambridge.

20

There seems to have been a somewhat spartan element in the daily ritual at Kew. Every morning, at six of the clock, the Queen would visit the nurseries to see her babies bathed; and winter or summer, at Windsor or Kew, the King rose at four, lit his own fire, made his own tea, and rode in his parks at dawn. The Princes were commanded to ride with him. No quarter was lent to a laggard, nor to any lie-abed excuse. Never mind the weather, rain, snow, or shine, up they must be with the King and the sun, and Mr. Montague, their riding-master, too.

Their father encouraged all outdoor pursuits; his passion for agriculture is proverbial. And so we have it that at Kew, in those pastoral surroundings where green fields dipped to the river bank, the two elder Princes tended each his own allotment. Together through the seasons, muffled to the eyes against the frost, or open-shirted and perspiring under an August sky, George and Frederick would toil, dig, sow, and reap their lean harvests; and having threshed and separated the corn from the chaff, would finally superintend the baking of some curious little loaves which they served to their parents on a platter.

None came to trespass on their privacy, save when twice a week the King flung open to the public the gates of Kew Gardens. Then, with noses pressed to the window-panes, the children of the King watched, doubtless with some envy, the comings and goings of the children of the people, whose lives were as remote from theirs as are those of Satan's imps from Heaven's cherubs.

It must have been daintily rustic, if not quite paradisiacal, to see the angular, plain little Queen in her enormous hoop with a flutter of daughters, some in their toddling stage, at her heels, moving among the flowers in her private garden. We can picture her there in her broad-brimmed hat with her wide smile and her basket on her arm, pausing to snip at a rose, stoop to a weed, pluck a pale orange–she grew oranges–, or turning, eyes busy, to hasten a loiterer, or hush too boisterous a giggle.

Although the King and Queen cared nothing for society, the Prince of Wales and his brothers, and any sister old enough to stand, were forced to attend twice a week those formal evening gatherings, where a select few would be invited to a mild game of cribbage or to listen to the chamber-music played by Mr. Cramer at the harpsichord; the Cervettos, father and son, joint rivals to Mr. Crosdill, with their violins; or Mr. Papendiek, the King's flautist, with his flute. There, surrounded by a funereal circle of ladies, the Queen would sit at her embroidery, while the King beat time to the gentle strains of Handel and listened to the whispers in his head.

In this rarefied atmosphere the boyhood of George Augustus Frederick was nursed. No blight must impair the bloom of his youth, no blast from the outside world. Eminent tutors cared for his mind. His first instructors, Lord Holderness and Monsieur de Salzes, were succeeded by the more scholastic Dr. Markham of Westminster, his assistant, Dr. Cyril Jackson, and the prophetic Bishop of Worcester, Dr. Hurd, who, when asked his opinion of the fifteen-year-old Prince, replied: 'He will probably be the most polished gentleman or the most accomplished blackguard in Europe. Possibly both.'

Lord Bruce, whose knowledge of the classics was somewhat below the level of his pupil's, taught him Greek, and received an earldom for his pains on his retirement.

Although the King had been born an Englishman, that despotism which, with equal pertinacity, he imposed upon his Ministers and sons, was entirely Teutonic. The future of each had been decided by their father in their cradles. All, with exception of two, were set aside for the Army before they could speak. A third son, William Henry, who more than half a century later followed his brother to the Throne, an eventuality that none but the Fates could have foreseen, was destined for the life of a sailor, in his case a felicitous choice; and to give them their final polish the younger princes were to tour the Courts of Germany, a diversion from which the Heir Apparent was excluded. No military career or Grand Tour for him as guest of small Electors and Great Prussians. The future Sovereign of Britain must never be allowed to leave the country.

Thus, from the first, the King's attempt to graft his bigoted autocracy on the independent spirit of his eldest son shows a lamentable lack of intuition. Continuous repression caused eruptive smoulderings. Even as a child he had an ungovernable temper. At the age of seven, in heated defiance over some or other punishment administered, we find him kicking at his father's door and yelling, 'Wilkes for ever! And the forty-*five*!'

That story has been floated into legend.

John Wilkes, a vigorous supporter of the elder Pitt, had married a wealthy wife some several years his senior, and at her expense he exploited himself as a fashionable rake and a candidate for Parliament.

He was hideous and cross-eyed, yet possessed of a certain attraction, in particular for the tenderer sex. He was also the founder of a political rag known as the *North Briton*, in which he trained his most abusive batteries on Bute and his Ministry. In the forty-fifth number of the paper, issued after Lord Bute's resignation, he turned his invective on the King to attack his speech from the Throne, which he denounced as 'the most abandoned instance of ministerial effrontery ever imposed on mankind'.

Whereupon offended Majesty ordered a warrant for his arrest on the grounds of treasonable libel. His subsequent examination before Lords Halifax and Egremont, Secretaries of State, resulted in the confiscation of all papers appertaining to John Wilkes, and the commitment of his person to the Tower.

The country rose in protest. Public opinion, ever in favour of fair play, declared Wilkes to have been unjustly victimized. The cry, 'Wilkes, Liberty, and the Forty-five!' was bawled in every gutter in the town. The King took alarm and Wilkes took advice. Brought up for trial in the Court of Common Pleas, he was granted heavy damages for false imprisonment and immediately released.

From that time forth the name of Wilkes represented to the Sovereign synonym for Beelzebub. The youthful Prince must have kept his ears wide open while his Gentlemen-in-Waiting, in those houses on Kew Green, discussed between themselves the Wilkes affair. The Prince's intelligence was far beyond his years, and his memory had always been retentive.

That assault upon his father's door and dignity is not the only evidence of insubordination. When in his teens he was compelled to wear a childish frilled collar which he thought to be too young for him, he tore it off and turning on his servant in a passion and with, possibly, more kicks, screamed: 'See how I am treated!' These and sundry other incidents caused the King to exert every tyrannical means to suppress any sign of insurgence. Friction between the two resulted: on the one side an increasing detestation of his father, his piety, his principles, his trick of repetition, his 'Hey–what, what!' which the Prince did not scruple to mimic: on the other an abuse of authority which may have nurtured paranoia in the son. All his life he was sensitive to ridicule.

His fledgling wings were clipped, and he, with the surge of pulsating desires and mounting young perplexities, was caged within the bars of harsh restriction. His tutors reported him 'slothful'. The King insisted on eight hours' study a day, but in half that time he had learned more than his masters could teach and sat yawning while they droned. When they took their complaints to his father they were bidden: 'Then flog him.'

They flogged him; and flogged into him more red-hot hate against godhead and King, against all that held him captive from each visionary delight that floated with tantalizing siren-lure before his eyes, within his dreams, in those sanctified cloisters at Kew.

Who can tell, while he browsed in forest deeps of learning, what equivocal fantasies he conjured? A natural scholar, he drank at the fount of the classics. At first a timorous guest at the feast of Virgil, Horace, Homer, Aristotle and Euripides, he became host in their stead, invited them at his will, to his board. He flirted with the gods, bestrode Olympus; or, in his rambles along gaunt Windsor's galleries, he may have glimpsed a lifted new horizon in magical device of line and colour; the pencilled exquisite portraiture of Holbein; the breath-taking, forgotten splendour of Vandyck, or some quaint procession of small dancing figures delightfully imposed on the panels of a Florentine marriage-chest; all such discoveries were his to hold and cherish—for the moment.

He was at that age when life is either radiant or agonizing; when a pimple on his chin, a rent in the Mechlin at his wrists—a false note from Mr. Papendiek's flute—Mr. Papendiek's everlasting flute!—or some sun-lost autumn afternoon, sodden with mist from the river, dreary with the slow death-fall of yellow leaves—any one of these may have cast him from the heights of incalculable glory to the depths of irrational despair.

It is perhaps in some such mood of melancholy that he construes, very freely, this letter from Servius Sulpicius to Cicero on the death of Tullia, Cicero's young daughter.

'What is there now which could make her so much regret the loss of life?' cries George Augustus Frederick Sulpicius. 'What affairs?' (What indeed? When any Page of the Backstairs was permitted the joys of the alcove so sternly denied him?) 'What hopes? What prospects?'

This dirge may have been prompted by the boastful accounts of naval exploits retailed by his scrubby brother William, who just about this time had returned on his first leave from Digby's flagship. Spain had recently joined with France in the general upheaval that followed rebellion in America; and William had already been in action.

On his own showing, and according to Digby's report, he had been present at the capture off St. Vincent of a Spanish convoy carrying provisions to Cadiz. A chase ensued led by Rodney in the *Sandwich*. One of the enemy's ships was sunk, one got upon the rocks, another was run ashore and lost, and a fourth, the *Guipasciano*, was seized, re-manned and re-named the *Prince William*, 'in whose presence,' Digby wrote, 'she had the honour to be taken'.

Bitter hearing this to him, who was not allowed unattended outside the palace gardens or the walls of Buckingham House. Still, the King could not imprison a spirit, that, now identified with Servius Sulpicius, sailed the seven seas—a longer voyage than any on which William would be likely to embark.

'... From Aegina to Megara I began attentively to view the countries that lay around me. Behind me was Aegina, before me was Megara, on my right lay Piraeus, on my left Corinth. These cities, at one time flourishing, are now desolate, in ruins. Thus I began to ruminate within myself. Alas! do we poor mortals resent it so much if one of us dies, whose life is of such short date? . . . .'

Short! When every day was a month, and every month a year, in a desert waste of time hemmed in by petty barriers. And of what use this tedious history, this pedantic sermonizing of a Roman philosopher long dead? Why weep for a girl whose bones, for almost eighteen centuries, had lain in the dust? When here, at his father's gates, were girls alive and eager for him whose history was in the making. . . . But not perhaps as he would have it made.

* * *

Revolt was in the air, not only on the home front at Kew Green, but in pastures much farther afield. From time to time, during these first two decades of King George's reign, the American colonists had shown symptoms of dissatisfaction. While the King's eldest son hurled suppressed defiance at his father, those transatlantic younger sons of Britain had flung an open challenge from Boston Bay into Westminster Hall.

The Act imposing export duties on America, for which Lord Townshend, Chancellor of the Exchequer, had been responsible, and whose timely demise occurred before he could commit any more inexcusable blunders, had aroused a storm of protest from the Colony. But not until the famous 'Olive Branch' had been offered by Congress and rejected by the Crown, did war with America appear to be inevitable.

Every effort had been made to avert it. From the Opposition benches Burke was thundering: 'You cannot content such men at a distance. Who are you to fret and rage and bite the chains of nature? In all such extended empires authority grows feeble at its extremities.'

Feeble indeed was Authority at his extremities as he shuffled up and down the terrace of his Castle, his gooseberry eyes peering sideways at his 'good Lord North'.

Elected First Lord of the Treasury in 1770, North was His Majesty's ideal of all that a Prime Minister should be; not so in the opinion of his colleagues. Dutiful certainly he was, and conscientious, but inclined to sleep through the hottest debates, deaf to all invective directed at himself. Also he was strangely absent-minded. The story went, which may be pure apocrypha, that once he had seized in mistake for his own, the wig from the head of a Naval Secretary next to whom he happened to be seated. He was pippin-faced, cherubic, with a nose too short and a tongue too long that caused him to slobber when he spoke. Yet he could speak,

25

when he chose, to advantage; and when he spoke the King listened—to hear his 'good Lord's' report of Burke's latest harangue.

'Do not appear in the character of madmen as well as assassins, violent, vindictive, bloody, tyrannical. . . .'

Shocking language! Most unparliamentary. And here was King George's dream of himself as the Father of Peace clasping hands across the sea, swept away in that volley at Lexington!

North, on the verge of a nervous breakdown, sent in his plea for resignation. He had been handed a burden too great for him to bear, and he wished to shift it to shoulders more worthy of its weight before 'he and the nation were undone'. He wrote to the King; he begged for another to succeed him. Why not Lord Chatham, who, as William Pitt, had so decisively settled the Seven Years' War? But Pitt was seventy, riddled with gout, and dying. . . . Pitt was dead; and the King, who had always disapproved of his Whiggery, took umbrage at the demand of the Commons for a funeral in the Abbey, and a monument raised to his honour.

Nevertheless the Commons won the day. Pitt was duly interred at Westminster; and a tall, gawky, sallow-faced boy, Lord Chatham's younger son, chief mourner in his brother's absence, stood at his father's grave in tears. Yet neither North nor anyone who watched beside him there, could have foretold how, in a few years' time, that young lad's name would ring throughout all Britain in a jingle charged with wonder.

'A sight to make surrounding nations stare,
A Kingdom trusted to a schoolboy's care.'

That other schoolboy on Kew Green, with far less opportunity for exploitation of his gifts than William Pitt, 'the Younger', had turned from the study of the classics to the more absorbing study of himself.

His childish treble deepened to a harsh distressing croak. His letters, not now construed from Latin, were out-poured in fervent English, and to Mary Hamilton, attendant on his sisters. But despite the locks of hair, mottoes, vows, and hints of marriage showered on this 'Dearest Friend', we gather that his heart was still his own. He had a strong suspicion that she thought him, Prince or future King or nothing, much too young for her; for she was three and twenty, he barely seventeen; and then there were those pimples on his face!

Heaven knows if it were self-conceit or self-defence against youth's temporary, if none the less humiliating, blemishes, that made him pen this panegyric of his charms to Mary Hamilton, in which he tells her that his limbs were 'well-proportioned', his features 'strong and manly,' his forehead 'well-shaped', his mouth 'rather large', his teeth 'fine', his eyes

26

'grey and . . . tho' none of the best are yet passable'. He is obviously proud of his 'petit nez retroussé,' and adds, as modest afterthought, that he has 'very ugly ears'.

He had arrived at that exciting no-man's land of adolescence, when impatient boyhood, marking time on the threshold of experience, finds each facet of his consciousness extravagantly multiplied. Yet, in the ready flux and flow of swift impressions, his life had little contact with reality. The sycophantic courtiers in St. James's drawing-rooms, the wax-light radiance, the crystal lustres, the decorative 'heads' dressed high with flowers, jewels, the sheen of satin, of woven gilt brocade, the powder plastered thick upon white lead to hide the pock-marks—what were these? The tinsel décor of a puppet-show controlled by its kingly Master with much pomp and meagre circumstance.

Seated in his regal state, glittering with orders, pop-eyed, red-faced, sweating in the crowded warmth of candle-glow, the King pulls strings and calls the measure; a minuet, no prancing, no gavottes. Point the toe, bow, chassé, touch finger-tips; no more. Quickening fan-flutters hide airy innuendoes, the gay seduction of a smile; a promise, light as thistle-down, caught back upon a whisper. The Master's all-pervading eye can read the movement of a lip; he can hear, beyond the orchestrated music in his head, the smallest word, low-spoken. . . . Curtsies, bow again, another dance; another partner. The First Gentleman in that long cast is forbidden to dance twice with the same girl. Then to the buffet—welcome interlude. Brandy and rum punch are a sure antidote to boredom. But he cannot quite, at this age, hold his drink.

He practised singing; joined a glee-club; read the poets; studied science; yet we hear him plaintively complaining: 'I have nothing to do. Won't anybody tell me what to do?'

As might have been expected, he soon found what to do.

The moonlit glades of Richmond, a dusky dell at Kew, were the scenes of early amorous adventure.

Gross exaggeration has been lent to these with no brief recorded to youth's reckless bid for freedom, the natural sequence of too stern restraint. What if his first were the wife of a groom—, 'a dark-eyed slattern'? She was lovely. But his fastidious recoil from her coarseness and vulgarity –her manners were atrocious and she very seldom washed–drove him from her tutelage, a disillusioned tyro, to the capture of Harriot Vernon.

She was raven-haired and fragile, enchanting in her shy–and slight –resistance.

The Prince's apartments in the Household overlooked those allotted to his mother's Maids of Honour of whom Harriot was one. The Queen, heavy with the pending birth of yet another Prince,[1] had doubtless not observed this Maid's particular attraction. Queen Charlotte's choice of virginal attendants was judicious. No temptation must be offered to her sons; and hitherto there had been none among the Queen's young ladies who could have hoped to win a glance from the Prince of Wales at his window. Harriot, however, invited more than glances. Signals passed, and notes: an assignation arranged through the medium of Frederick, the Bishop.

The locality selected was a leafy copse in the remotest part of Kew Gardens–'after sunset'. And never did the sun linger more upon his journey to the west. At last when evening fell and colours faded, and the glistening river blanched beneath the newly risen moon, the Prince, disguised in a cloak borrowed from his equerry, Lord Malden, hastened through the gloaming to his tryst.

There must have been some pretty palpitations when she greeted him, breathless with her hurry, hooded, masked, tremulous, and yielding. . . . How unfortunate that just at the crowning peak of mutual delight the King should have decided to play chess. The Prince of Wales was commanded to play with him. George! Where was George? . . . Nowhere to be found.

A page went searching. The Prince Bishop went out. He ran panting through the gardens to interrupt an idyll, to bring his brother, cursing, to his feet, and the shameless Miss Vernon to her senses.

The scandal was up and down the Palace in an hour, and caused the subsequent expulsion of Miss Vernon from the Court, 'after she had sacrificed', so Mr. Huish informs us, 'all that was most dear to her on earth'.[2]

But that episode was speedily forgotten in the track of more exciting game, not to be found on the greensward at Kew, but on the green baize at Pall Mall. There the Prince was introduced by his uncle Henry, Duke of Cumberland, to the persuasive joys of faro.

No influence could have been more meretricious than this of his father's younger brother. His escapades drove the King frantic. In 1770, at the age of twenty-five, he had been defendant in a case brought against him by Lord Grosvenor for damages on the charge of adultery with the plaintiff's wife. Letters from the Duke to Henrietta, Lady Grosvenor, when read aloud in Court, caused vast amusement to the public and a brainstorm to the King.

Reports of the Duke's correspondence, addressed to the 'Angel of his Soul', were brought to his horrified Majesty. These included the descrip-

[1] Octavius, born 1779, died 1783.   [2] Memoirs: George IV, Vol. I.

tion of a dream of his beloved, in which the Duke confessed to having 'laye down and kissed her dear little hair . . . and had her on the couch ten thousand times'. Possibly the most expensive dream on record, since the sum total of damages awarded to Lord Grosvenor amounted to ten thousand pounds: appalling enough, but worse followed. Henry, off with the old love, was instantly on with the new!

Anne Horton, an attractive young widow and daughter of Lord Irnham, had, so Mr. Walpole assures us, 'the most amorous eyes in the world and eyelashes a yard long'. Those eyes, if not the eyelashes, proved too much for the susceptible Henry. He was caught and married after an uproarious week in her company at Calais.

The King was beside himself. The pair had been irrevocably tied by Holy Church, and short of divorce, which was unthinkable, nothing could be done to untie them; but at least this shocking Henry could be punished. His Majesty instructed the Lord Chamberlain to ban from the presence and St. James's, any person known to visit the Duke's house.

Yet still more trouble for the King was on the brew; this time from a favourite brother.

William, Duke of Gloucester, diametrically opposed in character to Henry, was a serious grave young man, one after the King's own heart; indeed, he greatly loved him. William, however, was not what he seemed, and the shock of this discovery which came hard on the death of the King's mother, the Dowager Princess of Wales, almost brought about a second mental lapse. William had been married. Secretly. These six years. And to Lady Waldegrave; another widow.

Certainly in this case there was no hint of any liaison, no imputation on the lady's virtue; but the accident of birth, without the sanctity of wedlock, branded her the daughter of Sir Edgar Walpole[1] and a little milliner from nowhere. . . . Incredible apocalypse! Not only had his pious brother William been guilty of abominable deceit, he had married a bastard and no Royal one at that. Moreover his Duchess was now pregnant.

Then the King, who had 'cried and been awake all night', determined to take steps which would prevent any such calamitous occurrence from marring the happy future of his sons.

Thus, in 1772, had been passed the Bill which forbade the union with a commoner and without the King's consent, of any Prince or Princess of the Blood.

But to George Augustus Frederick in his schoolroom, the Royal Marriage Act held no ominous portent. Its effect upon his life had yet to come.

[1] Brother of Horace Walpole.

Small wonder, then, that the house of his wicked Uncle Henry, which by the King's decree had been kept strictly out of bounds, drew the Prince from the hallowed precincts of his father's palace as surely as a magnet draws a pin. The fact that he trespassed upon forbidden ground may have added piquancy to contraband adventure. The joys and mysteries of gaming offered endless fascination, as also did his uncle's pretty wife. She could tell a ribald story with an air of wide-eyed innocence that convulsed the Prince and all the company with laughter.

The gay Cumberlands had gathered round them a host of pleasure-seeking friends who, on the whole, were a disreputable lot. The graceless Duke and his fair Duchess cared nothing for the morals, rank, or virtue of their guests. Any man willing to play high or to drink deep could obtain an invitation to their board. And besides these merry gentlemen there were ladies—some from the high world, some from the low world—and every one of them a charmer, chosen less for her wit than her face value.

But not all the guests who jostled shoulders at Duke Henry's gaming-table were of questionable origin or character. One frequent visitor who might often have been seen to throw and win or lose there with the worst of them, was a dynamic personality in Parliament. His memorable speech against the coercive measures adopted by North's Government in pursuance of the war with America, had brought him to the front rank of the Opposition Benches. His passionate orations shook the House and stupefied the Tories; he had no fear at that time of a rival. The pale lad, who later proved to be his deadliest opponent, was jogging back and forth to Cambridge in a coach.

And from that nightly saturnalia over which his uncle Cumberland presided, from the spell of dice and faro, hazard, loo, and courtesans, the Prince of Wales turned to find a friend.

It is scarcely feasible that at this age—seventeen—he could have recognized the qualities of greatness that outweighed the many scandals of drunken orgies, gambling, and unsavoury intrigues attached to the name of Charles James Fox. Indeed it is more likely that these rumours, in conjunction with Fox's political views—he was acknowledged leader of the Whigs and the King's avowed enemy—may have contributed to the Prince's hero-worship. Yet there was nothing in his outward person to inspire admiration in the critical young Prince. Precise in his dress and a sybarite for cleanliness in an age when daily baths were rarely taken, he surely must have shuddered at the slovenly habits of his 'Dear Charles', the recipient of so many eager letters.

Fox, younger son of Lord Holland, at thirty looked much older.

Although in his vacations he played cricket and shot partridges, over-indulgence in food and drink had coarsened him. Gross-bodied and paunchy, he carried two chins which he was not particular to shave; but his eyes, keen, humorous, beneath their beetling brows, held sparks as if lit by inward flame. Save in his speeches, however, he offered no sign of internal eruption. He was lazy. He would go to bed in the dawn, get up in the afternoon, and stroll into Brooks's to lose twenty thousand guineas at a sitting, then home to read Herodotus all night. He seldom changed his linen, and received his guests in a soiled dressing-gown. And this was the man the Prince took for his model, and whom, after himself, he came to love—for a time—more than any being in the world.

The influence of that foolish sot, his uncle Cumberland, was a passing phase of which the Prince soon tired; the influence of Charles Fox was vastly more pernicious; and as the strange friendship deepened, so did the Prince whole-heartedly succumb to that irresistible attraction. Always hypersensitive, he could not have failed to appreciate, if not to reflect, something of that peculiar brilliance which, when not clouded by the fumes of alcohol, shone with a light akin to genius. While Fox nourished this young infatuation which he knew he could turn at his will to his advantage, his preliminary overtures were cautious. He played the friend, the sympathetic confidant for fierce outbursts of complaint against the leading-rein, as his first rôle; no more than that. The Prince was still a minor, but as future Monarch he might prove to be a considerable factor in a joint alliance against obstructive Sovereignty. The King, as Fox was well aware, looked on him with loathing and contempt. Nothing, therefore, could have offered more subtle opportunity to avenge those insults, sparsely veiled, heaped upon him by his Monarch through the mouthpiece of his Party, than that this boy should have fallen, a ripening plum, at his feet.

And in the year 1780, at the age of eighteen, the Prince of Wales attained his legal majority as Heir Apparent to the Throne.

The question then arose whether he would or would not be given a house of his own and an income worthy of its maintenance. But the King, determined to keep him under his roof and his eye, conceded him the smallest personal allowance, a few horses and a suite of apartments at Windsor and Buckingham House: a niggardly concession which sent Mr. Walpole hurrying to dip his quill again.

'The Prince has been given a bit of an establishment; yet his Court is still kept in the nursery. However, there will be a little more room, for the Right Reverend Father in God, Prince Frederick, is to be weaned and sent abroad.'

The Prince of Wales must have missed him. There are accounts of prankish interludes, when parental supervision was temporarily suspended by that woeful transatlantic war which drove all other matters from his mind. The Princes took advantage of the loophole.

From Buckingham House to Vauxhall was no distance. We hear of 'broils' after dark in those gardens by the river; a masquerade in which 'Midshipman Guelph', home on a month's leave, took part, ineffectually disguised as a sailor. His elder brother, George, decked out as a Spanish grandee and attended by four of his squires, came to words with William Henry, who had sneaked out in the wake of his elders and was making gallant headway with a nun. But when the lordly Spaniard, feigning not to recognize his fifteen-year-old brother, cast doubt upon the morals of the sailor's pretty novice with allusions, in no choice terms, to the 'ladies of Portsmouth Point', affronted chivalry demanded satisfaction.

William, who had learned to use his fists at sea, used them to such good purpose that the constables arrived upon the scene to stop the row. The sailor and the don were marched off to the watch-house, where they were curtly requested to unmask. The consternation of the officers when they recognized the battered pair, was appeased by roars of laughter from the sailor, and a guinea all round from the Spanish grandee.

That episode and others were carried to the King and gave him 'ten nights without sleep'.

Thereafter, while Vauxhall and its temptations were taboo, the more reputable Ranelagh was not. No objection could be raised to that favoured resort of the *ton* where, accompanied by his guardians and surrounded by a circle of admirers, the Prince joyed to promenade dressed to kill.

He must have been bewitching at eighteen. His skin had cleared, and he had not at this age run to fat. His swift ingenuous smile lent vivacity to features a trifle stolid in repose, modified the supercilious tilt of lips, blunt-cornered, the evasive indolence of eyes more grey than blue, set wide apart beneath brows darker than the gilt-blond lightly powdered hair.

His gifts were undeniable. He spoke French and German with bilingual ease, was the possessor of a remarkably good voice, and already displayed that perceptive rare appreciation of the finer arts, which in later life gave him his connoisseur's collection picked from the treasures of the world. His grace of manner, allied to his capricious versatility, did, in part, fulfil the famous oracle uttered by his former tutor, Bishop Hurd. If not the most 'polished gentleman in Europe', there was none who could challenge his charm: that fatal charm which all his life made fools

PORTRAIT OF H.R.H. GEORGE, PRINCE OF WALES, IN UNIFORM AS COLONEL OF THE IOTH
LIGHT DRAGOONS, BY BEECHEY

From the Royal Collection at Windsor Castle, by gracious permission of Her Majesty the Queen

of his men and slaves of his women; and, when turned full force across the footlights of Drury Lane theatre, ensnared the loveliest little play-actress in town.

★   ★   ★

Her career was not unchequered. Adversity had spurred her on the hard way to success. Her father, Captain Darby, a seafaring gentleman of Bristol imbued with eccentric ambitions, had come to grief in his attempt to establish a whale factory off the coast of Labrador. Compelled to quit the country in some haste, he left his wife with a bill of sale on his house, two children on her hands, and very little else beyond his debts.

Driven by the importunities of her husband's creditors, Mrs. Darby cut her losses and departed with her boy and girl to London. Mary, soon to be the breadwinner, was sent to school at an establishment near Mary-le-bon Marshes.

According to her own account Mary must have been an infant prodigy. She could recite Pope at length before she was seven, and was singing Gay's ballads at eight. At thirteen she received a proposal of marriage. A year later her dancing master, Mr. Hussey, who was also Maître de Ballet at Covent Garden Playhouse, recognized her histrionic possibilities. Through his intervention, Thomas Hull, then assistant manager of Covent Garden, heard her recite an act from *Jane Shore*, and brought her to David Garrick. So impressed was he by her appearance, if not so much by her ability, that he offered her the part of Cordelia in his forthcoming production of *King Lear*. But before the agreement could be signed, little Mary Darby was wooed and won and married.

Her husband, Thomas Robinson, an old Harrovian and articled clerk to an attorney, having fallen crazily in love with her, represented himself as a gentleman of means with 'great expectations from an uncle'. The 'uncle', however, proved to be his father, and Thomas his natural son. Poor Mary's visions of 'great expectations' vanished before her disillusioned eyes. Yet if Mr. Robinson had no name he had at least some credit that enabled him to rent a house in Hatton Garden and to enjoy, with his presumably fifteen-year-old bride, a luxurious and haphazard existence. He paraded her at Vauxhall and the Pantheon where her childish airs and her pink satin gown trimmed with sable, created a sensation. Soon all the most prominent rake-hells in London thronged to the house in Hatton Garden. The admiration she excited among her husband's so-called friends, and to which she modestly admits she 'never thought herself entitled', she attributes to 'my youth, my inexperience,

33

my girlish simplicity, and the lavish style in which Mr. Robinson lived', –and which inevitably landed him in gaol.

To the King's Bench Mary with her baby daughter followed him; and there the three of them remained for near upon ten months. She spent her leisure hours writing poems. One of these, an 'Ode to Spring', she published some years later in the *Morning Post* under a pseudonym, 'Tabitha Bramble'.

Compelled now to support not only her child but a husband whose most frequent visitors, we are informed, 'were of the Jewish tribe', Mary sought again the influence of her theatrical acquaintances, with the result that Sheridan, part manager of Drury Lane, engaged her for the season.

Her success was instantaneous. The dainty little creature took all London by storm, to star at the Theatre Royal for three years.

It is evident that for some months before his first meeting with Mary, the Prince of Wales showed her marked attention from afar. Notes and ardent letters, *billets doux*, followed his first sight of her as Perdita at the command performance of *A Winter's Tale*.[1]

'As I stood in the wing opposite the Prince's box, waiting to go on the stage,' thus Perdita's own version of that memorable night, 'Mr. Ford the manager's son, presented a friend who accompanied him; this friend was Lord Viscount Malden. . . . I hurried through the first scene, not without embarrassment, owing to the fixed attention with which the Prince of Wales honoured me.'

So fixed indeed was his attention that the whole house observed it, with the possible exception of their Majesties whose box was not shared by the Prince. 'On the last curtsy', Mary tells us, 'the Royal Family condescendingly returned a bow to the performers, but just as the curtain was falling, my eyes met those of the Prince of Wales, and with a look *I shall never forget*, he gently inclined his head . . . I felt the compliment and blushed my gratitude.'

Within a few days Lord Malden paid a visit to her house, at a favourable moment when her husband was from home. She received the 'Lord Viscount' with more blushes, but: 'His Lordship's embarrassment far exceeded mine. He attempted to speak, paused, hesitated, apologized; I knew not why. He hoped that I would pardon him, that I would consider the peculiar delicacy of his situation and then act as I thought proper.'

We can fancy him there with his hems and his haws, and Mary in the trembles. She may or may not have guessed what was coming, till: 'he drew a small letter from his pocket. I took it, and knew not what to say.

[1] December 3, 1779.

It was addressed to PERDITA. I smiled, I believe rather sarcastically, and opened the *billet*. It contained only a few words, but those expressive of more than common civility; they were signed FLORIZEL. . . .' The first of many others that for months were showered on her daily.

In common with her numerous successors she was 'not insensible to his powers of attraction, the beautiful ingenuousness of his language, his warm enthusiastic adoration. . . .' There is no end to her raptures. And so it goes on, with Florizel frenzied and Perdita coy.While she denied any 'sordid or interested thought', she begged him to be patient until he became his own master, when doubtless she hoped to share that 'bit of an establishment', due to him in August of that year.

At last the lovesick Florizel, who, if not his own master had been grudgingly accorded his own suite, was in a position to request that his Perdita should visit him privately at Buckingham House, and, for some reason best known to himself, dressed as a boy.

But if Florizel had lost his head Perdita kept hers.

'The indelicacy of such a step as well as the danger of detection, made me shrink from the proposal.' And threw Florizel into a state 'of the most distressing agitation', which brought Malden to her doorstep once again.

Perdita now found herself caught between two fires. Lord Malden, she declares, conceived for her 'so violent a passion that he was the most unfortunate and miserable of mortals'.

How she dealt with the love-pangs of this most 'miserable of mortals', Perdita does not reveal. She hastens on to tell us that while her husband remained ignorant of her 'epistolary intercourse' with the Prince of Wales, his conduct was entirely neglectful. She seems, indeed, to have been sorely tried. Mr. Robinson, when not engaged with his 'bearded friends' in the parlour, was engaging Perdita's maid in her bed.

'Plain even to ugliness, short, squalid, dirty', is Perdita's description of this damsel, who may not have been quite so plain as she is painted, but who, with others, served her purpose to allay any qualms which might have troubled Mrs. Robinson's wifely sense of duty. 'I admired the Prince. . . . His ardent expressions of adoration, his eloquent letters, the exquisite sensibility which breathed through every line, combined to shake my feeble resolution.'

As, doubtless also, did his 'highest token of esteem' expressed in 'a Bond of the most solemn and binding nature', containing a promise of twenty thousand pounds to be paid by the Prince to Mrs. Robinson so soon as he should have command of such a sum.

Florizel was asked to wait no more.

Accompanied by the 'Lord Viscount', with whom she dined at a river-

35

side inn on an island between Brentford and Kew, Perdita in the flutters and his lordship in the sulks, watched for the pre-arranged signal from the opposite bank which would herald the Prince's approach.

An early moon crept up above the black-plumed tree-tops, drained of sun, and dark against a saffron-tinted sky. The call of an owl pierced the breathless pause that followed a bird's last evensong; then nothing stirred save the blind flurry of bat-wings, the scuttle of some scared creature in the long grasses at their feet. And as twilight spread its bridge of dusk between the night and the ended day, a ghostly handkerchief was seen to wave from the mists on the farther shore.

Malden unfastened the boat that lay moored to a jutting snag. Silently Perdita stepped in; and now no whisper, not a sound save the plash of oars, broke that furtive stillness as she was rowed across the water to her Prince.

Soon the whole of London had wind of the affair. Prints and lampoons, damp from the press, were dangled in her face as she passed to and from her carriage on shopping expeditions. She could not visit her milliner without a crowd at her heels to follow her and peer in at the windows. But the publicity that linked the name of Florizel with Perdita neither embarrassed nor dismayed her; she enjoyed it. While, from the Clubs of St. James's to the stews of St. Giles's the tongues of the tatlers wagged, Perdita flaunted, demurely, her conquest.

With Florizel beside her she drove in Hyde Park in her carriage, painted scarlet, silver panelled, for which the Prince had paid—or owed—nine hundred guineas. She wore exquisite clothes to the envy of the ladies, who lifted chins and noses at the sight of her; not so the gentlemen; they, in gallant recognition of her peach-bloom loveliness, swept hats to the ground as she passed. She never appeared twice in the same costume. On one day she would be powdered, patched, as a Lady of Quality in a towering 'head' topped by a basket of flowers, a bright-plumaged bird, or a ship in full sail. On another occasion she would be a simple shepherdess with artfully gold-dusted curls; or again, as if that moment dismounted from her horse, she would astonish beholders as an Amazon, rakishly habited in riding-suit and three-cornered hat, her hair tied *en queue*, and a diamond flashing in the fall of lace at her throat.

This trinket and others, bought of Gray's, the jewellers, and presented to her by the Prince, she disdains as 'trifling ornaments, the whole in value not exceeding a hundred guineas'. And these, when they parted, she returned—with one exception: a locket containing a miniature of Florizel and a heart cut out of paper, inscribed on the one side: 'Je ne change qu'en mourant', and on the other: 'Unalterable to my Perdita through life.'

Unalterable certainly he was for two years, and then:

'At the moment when I looked impatiently for the arrival of that day when I might enjoy the public protection of him for whom I had given up all, I received a letter from His Royal Highness, a curt unkind letter, briefly informing me that we must meet no more . . .!'

She was shocked, amazed, incredulous. Only two days before she had seen him at Kew, 'when his affection appeared to be boundless'. . . . Nothing would induce her to accept such unwarranted dismissal. She wrote to Florizel, and received no answer. She could not fathom his silence, unless he had taken leave of his senses—or come to them.

Full of fears, misgivings, trepidations, but determined to solve the mystery, she set out in a small pony-phaeton for Windsor. The Prince had removed himself from her reach in the belief that she would not dare pursue him to his father's Castle. Tears gave way to indignation. She would! She could! And insist upon an explanation of his conduct!

Her journey was not without excitement. Unattended, save for a nine-year-old postilion, she encountered a footpad at Hounslow who rushed from the bushes to grab at the leader's rein. This diminutive nine-year-old seems to have shown remarkable courage and presence of mind when he whipped up his pony and drove hell-for-leather to outspeed the 'assassin' at her wheels.

Poor Perdita! She might have spared herself much heartache, to say nothing of the fright she had sustained, if she had shown a little less precipitance and more circumspection. On her arrival at Windsor, Florizel refused to see her. . . . Cruel! And as, despairingly, she jolted back to London, she may have wished a dozen more 'assassins' would assault her. Sudden death would have been better than lingering uncertainty.

One interview only he gave her to buoy her sinking hopes, when 'we passed some hours in most friendly and delightful conversation, and I began to flatter myself that our differences had been adjusted'.

But he cut her dead in Hyde Park the next day.

Was it caprice or something more—a trick-light flash from depths concealed, where grievance brooded to avenge his youth's frustration in perverted torment of another? Or had he merely tired of her pretty little-girlishness, her studied coquetries, her yearnings, her surrender? Or had his headlong chase of beauty led him to the feet of—Sarah Campbell? He met her at his birthday ball: sat next to her at supper, walked with

37

her in the moonlight, took her to an arbour; and when the guests had departed he went to his room, and, giddy with wine and emotion, wrote this.

> 'Oh, Campbell! the scene of tonight
> Has opened the wound of my heart;
> It has shown me how great the delight
> Which the charms of thy converse impart.
> I've known what it is to be gay,
> I've revell'd in joy's fleeting hour,
> I've wished for the close of the day
> To meet in a thick woven bower.
>
> 'Twas there that the soft-stolen kiss,
> 'Twas there that the throb of our hearts,
> Betrayed that we wished for the bliss,
> Which love, and love only, imparts.
> But Fate will those hearts oft dissever,
> By nature designed for each other;
> But why should they part? And for ever?
> And force their affections to smother.
>
> Now, sweet be thy slumbers, my friend,
> And sweet be the dreams of thy soul;
> Around thee may angels attend,
> And visions of happiness roll.
> Whilst I ★ ★ ★ ★ ★'

That abrupt termination to the elegy may be due less to desertion of his muse than to modesty on the part of his recorder, Mr. Huish, who vexatiously forbears 'from particular motives' to give us the conclusion.

Unfortunately, the recipient of this doggerel to whom it was delivered the next day, did not respond with quite the same warmth that its author had hoped to inspire. His Campbell may, indeed, have been more furious than flattered at the nostalgic allusions to 'the wound of his heart' and his 'smothered affections', which looked to be divided between herself and Perdita.

Florizel's ardour was quenched by a series of gentle rebuffs; or by this time his 'revels in joy's fleeting hour' may have palled.

At nineteen he still could find nothing to do. Drink, faro, dice, the invention of a new shoe-buckle that made a stir at Ranelagh and was copied by all the young bloods, were the flimsiest alternatives to idleness enforced. Even Fox could offer him little more than sympathy. The Prince of Wales must take no part in politics until he should attain the age of twenty-one, when, as Duke of Cornwall, he would sit in the House of Lords. That was two years yet to go.

In a vain attempt to find some occupation he entreated his father to grant him an active commission in the Army, other than his honorary rank of Colonel of the 10th Light Dragoons,–an appeal that was peremptorily refused. And now, turned in upon himself, more than ever did he seek the company of Fox.

He dined with him, wined with him, played cards with him, and through him met two valued new acquaintances.

He, who has been perpetually reviled for his low associates chose, while still in his teens, a triumvirate of intellect unequalled in his or any other age. From Fox he took his politics; from Sheridan that rapier-edge of Celtic satire upon which he sharpened his wits; and from Burke, another Irishman, his ironical philosophy. But it was to Fox he turned when Perdita, from whom he had heard no word since her dismissal, demanded the premature repayment of her bond, or, as alternative, the publication of his letters.

Twenty thousand pounds! . . . He had not that sum in pence, for he still lived on the niggardly allowance doled out by his father, and which would not be augmented until he reached the age of twenty-one.

How he must have groaned to Fox and cursed himself for that infatuated promise. And those letters! To what other follies had he been committed? If he refused to pay, would she flourish his besotted ravings in the face of a judge and jury to be read in open Court? Would he be pilloried before the whole of London–a target for every mud-slinger? His uncle Cumberland had been given a taste of that; but Cumberland was not the Heir Apparent, nor had a few more splashes of dirt affected his bedraggled name. And even if this last extreme might somehow be avoided, what if the King should come to hear of it?

The King did come to hear of it, and wrote to Lord North:

. . . 'My eldest son, got last year into a very improper association with an Actress, a woman of indifferent character. Through the *friendly* assistance of Lord Malden, a multitude of letters passed which she has threatened to publish unless He, in short, bought them of Her; He has made her very foolish promises. . . . I have thought it right to authorize . . . Lieutenant Colonel Hotham on whose discretion I could depend, to get these letters on her receiving £5000, undoubtedly an enormous sum, but I wish to get my son out of this shameful scrape. . . . I am happy at being able to say that I never was personally engaged in such a transaction, which perhaps make me feel this the stronger. . . .'

But not so strongly as did Florizel. Looking ahead to his twenty-first birthday, when he hoped to be given something more than a 'bit of an establishment', he may have deemed it wiser to behave himself. He did, for quite a while; and then he was no longer fancy free.

On a Sunday in September, 1783, he paid a visit to his Uncle Cumberland, who, with his Duchess, had recently taken a house in a Sussex fishing-village. Thereafter at the most unconscionable hours – and sometimes at the crack of dawn – he might have been seen bowling gaily along the road from London to the coast. He drove a phaeton drawn by three horses in the fashion of a wagon team, and was attended only by an equerry and one postilion.

The wondering natives clustered in their doorways may or may not have recognized the hatless flushed young gentleman with the wind-tossed wild hair, who clattered so furiously down the narrow crooked street to the shore. And as he strolled there on the pebbled beach with the green downland behind him, the curve of the Channel before, and on his lips the salt tang of spray that was sweeter than the kiss of any girl, he may have dreamed to build him a home here in this very small sun-dazzled place with the long unpronounceable name: Bredhemsdon, Brighthelmstone; Brighton . . . for short.

He had fallen in love with the sea.

CHAPTER TWO

1783–1785

TWENTY-ONE! . . . And release from bondage as his birthday gift. A joyful year for Florizel was 1783; for his father a year of tribulation.

The war with America had dragged to its disastrous end in 1781 with the surrender of Yorktown to George Washington; but not until December, two years later, was the final Treaty signed that severed for all time Britain's most valued colonial possession from the motherland. The King, upheld by his indomitable faith in the Divine right of Sovereignty, accepted his defeat as a test of his endurance. The inscrutable jurisdiction of Almighty God must not be questioned. His own ill-placed judgment, however, was soon to be called to account.

During the crises and confusions that preceded the signing of Peace and the collapse of North's administration, the King had attempted to reset the Parliamentary chequer-board in a series of unfortunate gambits. His pawn Rockingham had fallen in two moves. The second Rockingham Ministry, terminated by the sudden death of the Premier, brought Shelbourne into office for eight months. North, who meantime had been held back in an indeterminate position, moved up to call check to the King in a coalition with–of all men in the Government–Fox!

Omnipotence was shattered. North! His 'good Lord', his cherished adviser, his most intimate counsellor and friend, had gone over to the enemy! Such merciless disintegration of his fond belief in this unfailing prop completely crushed him. He would abdicate. Let his son sit in his place and hasten his country's downfall and his father's end. Let him die –or return to the Hanover of his forbears. 'This sorrow', he wailed, 'will prove fatal to my health.'

His anguish, relieved by tears, a never-failing refuge of the Hanoverians, wept itself out at last. Courage, or his native obstinacy, rose to the bitter occasion. Though galled to the marrow he was bound to acknowledge the Fox-North Coalition; yet onlookers observed that His Majesty 'laid his ears back like a horse at Astley's', when Fox approached to kiss the Royal hand. Then, while the King rallied his forces to attack, he was bothered again by his reprobate son on whose behalf the loathly Fox was pressing him, through the glib persuasions of the Duke of Portland, to grant the Prince of Wales an allowance of £100,000 a year. A hundred. . . . *What!* Was this to be believed? Had his ministers run mad or was he? And these debts—the Prince's debts? Thirty-nine thousand pounds owed to tradesmen, for wine—that headed the list—jewellers, tailors, hosiers—there appeared to be no end to this wasting of money on drink, for the worst part, and women. Merciful Powers! He 'wished he were eighty or ninety or dead!'

In the end it was agreed that the Prince's debts would be paid, and that he should receive a yearly allowance of £50,000 which, with his £12,000 a year from the Duchy of Cornwall, would bring his income up to £62,000—and quite enough, too.

But not enough for Florizel, who, in addition to these Royal concessions, now demanded his own residence. After further parley the King agreed to give him that 'derelict barn' uninhabited since the death, eleven years before, of the Dowager Princess of Wales.

Carlton House.

Derelict it was indeed. Built for Lord Carlton in 1709 it stood where Waterloo Place now is, on the site of the United Services and Athenaeum Clubs. The grounds, laid out after the style of Pope's garden at Twickenham, extended along the Mall to Marlborough House, and enclosed within their walls a fountain, a marble-paved temple decorated with indifferent frescoes, several fine elms and a few mouldering statues. But the Prince, who recognized its possibilities, moved in so soon as the King had notified Parliament of his intention to make 'an immediate and separate establishment for his beloved son'.

The King's 'beloved son' was running no risk of a parental change of mind. Carlton House had been promised him and Carlton House he would have, rat-infested, mildewed, damp and awful though it was. Once installed there he could make his alterations. He chose Henry Holland as his architect, and Gaubert, a Frenchman—formerly a cook—to redecorate the interior. Plans were submitted, discarded, accepted. The Prince would have this or he wouldn't have that. The entrance hall and staircase did not need much alteration, but the ceilings of his apartments on the ground floor must be raised, the walls panelled, repainted, regilded.

Improvements went apace. All through that autumn, when he was not tearing off in his phaeton to Sussex, he was striding about his domain interviewing mercers, buying brocades, velvets, satin, plush, selecting *objets de virtus*, porcelain, pictures. He would have a drawing-room hung with yellow silk—*Chinese* yellow—and furnished in the Chinese fashion;

the first inception, surely, of his later craze for Chinoiserie. His dining-room must be walled with silver and supported by columns of red and yellow granite; his hall with pillars of porphyry. There must be niches to hold busts, statues, griffins, urns; and his bed-chamber must have a bow window with a communicating dressing-room and bath. He *must* have a bath-room. . . . Amazing innovation! Nor was his domestic staff forgotten. Under his grandmother's régime their quarters had been dingy and horrible. New kitchens must be built, a scullery, pantry, servants' hall and maids' rooms in which they could live and not suffocate or shiver.

For the next two years the walls of Carlton House resounded to the ringing of hammers, the scraping of chisels, the tramp of hobnailed boots, and the Prince's voice with its engaging, slightly hesitant drawl, endlessly ordering this or that and cancelling that or the other. Then the exterior must be altered and a Corinthian portico and a row of Ionic pillars added to the frontage that overlooked Pall Mall.

These classic ornaments, which occasioned much ridicule in Clubland, were removed on the accession of George IV, and now support the entrance to the National Gallery. But not all the *ton* scoffed at the Prince's extravagant tastes, nor at his decorations. When, in 1785, Horace Walpole paid his first visit to Carlton House–'it will be', so the epicure of Strawberry Hill wrote to Lady Ossery, 'the most perfect in Europe . . . I expected a more tawdry assemblage of fantastic vagaries. . . . I beg his pardon. In all the fairy tales you have been in you never was in so pretty a scene. . . . How sick we shall be after this chaste palace of Mr. Adam's gingerbread and snippets. . . .'

His home-building activities occupied every moment of the Prince's time and energy until, in November 1783, he took his seat in the House of Lords.

He was tremendously dressed for the occasion.

Disdaining the insignia of scarlet and ermine, he chose instead black velvet lavishly embroidered in gold, lined with pink satin and strewn with pink spangles. His shoes had high pink heels to match; and to complete the astonishing picture, his hair, very much frizzed at the sides, was ornamented with two coquettish little curls.

The dazzled Lords could scarcely take their eyes off him.

Having made his sensational entrance he was duly sworn in; then, as soon as he could get away, he rushed off to the House of Commons to hear the speech of his 'dear Charles'. The House at this time was in continuous debate. The King who, as Tory Master of the Whig hounds, had been avidly awaiting his chance to run 'that Fox' and his cubs to a kill, saw a clear field before him when Fox introduced his East India Bill.

This, which proposed to place the affairs of the Company in the hands of certain directors to be appointed by Parliament, and—offensive afterthought, or so Majesty took it to be—without the sanction of the Crown, was presented in November. Forcefully opposed by young William Pitt and vigorously supported by Burke, the Bill was passed through the Commons and thrown out by the Lords.

The King had his moment of triumph.

True, there were opprobrious murmurs from those who believed the defeat of the Bill in the Upper House had been obtained by a trick on His Majesty's part. Damning evidence had been produced by Lord Temple—late Lord Lieutenant of Ireland—to the effect that any peer found voting for the Government would forfeit the friendship of the King. But he who had led his son by the nose, did not scruple to tie a noose around the neck of any other who defied him.

Those few who might have defied him considered the threat and decided to withdraw half-promises made, and vote against the Bill in exchange for Royal favour. The Prince of Wales refused to vote at all.

It was clear after this kingly coercion that both the Bill and the Government had received their death-blows. 'We are not out yet,' Fox dolefully recorded, 'but we shall be by to-morrow.'

They were out before 'to-morrow'.

The King sent his orders to Fox and North that they must surrender their Seals of Office at midnight. Fox delivered his on the instant. North had to be dragged from his sleep, and told the King's Messenger who stood at his bedroom door—while his lordship, in his shift, searched for the Seal—to 'come in and see Lady North too'.

The next day the frail boy, whose parliamentary genius has, in near upon two centuries, only once been equalled and never yet surpassed, kissed hands as Prime Minister of England at the age of twenty-four.

*   *   *

During the few months that succeeded Fox's ignominious defeat, the victory in the battle of wits between two powerful rivals went to the younger. Courageously sure of himself, Pitt demanded of the King a dissolution.

Overjoyed was beaming Majesty to grant his 'good Mr. Pitt' that request. He had implicit faith in the wisdom of this sober, dignified, elderly young man, so aged in spirit, so youthful in bearing. Royal assent was speedily followed by a General Election—the most bitter Party feud ever fought. Fox, again candidate for Westminster, was daringly championed by the Prince of Wales. He drove through the streets wearing

Fox's colours in his hat; he turned Carlton House into Committee rooms for the Whigs. Short of canvassing votes there was nothing he would not have done for his 'dear Charles'—if for no other reason than to infuriate his father.

Georgiana, Duchess of Devonshire, and other lovely ladies who had fallen victim to the charmful persuasions of Charles, enlisted themselves as his eager disciples. With his emblem, a fox's brush, in their caps, and his colours, buff and blue, floating in scarves from their shoulders, they combed every street, every alley, every house in the borough, begging votes.

The Duchess scored the most. Strikingly habited in scarlet, a cap of fox fur on her red-gold curls and her hands in a muff of the same, she worked all day and every day buying votes from householders and shopkeepers with the promise of a kiss. Fox's victory was certain from the moment the exquisite Georgiana set her dainty foot in 'the most blackguard houses of Long Acre'.

Undaunted by the stench and refuse in the gutters, unabashed by the gaping crowds that followed her, the Duchess won a vote on every doorstep. A butcher, a blacksmith, any man of them who wavered, was offered the same irresistible bribe. But although the majority of 236 with which Fox had been returned can scarcely have justified the bounty of the Duchess, it caused enormous excitement among his supporters. The 'Man of the People'—self-styled—was the centre of a triumphal procession led by a drum and fife band. Carried through the shouting streets in a laurel-decked chair, he had for his escort the Duchesses of Devonshire and Portland driving beside him in their coaches, waving banners, flinging flowers, cheering him merrily on.

Before him rode a cavalcade of military gentlemen in uniforms of buff and blue; behind him stormed a raggle-taggle mob. Heads popped from every window. The ladies were hysterical; his reception was terrific. So, flushed with wine and victory, the successful candidate came to Devonshire House, where he was received by the Prince of Wales who stood on the top of the wall and yelled himself hoarse at the sight of him.

The next day a garden fête was held at Carlton House in celebration. Festivities began at noon and went on until six in the evening, with four bands all playing at once, nine marquees, much rioting, revelry, dancing, and drink.

It must have been a breath-taking spectacle—that brilliant fragmentary pattern of gold and scarlet, buff and blue, its sun-pointed sparkle of jewels; the glitter of a diamond knee-buckle, the satin lustre of swinging hoop or quilted petticoat, the frills of cobweb lace edging the gentle hare's foot blush of cheeks, rose-tinted under the wide befeathered hats.

Gracefully poised with an eye to effect, in lively contrast to the grey of mouldered statuary, shrub green, or moss-grown baluster, the Prince, in his gala suit of 'pearl-coloured silk, embroidered with silver, pearl and foil', received his guests. The most gallant of hosts, he drank to the ladies, cracked jokes with the men, laughed more loudly than any at his own, sang glees, and whispered in the ear of his 'ever dearest Duchess', Georgiana, the words he had penned to her the night before: 'I consider this to be one of the luckiest days I have spent for ages!'

He might not have thought it quite so lucky had he known that the King, driving in his coach along the Mall to open Parliament, could hear the braying of those bands, and the songs and the cheers, could see the waving of pennons from those nine marquees, and guessed in whose honour they were flying.

That same night the Prince, with Charles and a few intimate friends, drove to the house of Mrs. Crewe, one of Fox's most ardent admirers. All the company wore buff and blue for Fox. The feasting went on until daybreak. By this time the Prince had reached that stage of convivial well-being when laughter flows more readily than words. Raising his glass he carefully pronounced his famous toast: 'True Blue–and–Mrs. Crewe!' To which the lady, no less carefully, replied: 'True Blue–and all of you!' Then the party broke up and the Prince went home. . . . It had all been immensely amusing.

That August the birthday of the Prince of Wales was for the first time ignored by his parents. He failed to understand why. . . .

Nor did he very much care. He had cast off the shackles; life was gloriously free. The days stretched before him in a multi-coloured pageant brushed with magic. The hilarious racketings at Carlton House, the festive board, the wit that flashed around it, the foibles and follies of its youthful host, set the whole Town talking. While the Prince's loyalty to his 'dear Charles', his charming 'Sherry', and his rip-roaring philosophic Mr. Burke remained unshaken, he picked from the Clubs of St. James's an exuberant collection of new friends. In addition to these most favoured of the Prince's boon companions was a certain Major Hanger, an eccentric dude given to practical joking; and that notorious couple, Sir John Lade and Laetitia, his hard-riding, hard-swearing good lady. Born in St. Giles's, she had been, before her marriage, the mistress of Jack Rann, the highwayman, who ended a rollicking career on Tyburn gallows.

Reports of the jinks and jollifications in which this distinguished company indulged, were not kept from the ear of the King. He fumed, and he cried, and he blustered. . . . What! A wager? A ten-mile race between turkey and geese, waddling twenty aside along the King's highway to Brighthelmstone? . . . Prodded on by the Prince who carried a–*what*? A pole with a piece of red cloth attached! . . . *Five hundred guineas* lost by the Prince, and his house full of prostitutes and drunkards! . . . The King fretted and fussed himself sick. 'The bile', he told his brother Henry, 'fell upon his breast.' He passed another ten nights without sleep and was 'unusually pensive, a prey to habitual dejection'.

He sought refuge from his worries at his harpsichord, in hymns, in prayer, in his hounds, in his farms, in the preparations of his 'Annals of Agriculture'. But the strain that his harassed Majesty had suffered, resultant on the antics of his son, was as naught to the horror yet in store for him.

'Oh, but the hubbub you are to hear and to talk of, and except which you are to hear and talk of nothing else!' . . .

The giggling Mr. Walpole found it vastly entertaining; and the ballad-mongers put it into song.

> 'I'd crowns resign
> To call thee mine,
> Sweet lass of Richmond Hill.'

★ ★ ★

Not all of Britain's victories, nor that recent mutilation on the other side of the Atlantic which had split the English speaking race in two; no inglorious scandal of turkeys and geese had aroused such stirring interest as that which focused now upon Maria Anne Fitzherbert.

Twice widowed, and certainly no 'Lass' at twenty-eight, she arrested the Prince's tempestuous youth at the height of its springtime fever. No passing fancy this, no 'shameful scrape', but a deep-hearted burning, that even when consumed left its ashes in his life and its scar upon his spirit, still unhealed.

How or where these two first met is buried in obscurity. Some insist that he saw her in a box with Lady Sefton at the Opera, and was so struck by her beauty that he followed her home. Or tradition may have twisted fact to lend romantic flavour to a meeting on the river-bank, near her house at Richmond. That neither recognized the other is unlikely. If he did not know who the lovely lady was, she surely must have guessed at the identity of the tall, slightly florid, slightly plump young gentleman who paused–then bowed with such exaggerated grace. How should she not have known him? Even on a country walk he could never be mistaken

47

for any other than Prince Charming, with the Star on his chest and his waist pulled in, his hair puffed out beneath the curving hat-brim. His face may have carried a patch or two, one under his eye and one near his mouth to accentuate a dimple; and he was almost certainly powdered. He loathed his high colour; he longed to be pale. Talk gave it that his surgeon, at his order, plastered him from time to time with leeches to obtain the much desired languishing effect.

As for her, she paid no compliment to fashion. She wore her magnificent hair in powderless honey-gold curls; her cheeks were unrouged; and *she* was deliciously pale, her eyes the darker, the more lustrous for the contrast. Her nose, to be sure, was a trifle too long, her bust just a trifle too large; yet these trivial defects served only to enhance her Junoesque stature. No simpering rose and white Miss was she, but a reposeful goddess, firmly modelled. Divine, disturbing creature!

The Prince swore he fell in love with his Fitzherbert at first sight; but he had fallen in love with so many at first sight. The difference between those others and the handsome widow doubtless was her worldly-wise sophistication. She knew precisely how to keep this amorous young buck at bay, believing, possibly hoping, that his passion would burn itself out. She had not, at that time, come to know or reckon with a nature in which quickened sense and incontinent desire conjoin to seize and savour every fluctuating, strangely new experience. Her worldly wisdom encompassed only the security of life in so far as rank and wealth provide it, and probed no deeper than the outer skin of this violent adorer who so madly offered her his heart, himself, his future–he was mad enough for that, too–if she would ease his torment.

The posturing, the patches, the love of dress, display, the mannered grace, the subtle connoisseurship, all this she could perceive and may have weighed it–with a balance to the favour of his unchallengeable heritage –on the scales of Propriety. She must care for her position, her family name. It was Smythe; possibly a derivation from a less distinguished form of spelling, when, under Charles II, her ancestral grandfather had become a baronet. Above all must she care for her Faith.

A widow and a Papist!

Hands and eyes were raised by every matron in the land, and by every maid who hoped to be a wife . . . the Prince's wife! That could never be; the Royal Marriage Act had laid a stern taboo on his union with any save a Princess of the Blood; but would a woman be so idiotic, or so tied to her religion as to refuse what the Prince was asking? And only God and Mrs. Fitzherbert knew what the Prince was asking. There were, however, quite a few who guessed.

One night, at a dinner party given by Lord Lewisham, the Prince, who had drunk even deeper than his wont, sank into melancholic reverie. When, after a while, he came to himself he began excitedly to rage against his most unhappy lot which appointed him heir to a kingdom. 'If I had been born a Duke, as Rutland here'– he turned to him–'or Devonshire there', he gestured, 'I could have been free as were they to marry the most beautiful, most wonderful of women.'

As for himself, he supposed he would be mated to and couched with some 'ugly German frau'. Could any prospect be more frightful? Then he called across the table to the Master of the Ceremonies: 'Rigby! What would *you* advise me to do?'

'Faith, Sir,' Rigby bowed, and guarding a hiccup, replied: 'I am drunk, but not drunk enough to give advice on the marriage of the Prince of Wales.'

Yet if Rigby refused his advice, there were others more ready to offer it. By this time the Prince had made known his intention to anyone who cared to listen. We can believe them argumentative and practical. Since marriage with Mrs. Fitzherbert was out of the question, the Prince must induce the lady to waive her prudish principles – and to surrender.

These advances from the lovesick Prince's emissaries, were received with indignation. Mrs. Fitzherbert made it clearly understood that she was not disposed to enter into any clandestine relationship with this impetuous young hothead, who wore his heart so blatantly on his brocaded sleeve. She would not–no, she would *not* forfeit her good name! And, she may have inly added, her two thousand a year left her by her second husband and likely to be swallowed by Prince Charming for his debts, if he could get near enough to lay his hands on her and on her income. . . . No, and no again!

Such determined opposition served not to cool but to inflame him. He was on his knees to her, and he was devastated. . . . His fervent protestations passed beyond the boundaries of reason, duty, sense. Vainly did she pray him to consider his exalted rank and her unblemished reputation. Would he slur it? Both her husbands, Edward Weld of Lulworth, her first, and Thomas Fitzherbert of Swynnerton, her second, had been men of high integrity. Must their names and hers be dragged through the mud for his pleasure?

She drove him crazy.

His friends again appealed. . . . Would she not consider her refusal? They greatly feared his frantic love had rendered him unbalanced. Far from their intention was it to connive at any morganatic form of marriage, but . . .

At these tentative suggestions she professed herself outraged. Not on her life would she countenance the semblance of a marriage without the sanction of her Church. To save herself from such disgrace she was prepared to leave the country. His Royal Highness must be told of her decision.

He was told.

Was it true? . . . He besought them all to tell him, *was it true*? She could never be so heartless. But if she went, he swore that he would follow her, forgo his future Crown, and hand his right in the Succession to Frederick.

Things were at a pretty pass at Carlton House when his advisers hit upon a scheme whereby they hoped to save the Prince from irrevocable folly, and overcome the scruples of the lady.

Accordingly, on a morning in November 1784, while Mrs. Fitzherbert was hurriedly packing her bags, four gentlemen alighted from a coach at the door of her Park Street house.

Summoned from her bedroom by an urgent message from the Prince, she hastened down to find Lords Onslow and Southampton, Mr. Edward Bouverie,[1] and the Prince's surgeon, Mr. Keate, standing in her parlour.

'The life of His Royal Highness', they nervously informed her—'was in danger. Goaded by her cruelty, he had stabbed himself. Only the immediate presence of Mrs. Fitzherbert could save him. He was dying. . . . He would die if she refused to go to him. This minute. Not a moment to be lost. . . .'

Unimpressed by this stammering recital, she turned to the silent Mr. Keate for confirmation. Was his Royal Highness's condition really serious?

The surgeon's guarded assurance that the Prince's state was critical, alarmed her; yet, even so, she must consider the proprieties. It would not be circumspect for her to visit the Prince attended only by four gentlemen. She insisted that a Lady of High Character go with her.

To find 'a Lady of High Character' in the vicinity of St. James's, and at such short notice, was a poser. Certain names were suggested and loftily disdained. . . . Mrs. Armistead? *That* person! To be known as the friend of Mr. Fox was enough to damn her in the eyes of the virtuous Fitzherbert. . . . Lady Sefton? Her own kinswoman. Certainly. But Lady Sefton was from town. Finally it was decided to call on the Duchess of Devonshire.

Georgiana professed herself delighted to act the part of chaperone in so intriguing an adventure. Thus properly escorted, and her social conscience salved, Mrs. Fitzherbert came to Carlton House.

[1] Second son of Viscount Folkestone, and later M.P. for Northampton.

All doubt of the Prince or his injury, was promptly dispelled when she saw him. He presented a piteous spectacle. He lay where they had found him on the floor of his bedchamber in a pool of blood and deathly pale. His suit was splashed with crimson; his eyes were rolled up and his jaw was dropped down, his pulse and breathing rapid, his plight indeed so parlous that she all but swooned away.

Lords Onslow and Southampton each supplied in turn a cause for his woefully moribund state. The Prince had fallen on his sword with intent to kill himself–he had vowed he would not live if she persisted in her merciless denial. In short, she had driven him to attempted suicide, that but for the grace of God. . . . And so on.

Southampton inclined in favour of a pistol shot. The Prince, fortified with brandy, a tumbler of which stood on a table near him, had turned the weapon to his temple, but luckily the bullet hit the bedpost.

Had the surgeon been asked he could perhaps have offered another explanation–that he had been called upon to bleed His Royal Highness, who had grabbed the cup, smeared himself with its gory contents, cut a hole in his coat, filled it with blood, and then sent for his lady to view the *mise en scène*

She viewed it aghast. She was stupefied; appalled. Yet, even as she knelt to support his dying head, he braced himself to tell her at his, seemingly, last gasp, that 'nothing on earth– would induce him to live–unless she would promise to be his wife– and allow him to put the ring–round her finger'. Let somebody give him a ring. Who had a ring? A betrothal ring? . . . Mrs. Fitzherbert had two, but it would scarcely have been tactful to have said so. The Duchess of Devonshire obligingly offered her own ring, which the tottering, blood-stained Prince 'put round' the finger of Mrs. Fitzherbert, and called all present to witness that this plighting of their troth proclaimed her indisputably his wife-to-be.

A deposition was then drawn up and signed by every member of the party; and after the trembling lady had been wildly embraced by her future 'husband', he permitted her to leave him and go home.

Later, when recovered from her fright, she disgustedly perceived she had been hoaxed–committed to a ceremony that could lay no more claim to a marriage than a pantomime; for which she blamed–not the Prince, who had sought death sooner than life without her. She blamed her own hard-heartedness and her misjudgment of his deep, his true affection. Had he not often threatened to kill himself if she refused him? But more than all did she blame the four 'gentlemen' who had plotted this vile conspiracy.

She had been most abominably used.

That same evening she wrote a letter to Southampton, flaying him and his associates for their connivance in the whole disgraceful business. She protested that she had been taken by surprise, and, in view of the Prince's supposedly serious condition, had been forced against her will to comply with his demand which she now repudiated.

Then she sealed and sent her letter and returned to her interrupted packing. She had made her decision.

She must go.

She went—where she knew that the heir to the Throne must not follow her—over the sea. At Aix-la-Chapelle she believed herself safe from pursuit.

After some weeks at the Spa she moved on to the Hague. The Stadholder, a grandson of George II, hopeful of an alliance between one of his daughters and the Prince of Wales, received her with overwhelming gush. The young Princess of Orange showed particular favour to Mrs. Fitzherbert. Confidences were exchanged or may have been extracted by the Prince's errant lady. Little did the naive would-be Princess of Wales know that she was pouring her most secret hopes into the sympathetic ear of a rival. At the Hague, an honoured guest of Royalty, welcomed, fêted, flattered, Mrs. Fitzherbert happily installed herself and kept a careful guard upon her tongue: a necessary precaution, since the Stadholder and his eager daughter perpetually plied her with questions concerning the Prince and his Family, of which—with one exception—she knew nothing, though she managed to convey that she knew much. But her sojourn in high places was curtailed by the news that Sir James Harris, recently appointed British Minister to the Hague, was due to arrive. Sir James, valued friend and adviser of King George, must surely have heard of Mrs. Fitzherbert and her share in that crisis at Carlton House. Come what may, Sir James must be avoided.

To the regret, therefore, of the House of Orange, Mrs. Fitzherbert announced her immediate departure. It was necessary for her health to visit Plombier; and by the time Sir James Harris came to the Hague she was bumping across Holland in a diligence. At Plombier she lived in strict retirement. Yet her self-imposed seclusion did not safeguard her from the attentions of a certain Marquis de Bellois, an impecunious and fascinating Frenchman, from whose pursuit she fled to Switzerland and then to Paris. She rested nowhere very long, for since the Prince had heard of her departure he was sending spies across the continent to track her; but still he could not find her. She was lost. . . .

And he was frantic. He 'cried', we are told, 'by the hour'. He went raging round to all his friends that he would follow her, bring her back, and in defiance of his father and every–unmentionable–law, he would marry her. In church: before a priest: or kill himself. There was no holding him. He drove in his phaeton down to Chertsey where Fox lived in blissful sin with Lizzie Armistead, whom he eventually married. Charles was not at home. His 'sweet Liz' received the Prince, and was treated to a frenzied exhibition, which in later years she vividly described to Lord Holland, her father-in-law.

'He [the Prince] testified to the sincerity and violence of his passion and despair by the most extravagant expressions and actions, rolling on the floor, striking his forehead, tearing his hair, falling in hystericks, swearing that he would abandon the country, forego the crown, sell his jewels, scrape together a competence, and fly with the object of his affections to America.'

It is doubtful if the 'object of his affections' would have agreed to fly with him to America or any other place, since she had so effactually flown from him and lay concealed he knew not where.

His next move was to find her, by hook, or by possible crook. To this end, and despite his 'hystericks', he systematically set to work.

Messengers were despatched far and wide, to no avail. He then appealed to that unpleasant friend of his, the Duke of Orleans, who sent him a hint that she might be found in Paris. Having traced her thus far he bombarded her with letters full of heart-rending appeals to pity his plight, to return or else–more threats–have his death upon her conscience.

He did not know himself ridiculous; he only knew himself in love. That his longing for this woman was genuine, profound, is undeniable. As always in his choice of loves she was his senior; but her detached, unpossessive domination bound him closer than all the imperious demands of her successors. Unremarkable for her intelligence, Mrs. Fitzherbert held an intuitive comprehension of the thwarted child that underlay the garish impulse of the man. The graceful Narcissus who loved to deck himself in harlequin array, who cultivated an elegant foppery of words, and whose pagan joy in food and drink was allied to a perceptive sensitivity, remained for her unaltered and unalterable, even when age and corruption had transformed him into a dropsical grotesque. And beneath that bloated mask, long after she had gone her ways, she saw him, as she had ever seen and cherished him; the boy whom she had mothered. So, for her indulgence, her innate and honest kindliness, and for his comfort, did he love and want her. Nor would he be deprived of her, though he flung away all hope of future glory, of a throne, to have just that which she alone could give.

53

Yet she appeared disposed to give him nothing. While day by day, and week by week, his panting couriers went galloping along the French highroads to Switzerland bearing sheaves of love-tormented letters, she maintained an inimical silence. He repeated, undaunted, his efforts. On and on came the couriers, faster and faster. So great was their hurry, so frequent their appearance on the frontier, with their steaming horses no less blown and exhausted than themselves, that three were detained and thrown into prison as suspected enemy agents. Only the intervention of the Duke of Orleans, who managed to convince the authorities that the messages they carried were romantic, not political, saved them from extinction.

Finding that this method of attack had no effect upon his lady's stern resistance, the Prince approached, a trifle tactlessly, his father.

In a carefully worded appeal to the King he announced his intention of giving up his extravagant mode of life and to travel abroad for a while, where he could live within his means.

The reply to this sudden urge for economy was distinctly discouraging and curt. After reminding his son that any such procedure 'would for ever blast his character in this country and in Europe, and that he would in every sense be ruined and lose the protection of his very affectionate Father', the King demanded a list of his debts.

Optimistically believing that his 'very affectionate Father' intended to disburse on his behalf, the Prince and his treasurer between them produced a full account of debts outstanding, with exception of one item for £25,000. Particulars of this the Prince could not–or would not–give, other than that it was 'a debt of honour'.

'Then, if it is a debt that my son is ashamed to explain', came the King's prompt rejoinder, 'it is one which I, his father, must not pay.'

It was evident now that his father had never entertained the remotest intention of paying. Having satisfied himself that the Prince had frittered away a colossal income in two years on women, drink, orgies, jewels, clothes, and those fantastic furnishings at Carlton House, the King retained the list for four months and returned it to his son without a word.

Enraged at the trick by which he had been induced to render his accounts only to have them thrown back into his face, the Prince declared 'he would reveal State secrets, for suffering as he did from the treatment he had received at his Father's hands, he was an object of suspicion and contempt to half the kingdom'.

But threats were not enough. He would now take action, make a bolt for it to Switzerland, Holland, France–wherever Fitzherbert had rested, there would he go.

To Sir James Harris, who happened at that time to be in London, he sent an urgent message to wait on him at Carlton House. Thither Sir James apprehensively repaired, and was startled to hear of the Prince's intention to visit the Hague. Would Harris be willing to present him as 'Lord Chester'?

Sir James was in a quandary. Well aware why the Prince intended to visit the Hague, although the name of Fitzherbert had not once been mentioned during the discussion, he played for time and temporized. 'Sir . . . your coming abroad without the King's consent implies that you will come after it has been refused you?'[1]

'Certainly.' The Prince, restlessly pacing the room, halted in his stride and faced the seated minister. 'Can't I travel legally *without* the King's consent? . . . I am ruined,' he dramatically declared, 'if I stay in England! . . .'

Sir James soothingly protested. Debonair, kindly, a trifle conscious of his exceptional good looks, he who had found favour with half the crowned heads of Europe and had effectually negotiated a delicate mission at the Court of the Empress Catherine at St. Petersburg, believed himself well qualified to deal with this impossible young man.

'Give me leave to say, Sir, you will find no relief in travelling the way you propose. You will either be slighted,'–the Prince glared–'or what is worse, become the object of political intrigue in every country you pass through. The title of Earl of Chester will be only a mask to cover the Prince of Wales.'

'You think I mean to go to France?' That was sailing fairly near the wind. The wily Harris had, however, come prepared for squalls.

'What I say applies to all countries, Sir.'

'But what am I to *do*? The King hates me. He won't even let Parliament assist me till I marry.'

'Surely, Sir, the King could not object to any increase of your income Parliament thought proper to allow you?'

'I believe he would. I tell you', the Prince vociferated, 'that he *hates* me. He has always hated me, from seven years old. The King has deceived me and made me deceive others. . . . I can't trust him.'

'Sir!' Harris exhibited shock. 'His Majesty may be displeased and dissatisfied with Your Royal Highness, but surely he cannot hate you . . . I am convinced nothing would make both him and the Queen so happy as to restore their affections to you; and I think Your Royal Highness should try every possible means before you carry into execution your plan of travelling. . . .'

[1] Diary and Correspondence of Sir James Harris, first Earl of Malmesbury.

This was all very well, but the Prince realized he had gained no more comfort from Sir James than oiled words. He terminated the interview with the frigid assurance that he would 'think it over'.

He thought it over for a month; then Harris was recalled and received by the Prince in his dressing-room and dressing-gown. His greeting was suspiciously effusive.

'If you are come, my dear Harris,[1] to dissuade me again from travelling, let me anticipate your kind intention by telling you I have given up the idea.'

Sir James received this intelligence with 'infinite satisfaction'—which he expressed at some length, and was interrupted.

'I am glad', said the Prince, 'to have pleased you at least, if I have not pleased myself.' But it was clear he had more in his mind than to pleasure Sir James, who in his turn 'anticipated', and then craftily produced his plan of action.

'If Your Royal Highness will give me leave I will propose to Mr. Pitt to increase your revenue to a hundred thousand a year'—the Prince visibly brightened—'on two conditions,' the suave Sir James added to sink him, 'the one that you will set aside fifty thousand of it to pay your debts, the other that you will cease to be a man of party and reconcile yourself to the King. I would have mentioned a third, Sir, but by declaring to me that you have given up all idea of leaving the Kingdom, Your Royal Highness has already subscribed to it.'

Fitzherbert! She, obviously, was the third condition. Not only would he be held a prisoner here in England, but must never set eyes on her again. . . . If so, to hell with James Harris and all the King's men, is what the Prince may have thought. What he said, cautiously, was: 'Your goodwill towards me deceives you. Pitt would not carry such a proposal to the King, nor would the King hear of it.'

'That, Sir,' returned the bland Sir James, 'is what I mean to try.'

'I thank you, but it won't do! I tell you the King hates me. He would turn Pitt out for entertaining such an idea. Besides I can't abandon Charles and my friends.'

'Mr. Fox and the Duke of Portland, Sir,' prevaricated Harris, 'have told me often that they by no means wish Your Royal Highness to condescend, on their account, to take any share in party concerns.'

'Well—admitting this'— his tone implied that he admitted nothing—'and supposing I can get rid of a partiality in politics, which you seem to condemn, I tell you the King will never listen to it.'

'Sir, I presuppose a reconciliation between you and His Majesty.'

[1] Diary and Correspondence of Sir James Harris, First Earl of Malmesbury.

'My dear Harris,' the Prince, with rising spleen, demanded, 'why will you force me to repeat that the King *hates* me! He will never be reconciled to me. If you don't believe me—take and read all his correspondence for the last six months.' Saying that, he went over to his writing desk, rummaged in a drawer, and produced a bundle of letters which he read aloud. Those of the Prince, Harris describes as 'full of respect and deference'; those of the King, 'harsh and severe, devoid of every expression of parental kindness'. It was evident that the breach between father and son had widened to a chasm. Seeing no hope of a peaceable adjustment, Harris steered a middle course.

'Sir, I am hurt to a degree at what I have heard, but surely the Queen must have your reconciliation so much at heart that through her and your sisters it might be effected?'

The Queen and his sisters, suggested the Prince, had nothing to do with the case . . .'Look ye, Harris! I cannot bring myself to say I am in the wrong when I am in the right. The King has used me ill, and I only wish the public knew what you know now, and would pronounce between us.'

'I should be very sorry indeed, Sir,' replied Harris with unease, 'if this were known beyond these walls . . .' He then committed a tactical blunder by assuring the Prince of his desire 'to relieve Your Royal Highness from a state of distress—I might say of discredit—and place you in one of affluence and comfort. May I suggest, Sir, the idea of your marrying?'

But this effort to make him see reason served only to make him see red.

'I will never marry! I have settled it all with Frederick. I *never* will marry.'

'Give me leave to say, Sir, most respectfully', urged Harris, 'that you cannot have come to such a resolution. You *must* marry, Sir. You owe it to your country. To your King. To yourself.'

'I owe nothing to the King! Frederick will marry and the Crown will descend to his children; and as for myself I don't see how it affects *me*.'

Harris, losing patience, and no longer 'most respectfully', proceeded to explain just how it would affect him. 'If you come to the throne a bachelor, and His Royal Highness, the Duke of York, is married and has sons to succeed you, your situation when King will be even more painful than it is now. Our own history furnishes strong examples of . . .'

His voice ran down in an affronted silence. The Prince, hugging his dressing-gown about him was striding furiously about the room. Harris, sensing thunder, sidled to the door.

'I perceive, Sir, I have said too much . . . I am sure I will be forgiven an hour hence.'

'My dear Harris',—the bowing Minister was treated to a glimpse of that celebrated charm—'you are forgiven now. I am angry with myself, not with you. . . . *Don't* question me any more. God bless you!'

Yet, long after Harris had left him, the Prince stayed there, sunk in gloom. No freedom, no redress while his father lived. . . . And then? Was Kingship but another form of slavery, or Almighty power, wielded, held? He could not know, could only dream of what might never be.

He drove down again to that Sussex coastal town and gazed longingly out at the sea. Only a strip of water a few miles wide, severed him from all that made life bearable. . . . Harris had told him he must marry. Well then, so *would* he marry—not some awful 'German Frau', but a wife of his own choosing. And since he must not go to her, let her come back to him!

Those extravagant messages carried full gallop over the poplar-lined roads of France, had avoided, hitherto, any promise, in writing, of marriage. Now the tone of his letters was altered. Henceforth he pledged himself solemnly to offer Mrs. Fitzherbert no burlesque of a ceremony as had been performed at Carlton House, but a union in its most complete sanctified sense.

She was melted; and, for the first time, returned an answer: 'If she did not marry him she would marry no other.'

She must have known that by such admission she was sealed, hand-fasted; his. Yet, still her Faith remained the one chief obstacle. By marrying her he risked the forfeiture of his Succession. A secret marriage, therefore, was the only possible solution. If her Church agreed to recognize her as his wife, then no longer could she justifiably resist. Nor could she have failed to realize the enormous advantage her resistance had, thus far, secured her. Marriage with the Heir Apparent though it must stay for ever clandestine, ignored, offered a prospect unique in its immensity. She, who held the Prince in the palm of her hand, might rise to unimaginable heights—behind the Throne!

So any woman placed in her position might have reasoned. Mrs. Fitzherbert, however, was less concerned with superlative issues resultant on the violent infatuation of a Prince, than with her honour. She was essentially a wife—and she was nearing thirty. In those days when girls married at fifteen, she could no longer be regarded as a—child. Also her enforced exile had become a bane. To be pursued by needy foreigners in every town and capital she visited; to live in a state of upheaval, packing and re-packing, jogging back and forth across the Alps in hired diligences, was no life for a lady of refinement. And she was very much a lady of refinement. A later age might have described her as 'genteel'. She longed for her peaceable well-ordered home; that she might be called upon to share her home with an irresponsible young lover was not included in her calculations. He had his own home, and the rumour had reached her that he was in process of taking or building another in some obscure coastal resort in Sussex. Well and good. He might if he wished build half-a-dozen homes, but she would not live with him in any one of them—unless her married state be publicly acknowledged. On that point was she determined.

Having come to this final resolution, Mrs. Fitzherbert posted from Paris to Calais, and boarded the packet for Dover.

*   *   *

She returned to her house in Park Street in the first week of December. The Prince, who had been told of her arrival—some said he had met her at Dover—showed significant signs of unrest. Those of his Household accustomed to his variable moods that changed in an instant from tears to loud laughter, were not prepared to find him secretive and sullen, sitting idle; or he would suddenly rush to his escritoire and write innumerable letters, poems—Heaven knew what—then would tear them up and send for Major Hanger, or 'Sherry', never Charles, and talk with them in close conclave for hours; very odd. Still more odd was it that he went to bed sober every night, attended no functions or balls, and seemed to shun society. When word filtered through that Mrs. Fitzherbert had come back to London, all Clubland was agog to know what next. Her homecoming might account for the Prince's repressed excitement and the long conferences with those few admitted to his presence. But why had he not called upon the lady at her house? Or perhaps he had.

The bloods of St. James's laid bets: five thousand to one the Prince would marry 'the Fitz.' He wouldn't. He couldn't . . . or could he? And was it true that His Royal Highness had split with Charles Fox because of pretty Mrs. Armistead, in whom the Prince confided all his troubles—and his hopes? Or did he avoid Charles for some *other* reason?

Only Fox could have answered that, which he was not disposed to do. But to the Prince he wrote:

'December 10, 1785.

Sir,

I hope that Your Royal Highness does me the justice to believe that it is with the utmost reluctance that I trouble you with my opinion, unasked at any time, much more so upon a subject where it may not be agreeable to your wishes.

I was told before I left town yesterday that Mrs. Fitzherbert was

59

arrived, and if I had heard only this I should have felt most unfeigned joy at an event which I knew would contribute so much to Your Royal Highness's satisfaction; but I was told at the same time that from a variety of circumstances, there was reason to suppose you were going to take the very desperate step (pardon the expression) of marrying her at this moment . . . If such an idea be really in your mind for God's sake let me call your attention to some considerations which my attachment to Your Royal Highness have suggested to me. . . .

In the first place you are aware that a marriage with a Catholic throws the Prince contracting such a marriage out of the succession to the Crown . . . The King not feeling to you as a father ought, the Duke of York professedly his favourite, and likely to be married to the King's wishes, and the nation full of its old prejudices against the Catholics . . . In all these circumstances your enemies might take advantage of any doubt of this nature as I shudder to think of. . . .

If there should be children of the marriage, I will not say how much the uneasiness of the nation must be aggravated . . . for if you should think proper, when you are twenty-five years old, to notify Parliament of your intention to marry (by which means alone a *legal* marriage can be contracted), in what manner can it be notified? If the previous marriage is mentioned or owned, will it not be said that you have set at defiance the laws of your country, and that you now come to Parliament for a sanction for what you have already done in contempt of it?

. . . It will be said that a woman who has lived with you as your wife without being so is not fit to be Queen of England, and thus the very thing that is done for the sake of her reputation will be used against it. . . .

The sum of my humble advice is this, that Your Royal Highness will not think of marrying till you can marry legally. . . . In the meantime a mock marriage (for it can be no other) is neither honourable for any of the parties, nor with respect to Your Royal Highness, even safe. This appears so clear to me that if I were Mrs. Fitzherbert's father or brother, I would advise her to prefer *any other species of connection with you* to one leading to such misery and mischief.'

To this sound reasoning the Prince at once replied.

'CARLTON HOUSE
Sunday morning.
2 *o'clock*
December 11, 1785.

MY DEAR CHARLES,

Your letter of last night afforded me more satisfaction than I can find words to express; as it is an additional proof to me (which I assure you I did not want) of your having that true regard and affection for me which it is not only the wish, but the ambition of my life to merit.

Make yourself easy, my dear friend. Believe me, the world will soon be convinced that there not only is, but never was, any ground for these reports which have of late been so malevolently circulated.

I have not seen you since the apostacy of Eden.[1] I think it ought to have the same effect upon all our friends as it has upon me—I mean the linking of us closer to each other. You will easily believe these to be my sentiments, for you are perfectly well acquainted with my ways of thinking. When I say my ways of thinking, I mean that of swimming or sinking with my friends.

I have not time to add more, except just to say that I believe I shall meet you at dinner at Bushey on Tuesday and to desire you to believe me at all times, my dear Charles,

Most affectionately yours,
George P.'

The omission of the word 'not' in the Prince's letter might have been, as his apologists will have it, a slip of the pen. But his irrelevant allusion to the apostacy of Eden, to which Fox had not once referred, cannot be so easily explained. This artless reply appears, therefore, to be a deliberate attempt to hoodwink Fox. For even while the messenger from Carlton House was on his way to Charles with the Prince's glib denial in his hand, the marriage had already been arranged.

Difficulties, which at first seemed insurmountable, had now been overcome. Since the law of England, at that time, forbade the union of a Roman Catholic with a member of the Established Church, any priest who so defied the law and performed the service was guilty of a felony. Thus, in order to ensure the legality of such a union, it was imperative to find a clergyman of the Church of England who would agree to marry them.

That the ceremony conducted by an Anglican priest between a Roman Catholic and a Protestant should be pronounced valid in the sight of the Catholic Church, and illegal under the statutory laws of England, presents a curious anomaly; for while the Pope sanctioned the marriage, the Church, under whose auspices it was solemnized, denounced it.

The first clergyman to be approached by Colonel Gardiner, the Prince's secretary, was the Reverend Philip Rosenhagen. This gentleman, whose reputation was as doubtful as his origin, ascribed his refusal to perform

[1] William Eden, afterwards Lord Auckland, who seceded from the Whigs to join the Tories.

the ceremony to 'motives of honour and duty'—which might, however, have been waived had he been offered some remuneration for his service.

The next application was made to the Reverend Johannes Knight, Rector of Welwyn in Hertfordshire. A sporting parson he, seen more often in the hunting-field and on the race-course than in the pulpit.

He was dining at Bushey Park with Lord North when a message came from the Prince desiring his immediate company at supper. Suspecting that something more than a desire for his company at supper was indicated by this urgent summons, Mr. Knight at once set out for London.

On his arrival at Carlton House another letter from the Prince, handed him by Edward Bouverie, informed the justly incensed clergyman that the party was 'put off', and that the Prince hoped to see him in the morning.

Mr. Knight, who had been interrupted at his dinner and was hungry, sought a meal at the Mount Coffee-House where he encountered and supped with his friend, Colonel Lake.[1]

In the course of conversation the Colonel gave it he was certain the Prince intended to marry Mrs. Fitzherbert, and significantly added that he 'trusted no clergyman would be found to perform the service'.

To this the Reverend Johannes cordially agreed; and, in a rare taking, walked home to his mother's house where he lay the night.

It was near upon mid-day when he presented himself to the Prince, who, as usual, received him in his dressing-room and dressing-gown and looked to have just got out of bed. After gracefully apologizing for having brought his 'dear Mr. Knight' all the way from Bushey and sending him off without supper, he spoke of his passion for Mrs. Fitzherbert and of all the taunts and miseries he had endured from the King. He then drew up his shirt and exhibited a scar upon his body, which he persuaded Mr. Knight to believe had been caused by falling on his sword in attempt to end his life for love of his lady. Having thoroughly exhausted that romantic theme, the Prince declared his intention of repealing the Royal Marriage Act the instant he came to the Throne; and further added that if Mr. Knight were really as attached to him as he professed to be, he would not hesitate to perform the ceremony between himself and Mrs. Fitzherbert.

The Reverend Johannes was greatly put about. He had no desire to make an enemy of so valuable a friend, still less did he wish to be involved in any disastrous consequence. He might even, should he lend himself to such a proposition, be defrocked. 'I used every argument I could think of to dissuade him from his purpose,' he declared in a letter to his daughter, 'but to no avail.' The Prince had the last decisive word.

[1] Afterwards created Viscount Lake of Delhi.

'If you refuse to marry me I'll find another clergyman who will.'

'His vehemence', Mr. Knight, with touching naivety, admitted, 'made me apprehensive that the Prince might get some clergyman to marry him for the chance of Church preferment'; a bait that proved too much for Mr. Knight's resistance. 'I could not bear,' he says, 'to see him miserable. He subdued me. I agreed. . . .'

But so soon as he had left the joyful Prince with that assurance, his Reverence walked home, again disheartened. To what imprudent step was he committed? What legal penalties would he not incur? 'And when just outside the door, my last night's conversation with Lake flashed across my memory. Too late I recollected I had tacitly engaged *not* to marry the Prince to Mrs. Fitzherbert' . . . What would Lake think of a man whose word was so easily broken? . . . 'Lake, whose good opinion I would not have forfeited for all the world' – or, possibly, future preferment.

In the end Mr. Knight, for his own peace of mind, begged the Prince to allow him to decline.

It is to the Prince's credit that he took the agitated gentleman's refusal in good part, and at their next meeting, shook him warmly by the hand and said with the gayest good-humour: 'If I had not let you off you would have had to fly the country.'

The Prince's strangely unaccountable high spirits at his failure to coerce the conscientious Mr. Knight, may have pointed to the fact that a substitute had already been found in the Reverend Robert Burt. With the promise of five hundred pounds, this newly ordained young curate was persuaded to run the grave risk of performing the ceremony.

On the evening of December 15, 1785, mysterious comings and goings might have been observed inside and outside the residence of Mrs. Fitzherbert in Park Street.

Dusk was closing in with shadows, and snow-clouds, thick and heavy, were threatening the sky when a carriage drew up before the house and there deposited two gentlemen, one elderly, one young. Soon after, in a chair, came another; all three were stealthily admitted. No light showed above the doorway, in the vestibule, nor at any of the closely curtained windows. The watchman had not yet started on his rounds, and save for an occasional coach rumbling over the frozen cobbles to and from the Oxford Road – at the corner of which stood Mrs. Fitzherbert's house – the street was empty: the hour six o'clock, when the Quality, bent on its joyful occasions, were at dinner, the Opera, or preparing for a rout.

The last arrivals, conspiratorially muffled, came on foot. The bulkier and taller of the two, with a furtive glance around his shoulder, ran nimbly up the steps. The door was again narrowly opened and shut.

A glaze of frost iced the slimy paving-stones, and snow began to fall in whirling flakes to cover all traces of footsteps and wheels. He who waited, shivered, and stamped his numbed feet as he perambulated back and forth gazing up at those black, inhospitable windows. But within all was warmth and fire-glow. Candles in crystal lustres shed a golden radiance on decorative panels, polished parquet, on the white-sleeved, white-faced young curate, and on the two who knelt before him to repeat their marriage vows.

'. . . Whom God hath joined, let no man put asunder.'

CHARLES JAMES FOX

From the portrait by R. A. Hickel in the National Portrait Gallery

CHAPTER THREE

1785–1789

IMMEDIATELY after the ceremony the bridal pair drove off in a post-chaise for the lady's house at Richmond, and were held up at Hammersmith by a heavy fall of snow. The horses floundered knee-high in a drift, the wheels of the carriage were blocked and had to be dug out, while the bride and bridegroom supped at the village inn.

Secure in their belief that they were man and wife in the sight of God, Mrs. Fitzherbert and her Prince were prepared to defy all opposition. Not only had their union been blessed by a priest of the Church, it had been witnessed by the bride's uncle, Henry Errington, and her young brother, Jack Smythe. Moreover, she held in her possession a certificate of marriage, signed by both, which she deposited for safety at Coutts' Bank. Many years later she cut from this document the signature of the witnesses for fear they should incur the penalty of the law; a chivalrous gesture which she afterwards had reason to regret. The name of a third witness might have been added had he been allowed to attend the ceremony: Orlando Bridgeman, the Prince's equerry, who on that freezing night had kept his faithful guard outside the door. But despite these elaborate precautions to hold the marriage secret, the news of it leaked out, giving rise to wildest conjecture. Mrs. Fitzherbert was in residence at Carlton House, living there with the Prince in flagrant delight. . . . She was his wife. She was not. He had said he would make her a duchess the moment he came to the throne, and had handsomely endowed her with an income of £6,000 a year. Impossible! Everyone knew *that* to be gross exaggeration since the Prince was up to his ears in debt. . . . And never had the pen of Mr. Walpole been so busy.

'Were rumour–aye, and much more than rumour, every voice in England–to be credited, the matter somehow or other reaches from London to Rome.' Yet even he could only guess at the truth of the 'matter', for: 'I know nothing', he wrote to Sir Horace Mann, 'but the buzz of the day, nor can say no more upon it.'

The Queen, however, to whom the 'buzz' was carried, had much to say upon it. She had carefully withheld from the King any hint of this latest cause for anxiety, fearing its consequence upon her husband's health.

His moods of dejection had increased to melancholia. He suffered from sleeplessness, was more than ever loquacious, bustling, repetitive. The Royal physicians tapped, purged, bled him: pulled long faces. Certainly the King was in no fit state to hear of this most recent 'shameful scrape'. But to her much loved so troublesome first-born, the Queen sent a message to wait on her at Windsor. She must learn from his own lips if there were any truth in these preposterous tales.

What the Queen learned from his own lips was worse than she had feared. Not only did he confess to his 'marriage' with Mrs. Fitzherbert; he swore that 'no power on earth could make him give her up'.[1] And he finally demanded that his mother must receive his 'wife' at Court.

It was too much for the poor Queen. These sons! . . . Only a week or two before she had been subjected to a painfully similar scene with William, or 'Guelph', as he insisted his shipmates should call him. William, now gazetted a Lieutenant in the Navy, lodged at the house of the Commissioner at Portsmouth. Post-haste, this third son of hers had come rushing up to Windsor, and had fallen at his mother's feet imploring her to intercede with the King on his behalf that he might marry the Commissioner's daughter, a young person of the name of Sarah Martin. To be rid of him—since he was shouting at the top of his voice for all the Queen's ladies to hear, that with or without the King's consent he *would* marry Sarah Martin—the Queen promised to speak to his father, and sent William back to Portsmouth that same night. She spoke to his father when he returned from hunting the stag in Windsor Park, and His Majesty promptly wrote to the Commissioner at Portsmouth to have his son removed to Plymouth. But the King could not remove his heir from Carlton House. Nor could he remain for ever ignorant of George's alleged 'marriage' which, in direct contravention of the Royal Marriage Act, could have no possible validity in law. And most emphatically did Her Majesty refuse to receive Mrs. Fitzherbert at Court. On that understanding she dismissed George from her presence, believing, hoping, praying that time would cure him of his mad infatuation.

The Prince drove back to Park Street determined to present his 'wife' himself. If the Queen would not receive her, every other lady in the land must be forced to do so. While he spent almost all his time at Richmond, he let it be known that he would accept no invitation to any private function unless accompanied by Mrs. Fitzherbert. He insisted also that she must take precedence above any lady of higher rank.

The leading Whig and Roman Catholic hostesses, only too anxious for favour, gave Mrs. Fitzherbert a cordial welcome. Balls and banquets were

[1] Dr. Doran: *Lives of the Queens of England.*

held in her honour. The Prince was constantly seen in her company at the Opera and playhouse. Never had the London season been so gay as in that summer of 1786. Never had the Prince indulged in such riotous extravagance. Generous to folly, he showered gifts on his 'White Rose', as he called her, as much for her cream and golden loveliness as for her Jacobite sympathies that she did not attempt to disguise. He loaded her with jewels, plate, carriages, horses, none of which was paid for. His debts increased; his lady protested. She had given herself to the Prince without any settlement, nor did she ask for it; but on her jointure of £2,000 a year left her by her second husband, she could not afford to maintain the semi-royal state to which she had been raised. At the Prince's request she leased a house in St. James's Square, where she could better entertain on the lavish scale he demanded. But although he paid the rent, her expenses as hostess and morganatic wife of the Heir Apparent were far beyond her means. Even with the most rigid economy she estimated that this palatial establishment would cost her another £3,000 a year.

The Prince, who had not the remotest idea of the value of money, would have given her twenty times that amount had she not restrained him. The house at Brighton, formerly the property of Thomas Kemp, and which in 1786 he rented and subsequently bought from Louis Weltje, a German pastry-cook,[1] was costing him a fortune in preliminary alterations. Again Holland was called in to transform that seaside villa–once a farm-house–into a Pavilion which later would assume a pseudo-oriental splendour. Two new wings were added to the circular room in the centre with its cupola above. On the second floor, consisting entirely of bed-chambers, a view of the sea could be obtained from every window. The Prince's bedroom was divided into three partitions hung with quilted chintz; the bed-curtains were of chequered green and white silk. And, as he lay there, he could see the Steine–as the primitive sea-front was called –could watch the fisher-folk hauling in their nets, and the motley parade of promenaders reflected in a mirror on the wall. Fashion had followed the Prince's lead to Brighthelmstone, which was in a fair way to become the most popular watering-place in England.

The result of this reckless expenditure was debt and still more debt; bills, long outstanding, came pouring in again, and other claims fell due. There was the case of Mr. Aaron who lived in Crutched Friars, and to whom His Royal Highness owed £10,000 on a post obit bond to be paid at the death of his father. But the actual sum received by the Prince was barely £7,500; the remainder had been supplemented in divers articles of questionable value. Not the least of these were three puncheons

[1] Weltje held the ambiguous office of 'Clerk of the Prince of Wales's kitchen'.

of French brandy distilled in Whitechapel; a diamond cross and rosary manufactured in Houndsditch, and two hundred silver [plated] tea urns which the disgusted Prince immediately sold to another gentleman of Mr. Aaron's persuasion. When, after three months, he was again compelled to call on the obliging Mr. Aaron, he found himself once more possessed of those two hundred tea urns. Having gone the round of Crutched Friars they had returned to their original owner and were used as before to make up the balance of the cash demanded. But what were a few thousand pounds to his credit when his debts totalled near upon a quarter of a million? . . . In view of this delicate transaction, and, on Sheridan's advice, the Prince appealed to Pitt. He might have stood a better chance of securing Pitt's support the year before, had he allowed Sir James Harris to approach the Premier on his behalf as, at that time, had been suggested.

The cautious young Pitt was so long considering the Prince's proposition that he decided once again to lay his case before his father: a bold move.

In July 1786, he wrote to the King that he could no longer delay 'the pressing importunities of many indigent and deserving creditors whose very existence depends upon a speedy discharge of their accounts. . . .' And he dropped a hint to the effect that 'any further procrastination might expose me to legal insult'.

He had, in fact, already been exposed to legal insult, when, for the comparatively small sum of £600 which he had been unable to meet, he had been forced to entertain the bailiff and his men at Carlton House. Not until his agonized appeals to all his friends had met with sufficient contributory response, was he quit of his self-invited guests.

While he refrained from giving the King a more explicit account of that unfortunate affair, he offered an alternative to the refusal of fatherly aid—which he may have guessed was a foregone conclusion. He would reduce every expense 'even those to which my rank and birth entitle me until I have totally liberated myself from my embarrassments'.

When, as before, the King vouchsafed no reply to his letter, the Prince determined to carry out his threat. He closed Carlton House, dismissed his servants, put his carriages and horses up for auction, and paraded his racing-stud through the streets *en route* for Tattersall's. A few days later he and Mrs. Fitzherbert drove down to Brighthelmstone in the public post-chaise.

This flamboyant display of economy enlisted the sympathy of the entire nation. The Prince was a martyr and His Majesty a monster, a despot, a skinflint, jealous of Prince Charming's popularity. When he attended the race-course at Newmarket, the Prince of Wales let it be known that Mrs. Fitzherbert had paid for the hire of their coach.

The King became uneasy. As 'Farmer George', who had so successfully played the part of an English country squire interested in cows and crops and psalm-singing, an affectionate parent and devoted husband–in short, a family man–he had earned the respect if not the love of his people. And now George, living in a state of exaggerated penury in some dreadful seaside hole, and driving all over the place with 'that Woman' paying his fares for all the world to see, had the country at his heels crying 'shame' upon the King. The Prince's private debts had become a public scandal, for which not he, but the King was held responsible!

Towards the end of August, when the Prince's retrenchment was the talk of the Town and the King in worst possible odour, one Margaret Nicholson, a servant-girl, sprang at the Sovereign with a carving-knife as he was entering St. James's Palace for a levee. The incident created a furore. Many people believed that the maid had been one of the Prince's staff, who, incensed at the King's cruelty to her master, had sought this means of vengeance; but medical opinion gave it she was mad. She had been shrieking that the Crown belonged to her and that she claimed the right to have it, when they took her. Throughout the whole occurrence the King had remained remarkably cool. The Prince showed dutiful concern. So soon as he had been told of the affair he drove at once to Windsor, asked to see his father, and was refused admittance. That rebuff finally induced him to bring the question of his debts before Parliament and let the truth be known. If the King were in such universal disfavour that even lunatics attempted to attack him, his son could be certain of fair judgment.

The time had come to strike.

During the interim before Parliament reassembled, the Prince had managed to secure to himself a strong supporting factor. Yet the House of Commons, predominantly Tory and adherent to the King, could present an equally formidable defence. Pitt, who had obviously no intention of acting as intermediary between the father and son, stood firmly by the Throne. The Prince, on his side, pinned his faith in his two most powerful allies, Fox and Sheridan.

On April 20, 1787, hostilities were opened by Alderman Newnham, one of the members for the City of London. Primed by the Prince's party, he wished to know 'whether it were the design of the Ministers to bring forward any proposition to rescue the Prince of Wales from his present embarrassed condition. It must be very disagreeable', the honourable member pointedly continued, 'for His Royal Highness to be deprived of those comforts and enjoyments which so properly belonged to him.'[1]

When Pitt answered curtly that 'he had not been honoured by any such command', Newnham gave notice that he would bring forward the motion again on May 4.

A few days later Pitt forestalled him with a statement sprung upon a crowded House, to the effect that 'the question of the Prince's debts, would necessitate an inquiry into their *cause*'.

While the King's party applauded, the Prince's supporters disdained the warning implied in those words. An acrimonious discussion followed, promoted by John Rolle, member for the county of Devon. With dogged persistence in the set of his jowl, and the West country burr in his voice, he called the attention of the House to the question which the honourable Alderman had proposed–'a question which immediately affects our constitution in Church and State'.

His words created a profound sensation and looked to bring the House about his ears. By that marked reference to 'Church and State', Rolle had made it clear that the rumours of the Prince's marriage with a Roman Catholic could no longer be ignored. Since Fox, unaccountably, was absent during this preliminary debate, Sheridan rose to parry Rolle's offensive in a masterpiece of blarney.

Professing a naïve misapprehension of the issues now at stake, he begged to 'differ much from those who represented that alarming consequences might arise from the present motion. Nor did he understand how the existence of *Church* and *State* could be in any way endangered by the Prince's debts. . . .' This thirst for information was instantly appeased by the stubborn Mr. Rolle.

'If the motion were to be urged, which he thought highly improper, the honourable gentleman would find that he would not flinch from his duty!'

Whereupon Pitt, perceiving a flutter of dismay among the Prince's followers, rose to express concern 'that he should be driven by the perseverance of the honourable member to the disclosure of circumstances which he would otherwise think it *his* duty to conceal. . . .'[1]

The fat was in the fire, but the fire did not burn. If Sheridan had called Rolle's bluff, the pale young Pitt had called his. While he refused to be drawn, Pitt hoisted a danger signal. Beneath that apparently innocuous question of the Prince's debts lay sinister undercurrents, which, if stirred, might sink the Heir to the Throne in a wave of disaster. For the moment, however, the subject was left in abeyance and the House proceeded with the business of the day.

[1] Hansard's *Parliamentary Debates*.

That same night Sheridan, a great deal more perturbed than he had led his fellow members to believe, went straightway to Carlton House, where, in a few dismantled rooms, the Prince was temporarily lodged. Without any bluff or blarney now, Sheridan gave a full report of the discussion in the Commons, and hinted at a possible crisis accruing from Rolle's interference.

The Prince received this information with the wildest dismay. What could have induced that Devonshire oaf to go digging into his private affairs, when all he asked of Parliament was the payment of his debts? Why had Pitt changed his tactics and insisted on a full disclosure of his marriage? And in any case how could he admit it with the King and all his men against him? What would be the effect on the country of such a confession? The 'No-Popery' riots, incited by the fanatical George Gordon only seven years before, were still a smouldering reminder of Protestant prejudice against the Catholics. If his marriage with a 'Papist' became known, another conflagration assuredly would flare from the ashes of those fires.

He raved up and down the room; he cursed the King for bringing him so low that he must send his friends to beg for him in Parliament. He turned on 'Sherry' with his parrot repetition–'What to do? For God's sake tell me what to do!' Should he confess to his marriage, imperil the Succession and bring about a dynastic upheaval? There were Jacobites enough in Scotland to endanger the House of Hanover. Charles Edward, though dying of drink was not yet dead, and there were many who would have the Stuart where the Prince of Wales hoped to be, and who raised their glasses secretly to 'the King over the water'. Even she, whom he had named his 'White Rose' for the clan that she openly favoured, would not hesitate–or would she?–to betray their so-called 'marriage' if she could, and bring about a rebellion in favour of Charles III . . .! There was no end to the fantasies he conjured. He rushed from extreme to extreme. The marriage was not legal. There had never been a marriage. The whole thing had been a mockery in law, as she would surely come to realize if the case were put before her. 'Sherry' must prepare her for the worst.

Confessedly the Prince in this emergency did not show to the highest advantage. He was pitiably frightened and anything but 'Charming'. Sheridan may have felt a faint disgust at the groans, the ravings, the hair-clutchings, the eternal 'I, I, I', with not a thought for her, his 'Dearest Love'–save that she must keep her counsel, hold her tongue.

Leaving the Prince to come to himself, Sheridan called upon Mrs. Fitzherbert. After he had given her a brief résumé of that day's debate in the House, he discreetly intimated that a public denial of her marriage had been threatened. Since neither she nor Sheridan knew of that letter to Fox written almost on the eve of the wedding, she could see no possibility of any such denial; nor could Sheridan bring himself to tell her that if a disclosure of the marriage were inevitable, the Prince would certainly disclaim her as his wife. All he could do was to warn her that if the subject were brought up again it might lead to a public inquiry.

Was ever woman caught in such a coil! To whom could she look for protection? Not to the reckless boy whose wife, for better or for worse, she believed herself to be. Nor to the young curate who had married them; she could not bring him forward who had risked so much for her; nor could she involve her brother and uncle as accessories after the fact. . . . She stood alone. 'I feel like a dog with a weight tied round its neck,' she said; and fell to sobbing. Would not Mr. Sheridan aid, advise, uphold her? . . . With her tear-drenched eyes, like darkest velvet, so imploringly upraised, and her face, bereft of all colour, framed in that powderless honey-gold hair, Sheridan went down before Beauty in distress. He would have been no Irishman if he had not sworn by every saint in the calendar and his own immortal soul to uphold and protect her with his life.

He left her comforted.

But Fox, who still remained an unknown factor, had made no promises to Beauty in distress; and this particular beauty was no friend of Mr. Fox. She, who could not dissemble, had never attempted to hide her dislike of him, his works, and his ways. He blasphemed in her presence, he drank to excess; she had seen him disgustingly raddled. He was dirty, untidy, uncouth, loose in his morals and odiously fat; and his influence upon the Prince deplorable. She greatly hoped to sever that too intimate connexion.

The Prince in fact had severed it himself; yet when ten days later Fox rose up in the House to deny the marriage, he denied it in good faith. He believed in the Prince's written word.

With scathing eloquence he began by attacking Rolle's previous allusion to 'something full of danger to Church and State'. He could only presume that the honourable gentleman referred to 'that low malicious falsehood which had been made the wanton sport of the vulgar. He hoped a tale only fit to impose on the lowest orders of the streets would not have gained the smallest portion of credence.'[1]

His scorn lashed the benches of the truculent Tory squires; his eyes, glowering under stormy brows, pinioned the impassive mask of the one among them all whom he knew to be more than his equal, whose youth-

[1] Hansard's *Parliamentary Debates*.

72

ful cold and calculating judgment he both applauded and feared. And to him alone he spoke.

'I am at a loss to imagine what species of *Party* it is which could have fabricated so *base* and *scandalous* a calumny. His Royal Highness had declared himself ready to submit his debts to the investigation of the House, and he was equally ready to submit the *other* circumstance to the same investigation if the consideration of a House of Parliament could with propriety and decency be applied to such a subject. . . .' Contemptuously he surveyed the pale narrow-chested youth who received this barbed challenge unmoved. 'Furthermore'–Fox paused a moment as if to weigh his words before he slowly and deliberately proceeded–'furthermore, His Royal Highness was prepared to offer His Majesty's Ministers the fullest assurance of the *utter falsehood* of the fact in question which never had, and which common sense must see, never *could* have happened!'

It was a tourney in which two champions met on Parliament's tilting ground, and the vizor of one was raised; the other lowered. Fox sat down amid a buzz of incredulity, hushed to an expectant silence as the Prime Minister stood.

Frigidly disdainful, his clipped clear voice that seemed to spurn his words, rang through the House in dignified cool contrast to Fox's spittle-flecked oration.

'It little became Mr. Fox', said Mr. Pitt, 'to throw out insinuations calculated to fall somewhere upon some person unmentioned, but whom he seemed to think the House would be able to discover. And since the honourable member did not choose to point his charge against any individual, he would not point it for him.'

The significance underlying this statement was unmistakable, and the House sighed its relief when the Prime Minister, turning to Rolle, enjoined the honourable magistrate 'not to force the discussion of a subject which was of all the *most* to be avoided.'

But Rolle, determined to get at the truth, refused to let the matter drop. He was on his feet again to tell his Chief, with clumsy eloquence, that 'the matter affecting Church and State had been discussed in newspapers all over the Kingdom. The Right Honourable gentleman, Mr. Fox, had said it was impossible to have happened. They all knew, that though it could not be done under formal sanction of the law, there were *other ways* in which it might have taken place.' He insisted that 'this matter must be cleared'.

Fox was up and ready for him. 'Sir, I do not deny the calumny in question, merely with regard to the existing laws–I deny it *in toto*. Not

73

only could it never have happened legally—in point of fact as well as in law—it never has happened at all! . . . I speak from *direct authority!*[1]

Such emphatic denial appeared to be enough to satisfy all parties, except Rolle. Sheridan, watching the open disbelief on the rubicund face of the Devonshire man, wondered uneasily how much he knew, or how much he guessed. The debate might have continued till midnight had not Charles Grey, a very young member just down from Cambridge, and a loyal friend of the Prince, burst forth in loud denunciation of Rolle's unmannerly and ungenerous conduct; and then he, who almost half a century later was to set his seal upon Reform, impudently turned upon his Chief to attack him for his 'veiled hints and menaces'.

Pitt, taking covert measure of young Grey, may have wished him on his right side instead of his left, while he curtly refuted 'any idea or intention of menace or threat'. . . . And put Mr. Grey in his place.

The House adjourned.

That evening when Fox strolled into Brooks's he was buttonholed in the entrance hall by the Prince's equerry, Orlando Bridgeman. 'Charles, I hear you have denied the Prince's marriage in the House. I can tell you that you are misinformed. I was present at the wedding.'

This was not strictly true, since Mr. Bridgeman had been tramping up and down outside in the snow during the service held in that Park Street drawing-room. But Mr. Bridgeman was a very honest and chivalrous young man, and devoted to Mrs. Fitzherbert. He let Mr. Fox know that he thought him a cad. Fox, however, was less concerned with Bridgeman's good or bad opinion of him than at the Prince's deceit. He had fully believed in his denial. Aware of the previous farcical comedy played at Carlton House, he did not doubt that some equally futile performance had been repeated, this time with the lady's consent. That the Prince had gone so far as to engage a clerk in Holy Orders to conduct the ceremony was utterly incredible. Yet here was Bridgeman swearing to the truth of it: and there was Fox—the dupe!

A note from the Prince awaited him on his arrival home. He may have read it with cynical humour. The Prince assured him he felt 'more comfortable by Sheridan and Grey's report of what has passed to-day, and I have had a distant insinuation that some sort of message or terms are to be proposed to-morrow'. He signed himself 'ever affectionately yours'.

From this letter it is evident that the Prince had no intention of quarrelling with Fox, whose friendship was far too valuable to lose. As for her who had been victimized, she must accept the situation. After all, her

[1] Hansard's *Parliamentary Debates*.

name had not been mentioned. But at least he had the grace to break the news to her himself.

Nothing in his greeting gave her any indication as to the reason of his visit. He took her hands and kissed them, and, with shocking nonchalance, he said: 'What do you think Fox did yesterday? He went down to the House and denied that you and I are man and wife! Did you ever hear of such a thing?'

If she had never heard of such a thing she heard it then, in silence; and stood so still, so very white, that he, fearing for her, faltered. If she had spoken, turned upon him with reproaches, he could have dealt with her; but this, her frozen calm, that dark unseeing gaze of hers, completely shattered him. Tears, ever his refuge, sprang to his eyes; he besought her not to break his heart. He was not to blame for Fox's treachery. He begged her to believe that he had never given Charles the least authority to make any such outrageous statement. She was not proof against his sobs, his protestations, his vows to see her righted; nor could she let him go without some reassurance. He was so young. . . . And so ingenuous.

Not until later, when the full report of Fox's speech was brought to her, did she come to know that her marriage, authorized by the Pope and by her husband's Church, had been denounced as false, denied–'*in toto*'.

In her fury she was terrible. The Prince, who had never known her anything but placid, acquiescent, was met by a raging virago. Unsparingly, she told him that her womanhood, her dignity, religion, and her pride, had been sacrificed, defiled. Fox and he together had conspired to bring her to this shameful degradation. Nor could all his frantic promises to clear her name of slander, to make her a duchess when he came to the throne, and every possible amend, mollify or soften her one whit. She ordered him away and he went, weeping. He sent for his friends; he called a consultation. If he could not, then a third party *must* make her see reason.

Their overtures were highly unsuccessful.

To Sir Philip Francis,[1] the first to approach her, she declared that Fox 'had rolled her in the kennel like a street-walker'; that 'every word he uttered was a lie–and so on', recorded Francis, 'in a torrent of virulence which it was in vain for me to counter . . . So I gave up the point and retreated.'

To Lord Stourton, the next intermediary, she vowed she would break off her connexion with the Prince. This message promptly delivered, threw him in a panic. He sent for Charles Grey and insisted he must find some means of modifying Fox's disclaimer. 'Charles certainly,' the

[1] Reputed author of 'Junius'.

75

Prince admitted, 'went too far . . . You, my dear Grey', he added vaguely, 'must explain it to the House.'

But Grey flatly refused to explain it to the House, and intimated that any further discussion would be most prejudicial to the Prince's interests.

Since the Prince's interests were centred wholly in the payment of his debts he was forced, with ill-grace, to accept Grey's refusal. Flinging himself on the couch in a pet: 'Very well, if you won't,' he said, 'Sheridan must.'

Sheridan, already pledged to protect the Prince's lady, reluctantly promised 'to do what he could'–if or when Fox should secure the payment of those debts. Pitt, who had been receiving hourly notes from the King at Buckingham House, called a council and waited on the Prince with every expression of good-will. All should be as His Royal Highness wished.

All was, most cheerfully, as His Royal Highness wished, except in the bedroom of Mrs. Fitzherbert from which he was unmercifully barred. Still, all so far had been so very good that he could only hope all else would be much better.

On May 4, Alderman Newnham withdrew his motion–no longer necessary in view of the King's compliance. And now came the moment for Sheridan to put in his defence on Mrs. Fitzherbert's behalf.

Yet even Sheridan, despite his impressive loquacity, had little to say upon a subject that had been so decisively closed. He spread his charming hands, smiled engagingly at the scowling Rolle, bowed with gentle irony to Fox, and announced that 'His Royal Highness felt the most perfect satisfaction at the prospect before him'–as indeed he might with something near upon £200,000 about to be placed to his credit. 'But', continued Sheridan, 'His Royal Highness did also desire it to be distinctly remembered that no attempt had been made to screen any part of his conduct, actions or situation from their view . . .' And he finished with a rather laboured compliment to 'a lady to whom it was supposed some late Parliamentary allusions had been pointed', affirming that 'ignorance and vulgar malice alone could have attempted to detract from a character upon which truth could fix no just reproach, and who was entitled to the truest, most general respect'.

At which there were quite a few sniggers.

Fox, who knew women and 'Sherry' too well, may have placed his own construction on this defence of and halo to Mrs. Fitzherbert, for whom he cared not a fig. He had accomplished his purpose, and the only debt outstanding to His Royal Highness's account should be one of deepest gratitude to him.

          *   *   *

This happy result of Parliament's tussle went far to heal the breach between father and son; but before the King would agree to the grant suggested by his Ministers, he demanded a full account of the Prince's liabilities–'if the same could be prepared with sufficient accuracy.'

To prepare the same with 'sufficient accuracy', was manifestly not an easy task. It is possible the Prince had been advised by his treasurer to delete certain items which might have led to some awkward inquiry. Under the ambiguous heading 'etcetera', the sum of £11,000 appears. Another 'etcetera' for £29,277, is appended obscurely to 'Household'. The full amount totalled £161,000 to be paid by Parliament, £60,000 of which was to be set aside for expenses incurred at Carlton House. When this had been decided, the King undertook to allow his son another £10,000 a year.

Once relieved of his immediate embarrassments, the Prince basked in the beams of magnanimity. A tearfully joyous reunion took place at Windsor. The caricaturists made fortunes. Gillray shows the return of a ragged prodigal with the Garter dangling from his knee, and the King and Queen coming out of the Treasury weighed down by bags of money. London looked on, laughingly indulgent. Florizel was once again the people's idol, and 'Farmer George', restored to popularity, had behaved as a loving father should. Taking their cue from parental beneficence, the doors of every hostess, Whig or Tory, were flung wide to welcome back their Prince.

Only one door stayed closed.

There followed the usual agonized scenes. Keate was sent for, found him in a paroxysm, bled him, and reported that 'His Royal Highness was not yet out of danger'.

So grave were the bulletins issued, that his adamantine love fearing, from previous experience, the consequence of her refusal to see him, relented in so far as to admit him to her presence. He came to her lachrymose; pale. He had been bled to the verge of transparency. Sobbing, he grovelled at her feet, implored her to be merciful. Must he be penalized for Fox's chicanery, of which he had known no more than she, until the man whom he had thought to be his friend had got up in the House to forswear, besmirch them both ? His tears fell upon her hands, her heart was wrenched. Even in his misery, whether genuine or feigned, he had charm to melt stones. He was forgiven, petted, loved again. The fiendish Fox had been the traitor, and this boy of hers, so wild-eyed and grief-stricken, the innocent victim of Machiavellian cunning. . . . Then they kissed and comforted each other, and were no more divided.

Next day he drove her to Epsom races in his phaeton, and the same evening accompanied her to the Duchess of Gordon's ball, where the Prince was seen to lead with her in almost every dance. After that avowal of reconciliation all society rallied round Mrs. Fitzherbert. Coaches and carriages lined up outside her house, with footmen on her doorstep to present their ladies' cards of invitation. The Duchess of Cumberland received her as a sister. The King's pious brother Henry, on holiday in Florence, sent her a letter full of affection, and 'a cestus done in oyster shell', which he 'hoped she would think pretty'. He wished her 'well and happy and that the Prince will be made easy now in his affairs'.

But despite these avuncular tokens of good-will and the homage of London's hostesses, Mrs. Fitzherbert was nothing so easy as her spouse. Gillray, who had spared the Prince, did not hesitate to point his wit at her. In a satirical print entitled 'Dido Forsaken', he depicts her perched on a funeral pyre of logs at the edge of the sea. The wind has torn the Crown and the Prince of Wales's feathers from her head, while sailing away in the distance is a little boat named 'Honour', steered by a very emaciated Pitt, with Fox sprawling in the stern and the Prince beside him shouting: 'I never saw her in my life!' To which Fox replies: 'No, damme, never in his life!'

Mrs. Fitzherbert accepted this unkindness as the penalty of fame; and as if to compensate her for the trouble he had caused, the Prince's devotion was boundless. In July he took her down to Brighthelmstone and installed her in a villa hard by his new Pavilion.

That summer and the few that followed were the happiest years of his life. It was his carnival era, bacchanalian, abandoned; yet, for all its paganism, the over-tones of the whole elaborate design are spilled from an artist's palette. Not entirely inconsequent, not without precision, placed with a master's eye to effect is 'that madhouse or a house run mad'–thus aptly is it stigmatized by Pasquin. In the perpetual process of rebuilding as caprice suggested, sunlight and ever more light, iridescent, tremulous, poured in at every window. Light, wan and greenly-blue as a world under the sea, was reflected from the harsher blue of corridors; light, coloured as in a stormy sunset, from the walls and ceiling of the dining-room; sunflower-yellow from the library.

But though he commanded 'let there be light', he had forgotten to let in fresh air. His dining-room, supported by four pillars in scagliolia, was so ill-ventilated that his guests were sadly over-heated and often overcome. Sheridan, a frequent visitor at the Pavilion, once asked Hanger, seated near him in the Royal oven, how he felt. 'Hot–hot–hot as hell!' gasped the perspiring Major. And Sheridan, himself parboiled, made his quick retort: 'It is right we should be prepared in this world for that which we know will be our lot in another.'

As the years sped on so did the Prince enlarge, improve, and reconstruct his sea-side palace until, at the turn of the century, it assumed its Asiatic-cum-Moorish confusion capped by a myriad miniature domes—'as if', said Sydney Smith, 'St. Paul's had gone to the sea and pupped! . . .'

To Brighthelmstone, or Brighton for short, as now the *ton* were beginning to call it, flocked all the Carlton House set. Besides the ubiquitous 'Sherry' and Hanger, Sir John and Laetitia Lade were frequent visitors. Fox alone, of all the Prince's friends, was noticeably absent. Still sore at the trick his 'ever affectionate George P.' had played him, he betook himself, with Mrs. Armistead, to Italy, there to seek forgetfulness from the ingratitude of Princes in the browsing contemplation of early Tuscan art.

While Mrs. Fitzherbert discreetly entertained ladies and gentlemen of impeccable repute, the Prince's gatherings were more hilarious than circumspect. A curious company attended his frolics, led by the three Barry brothers. The eldest, Richard, Earl of Barrymore, was known among his intimates as 'Hellgate', for his violent temper; then there was Henry, called unkindly 'Cripplegate' because of his club foot. The Honourable and Reverend Augustus, whose debts had thrown him in and out of every gaol in the kingdom, rejoiced in the name of 'Newgate', which according to popular belief was the only prison that had never housed him. Their tutor, who taught them everything but manners, was dubbed by his orphaned pupils 'Profligate'; and, for her filthy language, their little sister Caroline completed the quintet as Lady 'Billingsgate'.

The elderly inhabitants of Brighton who had been cutting their capers when the Prince had been cutting his teeth, were scandalized at the orgies that went on at the Pavilion. The Prince and his merry young gentlemen turned every night into day, played all manner of practical jokes on respectable householders, held shooting matches on the Steine, and drove a number of old ladies in terror from the town.

As we see him in his later twenties, the Prince had not completely run to fat, though he was plumper, more florid, full-chinned. He suffered from a glandular swelling of the throat, and in order to conceal it he introduced the ear-embracing high cravat to fashion. On the advice of his doctors he took to sea-bathing, and under the eye of one 'Smoaker', a beery old salt who taught him to swim, he bobbed and ducked in the water like a huge rosy porpoise.

In those early Brighton days his energy was tireless. He played cricket in the grounds of the Pavilion in a suit of his own creation; white beaver hat, short flannel jacket edged with blue ribbon, and white trews closely fitting his posteriority. Of his calves he was proud, but not of his bulk, that all his bobbings in the sea and his battings on the lawn failed to reduce. He hunted in the winter and went racing in the spring. His stud, sold at the time of his retrenchment, was renewed, and his colours appeared again at Newmarket. In 1788 he won the Derby.

With Mrs. Fitzherbert and a gathering of her friends, not his, of whom she strongly disapproved, he attended Lewes races.

Those meetings on the downs with the blue above, the green below, the butterfly-hued billowing of petticoats, the swing of padded hips, the dainty foppishness of satin coats, of silver-braided tricorne hats, tie-wigs, or sprinkled powder; the Royal gold and scarlet liveried postilions, the ceaseless flow and interflow of sunlit movement, held all the trifling, piquant grace of Watteau.

Herded respectfully, kept at their distance, the villagers, smocked farmer folk, the betting touts and gypsies—splashing red and yellow, green more emerald than grass, in every garish tint and stripe beloved of Romany—cheered the prancing horses, cheered the jockeys, picked the winner, lost, and cheered their Prince who from his coach waved hat in air to their God-blessings.

From France had come visitors too: men, high-nosed, lean-faced, ringed and ruffled, mincing, more resplendent in attire than any First young Gentleman; ladies in exotic silks, rainbow-shaded, shimmering, or hooped in muslin, daintily bepearled; or pastoral, simply, the latest whim from Versailles, with shepherdess crook and tilted hat and toy lamb tucked under the arm.

Joyously unconscious of doom swift-dawning, their slippered feet and buckled shoes trod the sheep-cropped turf; nor could some of those who stepped so lightly that the harebells scarcely suffered, know they never would tread English ground again.

Sharing the Prince's coach-box with Mrs. Fitzherbert sat Madame la Princesse de Lamballe, whose lovely head, stuck on a pike, was carried four years later through the howling streets of Paris.. . . .

Then, when the races were over, the horses led away, the winners jubilant, the losers glum, a long procession of chariots and coaches would go winding in the sunset back to Brighton.

It was after one of these race-meetings when Madame de Lamballe, and a few other Parisian guests were at supper with the Prince, that a message came from Windsor. The Duke of York had returned; he had been in Germany for seven years learning how to be a British soldier.

MRS. FITZHERBERT

Engraving by John Corde, after Richard Cosway, R.A., by courtesy of Brighton Art Gallery and Museu

Not the least of George III's well-meant but characteristic blunders had been the banishment of the Prince Bishop to those Prussian courts of *kultur*, where his study of martial tactics was enlivened by Neronian excesses. Yet, in that land of his progenitors, poised against the tapestried green background of Hanoverian plains and castled forests, one figure in perpetuity recurs.

Mounted on his white war-horse, frail, bent, but still impressive, he dominates the scene. His seared eyes watch the phantom march of vanquished armies, of ruthless victories, and spectacular defeats. Behind him the oft-repeated Electoral pattern of princelings, fat and bibulous, godlessly sportive in gilded seraglios, is revealed, a little tarnished, frayed; but that clear immortal silver thread weaves on throughout the ages when the world of Frederick, surnamed Great, has crashed.

To the Prince Bishop, however, the despotic old King with one foot in the grave and his head in the clouds, spouting excerpts from Voltaire, was ridiculous. Although Frederick feigned rapt attention to the lectures of his illustrious kinsman, and while his tutors professed to see in him a future Hannibal or Alexander, his military activities appear to be confined to the reviewing of troops in his uniform and attending social functions in his cups.

Immediately the Prince heard that Frederick was home again he excused himself to his company, ordered his phaeton, and drove post-haste through the night to Windsor. The meeting between the Princes, after so long a separation, was tearfully demonstrative. They fell into each other's arms and wept; the King wept; the Queen wept; the twittering 'Sisterhood' clustered round them with kisses and cries of joy. The King, excitedly trotting back and forth between his wife, his daughters, and his much loved Frederick–'the Hope of his Family', as he called him–was beatific. And when eventually these transports had subsided, the Prince hustled his Family's 'Hope' out of Windsor Castle down to Brighton, proudly to present him to his 'wife'.

If Frederick had thought to find in Mrs. Fitzherbert a more mature Perdita, he was agreeably surprised, although a trifle overpowered by her dignity and regal self-assurance. He may have noticed, also, that George when in her company was prone to be more silent and less jocular. Indeed the influence of Mrs. Fitzherbert on her rakish young 'husband' had been remarked in the Press. The *Morning Post* reported that 'His Royal Highness was much better than he used to be and certainly more sober in his libations to Bacchus'.

The increase in his income had enabled him to take a mansion for his 'White Rose' in Pall Mall, furnished regardless of expense. There she entertained in a fashion befitting her semi-royal state. Her servants wore liveries of green and gold; her clothes and jewels were fabulous. Attended always by an irreproachable Miss Pigot, her paid companion, Mrs. Fitzherbert received her guests in a drawing-room hung with blue satin. Pictures of the Prince adorned the walls of her dining-room; his bust in marble, pale and austere, stood by for him as deputy host at her assemblies. No doubt but that the Prince was entirely reformed–until the reappearance of the 'Hope'. Then comes a woeful regression. The two brothers, reunited, plunged into revelry unparalleled even in Florizel's wildest days. Nor was Mrs. Fitzherbert exempt from their clowning. The tale is told by the Duke of York that when the lady heard the Prince and his satellites come dashing up her staircase, she would hide herself under the sofa. Finding the room empty, they would proceed to make a search, poking behind curtains and in corners with their swords and canes, until at last 'they drew forth their trembling victim from her place of concealment'.[1]

She had troubles enough to contend with in those early years of her association with the Heir Apparent. That he had never been physically faithful she knew; but that she came before all others she believed. Fox, her chief rival for the Prince's affection, was still abroad: 'disgusted', he said, 'with the political situation', and more so with the way the Prince had used him for his purpose and deceived him.

Sunning himself in Italy with his flower-like 'Liz' Armistead, he wandered through art galleries and olive groves, drank Chianti and the 'Tears of Christ'; and, drugged with beauty, watched the fall of roses, red and white, in cyprus-shaded gardens bordering those vineyards on the terraced hills of Tuscany. He had left no address, read no news-sheets, heard no talk from London of another crisis clouding the monarchical horizon. Nor did he write letters or receive one, until he halted at Bologna where he was met with a message from Burke urging his immediate return.

> 'God bless you . . . Your business formerly was only to take care of your honour. I hope you will have now another trust. You are to act a great and though not a discouraging, a difficult part; and in a scene which is wholly new.'

★   ★   ★

The scene 'wholly new' was laid at Windsor.

For some time past the King's health had been causing his doctors much anxiety. His variable moods of exuberant mirth or melancholic silence

[1] Thomas Raikes: *Journal.*

were now more gravely apparent. He babbled incessantly, talked to himself, and was growing exceedingly stout. His protruding blood-shot eyes, his jerky gestures as he shambled up and down the terrace at Windsor in a uniform of his own design–blue coat with red collar and cuffs, white waistcoat, white wig, and cocked hat–his restlessness, his staring suspicious looks askance at his attendants, these, though minor symptoms, were significant.

His doctors advised a change of air and scene, and sent him to Cheltenham to drink the waters. While staying there the King and his Court paid a visit to Worcester. It was then that His Majesty began to exhibit more alarming eccentricities. On one occasion he went out unattended, strutted on the bridge followed by a crowd of inquisitive townsfolk, and jovially addressed them: 'Hey, my boys! What's this–a bridge? What–what!'– 'Yes, if you please, Your Majesty', was the wondering reply of a spokesman. 'Then let's give it a huzza!' cried the King, and snatching off his hat he cheered lustily three time three. Affable doubtless, but–unusual.

The next morning he got up at a very early hour, and while the Queen and the Household still slept, escaped unobserved and ran off to the lodgings of his equerries. Gleefully chuckling, the King trotted up the stairs, burst into the rooms of his shocked gentlemen, woke them with shouts and loud halloos, and crowing with laughter, hurried out again.

To be sure there was no harm in such gay familiarity, save that His Majesty had never shown himself gay or familiar with any member of his family, much less with any member of his Household. The Queen, who secretly feared that her husband was heading for another mental breakdown–she had unhappy memories of his first, soon after their marriage–watched, prayed and courageously smiled, ignoring the whispers of the Court.

Back again at Windsor, the King's young pages giggled to see his red-faced Majesty go puffing back and forth along the flagstones of the terrace, talking to himself and marking time in the air with his finger to music that none of them heard. The equerries were in a chronic state of nerves and apprehension. Once when driving the Queen round Windsor Park in his phaeton, the King suddenly pulled up the horses and exclaimed in delighted surprise: '*There* he is!' Then, handing the reins to his startled wife, he clambered out, darted over to an oak tree, bared his head, ceremoniously bowed, and seizing one of the lower branches went through an elaborate performance of shaking hands. The page in attendance, who, at a signal from the pale Queen, had hurried to his master's side, was angrily commanded: 'Go away! Can't you see I am engaged with the King of Prussia?'

He was got home and put to bed, purged, cupped, plastered, given James's powders. The Queen's scared ladies fluttered round their Royal mistress. The King, pitifully aware of the change in himself, greeted Lady Effingham with the announcement: 'My dear Effy! You see me all at once an old man!'

Frau–Madame–and now Mrs. Schwellenberg, between feeding flies to her toads and harrying Miss 'Berner', waddled in and out of the Queen's bedroom with consoling cups of tea. And that shrewdly observant, much younger Lady-in-Waiting on Her Majesty, loitered in draughty passages, and, with her nose to the casement, observed the comings and goings of the King whom she 'dreadfully feared to be on the eve of some severe fever'. . . .

And in her journal, on Guy Fawkes' Day, Fanny Burney writes:

'At noon the King went out in his chaise with the Princess Royal for an airing. I looked from my window to see him. He was all smiling benignity but gave so many orders to the postilions and got in and out of the carriage with such agitation that again my fear of a great fever hanging over him grew more and more powerful. . . .'

That same afternoon the Prince of Wales, having heard of his father's illness, arrived unexpectedly from Brighton. Two days later Miss Burney's fears were realized.

'Oh, my dear friends! What a history!' . . . She had been told how that 'the King at dinner had broken forth into positive delirium!' that the Queen 'had fallen into violent hysterics, that all the Princesses were in misery; that the Prince of Wales had burst into tears, and no one knew what was to follow. . . .'

The Prince may have guessed what would follow, for he was sending couriers to Italy to hasten the return of Mr. Fox.

On the advice of Sir George Baker, His Majesty's Physician-in-Ordinary, the King had consented to occupy a dressing-room adjoining the Queen's bedchamber. This change in their marital relationship brought him from his bed in the middle of the night, convinced that his Charlotte had left him. With a lighted candle in his hand he entered her apartment, and dragged aside the bed-curtains to the terror of the Queen and her Lady-in-Waiting; only after much persuasion from Sir George and Doctor Heberden, was he induced to retire to his room.

Hour after hour, his petrified wife and her attendants heard from behind the locked door that rapid, hoarse, piteous voice croaking to his doctors: 'I am not ill–I am nervous. If you would know what is the matter with me I am nervous–but I love you both very well–I love you–if you would tell me the truth. I love Dr. Heberden the best for he has not told me a lie. Sir George has told me a lie–a white lie he says–but I hate a white lie. If you will tell me a lie, let it be a black–a black lie.' So on and on unceasingly he raved, until for very weariness he could no more articulate.

Daily the King's physicians met in consultation. While the bulletins issued to the public were necessarily restrained, the dreadful nature of the King's malady could not be kept secret. More and more doctors were called in. Towards the end of November Sir Lucas Pepys, Doctors Addington, Reynolds, Warren, and the two Doctors Willis, father and son, were added to the list.

The Reverend Dr. Francis Willis, who had taken Holy Orders and medical degrees, specialized in diseases of the brain. It was in one of his more lucid intervals that the King inquired of Willis why he, a clergyman, should wish to practise medicine and *vice versa*. To Willis's reply: 'Did not Our Lord, Sir, go about healing the sick?' the King rejoined: 'Yes–but he didn't get six hundred a year for doing it!'

That sharp retort, while wholly inconsistent with his patient's pietistic principles, may have influenced Willis's hopeful prognosis. Modern medical science would have possibly attributed the King's condition to that of the manic-depressive which can recur after long intervals of apparent normality, and which Willis, far in advance of his time, had foreseen. His colleagues, however, disagreed. They took the gloomiest view of His Majesty's case and his constant lamentation on two themes: the loss of his American colonies and the disgraceful conduct of his eldest son, over which he brooded till one day he flew at the Prince's throat. Often, with a twist of macabre humour, he would say that 'the Prince was dead and women henceforth could be honest'.

Through all that dark, unendurable time, and despite malicious reports to the contrary, the Prince showed the tenderest concern for his afflicted father. Old feuds were forgotten; nothing of rancour or bitterness remained. Acutely sensitive to suffering–he could not bear to see a horse or dog ill-treated–all that was best in his paradoxical imaginative nature rose in filial anxious affection, and in pity the most profound. For the first time in his life he was faced with, and manfully shouldered, the full burden of responsibility. With Frederick always at his side he remained at Windsor, impatiently awaiting the daily bulletins. When at the end of November the Royal physicians decided to remove the King to Kew, the Prince superintended all the necessary arrangements, allotting to each member of the Household their respective apartments, and methodically chalking their names on the doors.

But despite this change of environment, the King's condition worsened;

and early in December his doctors pronounced His Majesty to be incapable of governance. On December 4, a Cabinet Council was called.

Fox, who, the moment he received Burke's summons, had travelled all haste to London pursued by letters from the Prince, demanded a full medical report on the state of the King's health. A committee of twenty-one members of each House was appointed to examine the report submitted which, swayed by Willis's opinion, inclined to the belief that His Majesty would regain 'the complete restoration of his intellect'. Only Dr. Warren stood firm in his diagnosis of incurable insanity.

On December 16, Pitt laid the report before the House; he then moved that another committee be appointed to search for precedents referring to the power exercised by a Regent. Fox hotly contended that 'any such motion would cause a waste of time, and that it was the duty of Parliament to provide some immediate measure to meet the exigencies of the moment . . . Was there not an Heir Apparent of full age and capacity, fitted to exercise regal power?' He accused Pitt of seeking no precedent but only the means of delaying what ought to be done—and at once.

Fox, in point of fact, was right. Pitt, fully aware that the appointment of a Regency would necessitate a total change of government, was not wasting, he was playing for time. Willis had told him, in private, that he held every hope of the King's recovery within a matter of weeks; in which event Pitt would guard the fortress against possible invasion—and his own downfall.

His next move was to introduce three resolutions affirming the right and duty of Parliament to deal with the present emergency. After a series of lengthy and tedious debates, spun out till the end of January, the Cabinet proposed to legalize proceedings by the issue of letters patent, and appointed Lord Chancellor Thurlow to affix the Great Seal to any measure passed by both Houses.

This final resolution brought howls of protest from the Opposition benches. Burke, in a volley of vituperative ridicule, denounced the Prime Minister as a 'Dictator', quoting to the impermeable Pitt the words of Macbeth to Banquo's ghost: 'Avaunt and quit my sight!'

No one stirred.

' "Thou hast no speculation in those eyes which thou dost glare with–" ' bellowed Burke. 'So in fact is this political spectre. Its blood is cold. It is a chimera, a monster taken out of Hell!'

If then, speculation did glare from the eyes of the Tories, it was repeated with doubt in the eyes of the Whigs, as Burke, borne on his hurricane rhetoric, continued to rant. They who saw and heard the massive Irishman's demoniac vehemence may have thought him more fitted to wear a strait-jacket than his ailing Majesty, the King. . . .

While the Prince's men were fighting for the Regency in Parliament, another fight was going on at Kew.

The Queen, who remembered the appointment of a former Regency Council when she had been one of those provisionally nominated to officiate, was bitterly offended that in this instance her name had been excluded from the list; for which oversight the Queen maintained the Prince was answerable. And she had other grievances.

After the King's removal to Kew, the Prince had taken the wise precaution, which Her Majesty deemed high-handed impertinence, of placing the King's personal papers and jewellery under lock and key. He had also been heard, inexcusably, to call the Princess Royal a 'bandy-legged bitch'.

All things considered, it is not surprising that the Queen received her eldest son in a 'degree of passion', which he declared, 'I never had witnessed, nor believed to exist in Her Majesty before'. She forbade him to enter his father's room, withheld from him the doctors' bulletins, and was so unaccountable in her behaviour that Frederick, who always championed his brother, told her bluntly: 'I believe, Madam, you're as deranged as the King!'

The rows in the Palace and the racket in Parliament found an echo in London society. Party rancour had never turned so sour as in the early weeks of 1789. Everyone took sides for or against the Prince of Wales. Those long-suffering vestals, the 'Sisterhood', clung to the Queen. The King's graceless brothers rallied round their nephew. All the Whig ladies wore Regency caps. On December 30, Pitt, in a formal letter to the Prince, communicated the terms which 'His Majesty's confidential servants humbly conceive to be proposed in the present circumstances'. While tactfully assigning to the Queen 'the management of His Majesty's Household and the direction of appointments of officers and servants therein'—a glorified housekeeper in fact—he made it clear that the Prince's authority would be restricted to that of a cipher under Parliamentary control.

The conditions proposed not only excluded the Prince from the grant of pensions 'or any office whatsoever except such as must by law be granted for life', but deprived him of the power 'to raise to the peerage of this realm any person other than His Majesty's issue'; a clever move on the part of the Premier, who would thereby secure for himself a certain majority in the House of Lords.

The Prince's first reaction to this ultimatum was to refuse point-blank

87

the offer of a Regency under any such restrictions. On further reflection, however, he decided to indite a protest which, at the same time, would leave him a margin for acceptance. In a letter written by Burke, altered and polished by Sheridan, and delivered to Pitt on January 8, he expressed himself 'compelled to remark that it was not necessary for Mr. Pitt nor proper to suggest to the Prince the restraint he proposes ... His conviction of the evils which would rise from the government of the country remaining longer in its present maimed and debilitated state, outweighs, in the Prince's mind, every other consideration.'

Yet despite all animadversions, when, on February 12, the Bill passed through the Commons, the Prince's party gave vent to wildest demonstrations of delight. Pitt would go out. Fox would come in. Mrs. Fitzherbert would be made a duchess, the Regent a Field Marshal, and the Prince Bishop Commander-in-Chief of the Army. There would be a new Government to build a new world, founded on Burke's theory of Reform . . . Then from these happy Utopian dreams the Whigs awoke.

The King's doctors reported a remarkable improvement in the state of His Majesty's health.

Not even Doctor Warren, most dismal of Jonahs, could deny a turn for the better, or, in the opinion of his colleagues, for the best.

Far less frequent were those lapses into melancholia or babbling delirium. Indubitably was the King more rational in his behaviour and more cheerful. True, his cheerfulness led him to a chase of Miss Burney in and out the labyrinthine pathways of Kew Gardens, calling loudly after her to stop . . . 'Heavens, how I ran!' she cries. 'My feet were not sensible that they even touched the ground.' And although the King's attendants and two doctors joined in pursuit of the terrified Fanny, she did not stay her headlong flight until a servant shouted that: 'the Doctor says it hurts the King to run!'

When, 'with all his wonted benignity of countenance', His Majesty approached, 'think of my surprise', trills Miss Burney, 'to feel him put both his hands round my two shoulders and kiss my cheek! . . . And what a conversation followed! He opened his whole heart to me—expounded all his sentiments—assured me he was well, as well as he had ever been. . . .'

Up and down the garden path the King, 'pressed close to her side', walked with Fanny, who notwithstanding her alarm was highly flattered at such Royal condescension. 'He asked after the co-adjutrix', (the hated Mrs. Schwellenberg,) and said merrily: 'Never mind her! Don't be oppressed. I am your friend. Don't let her cast you down—you've had a hard time of it, but don't mind her! . . . Stick to your father!'

While daily, almost hourly, the King's convalescence is hysterically noted by Miss Burney, she withholds from her journal a remarkable incident told by one of His Majesty's pages.

One Sunday, while the Chaplain was reading prayers in the King's apartment with his equerries and doctors, Sir George Baker and Willis, in attendance, His Majesty was moved to interrupt the service with stentorian hunting calls of: 'Tallee-*ho!* Go forward, Miranda! 'Ware fox! Halloo, Ranger and Swift—*Tallee-ho!* . . .' The Chaplain paused and looked at Sir George and Sir George looked at the Chaplain, then '*Risum teneatis amici*', they laughed . . . recounts the page, who prefers to remain anonymous . . . 'And Sir George said the prayers had done His Majesty a vast deal of good, and Dr. Willis said the same—and the King dined very comfortably and was cheerful.'

So cheerful indeed that he called for his flute and made Sir George and Dr. Willis dance the hornpipe. They danced till it was dark. And, 'Huzza!' cries the joyful Miss Burney, 'Heaven—heaven be praised!'

Soon all London was crying praise to Heaven. The King's Most Gracious Majesty was cured.

On the day following the announcement of his father's recovery, the Prince was visited by a deputation from the Irish Parliament offering him the Regency of Ireland. He was touched, elated, cruelly disappointed. Such a bitter anti-climax he could never have foreseen. Since the English Bill was certain now to be abandoned, he could not accept, he must decline—'the arrangement, but nothing', he wrote, 'can obliterate from my memory and gratitude the principles by which it was made and the circumstances by which it was attended'.

That allusion to 'the circumstances by which it was attended', is doubtless the series of banquets held at Carlton House in honour of the deputies. The most convivial of these was their farewell party at which were present the Dukes of York and Cumberland, Burke, Fox, Sheridan, and a hilarious assemblage of Irishmen. The Prince, who himself had supervised the decorations, paid his guests the graceful compliment of adorning his walls with harps and shamrock. The same emblematic plant festooned the dining-table and sprouted from the centre-piece—the arms of Ireland circled by a 'glory'. Wine flowed in torrents, everyone made speeches; and on the final rising of the company, the Prince called for the 'Landlord's Bottle'.

To the Tories that offer arriving too late was a source of exquisite amusement; and when full of love and drink, staunch to the last, the loyal deputies set sail for their island, the jeers of the rhymsters pursued them.

> 'Six rogues have come over our pockets to pick,
> And dispose of their second-hand ware,
> To play the buffoon, to jump, tumble and trick,
> But they've come – the day *after the fair*!'

CHAPTER FOUR

1789—1794

THE King was himself again and his people jubilant. With his safe return from that moon-distorted world where none could follow him, he had become once more their 'Farmer George', their good old King–prematurely old at fifty-one.

London turned out in full force to see the illuminations in honour of His Majesty's recovery. Royal crowns, portraits of the King surrounded by coloured lights, glittered and flared from the Bank, the Exchange, and the great merchant houses of the city. The gates of Buckingham House displayed a grand gold and purple transparency. It was 'magnificently beautiful', Miss Burney declares, 'a day of happiness indeed . . .' But Carlton House contributed nothing more magnificent or happy than a row of funereal flambeaux.

On April 23, when the King drove through the streets to attend a Thanksgiving Service at St. Paul's, he was greeted with multitudinous cheers; the Prince with a sinister silence. Unjust rumour, propagated by the Queen, condemning his callous behaviour during his father's illness, had been given ready acceptance by a credulous public and magnified out of all proportion, until their former idol stood revealed with feet of clay, greedy rival for the Throne of their King, a drunkard, fornicator, libertine –a Whig!

In view of His Majesty's Tory predilections, Pitt now was the popular hero that once the Prince had been. He had been offered proof enough of his fall from grace, when, driving to the Opera shortly after his father's recovery, his carriage was held up by a crowd of hooligans. Hurling themselves at the doors of his chaise, they pulled them open and threateningly accosted him–'Cry Pitt for ever!'

Furious, but unafraid, 'Damn Pitt!' the Prince retorted, 'Fox for ever!'

They fell back and the carriage rolled on. . . . It had all been immensely unpleasant.

The Queen, who throughout the Regency campaign had been wholly guided by Pitt, carried complaints of her son to the King. The Prince retaliated by accusing her of 'favouring his father's enemies, of destroying and disgracing him and all her children'. The Queen lost her temper:

the Prince kept his. When the Queen gave a fête at Windsor to celebrate the King's homecoming, she intimated to the Duke of York that both his and his brother's presence would be regarded as superfluous. She 'wished only to entertain', she said, 'those persons and Ministers who had voted for the King and herself'. Ignoring this strong hint, both sons attended in full gala dress, and, to the Queen's vexation, were affectionately welcomed by their father.

The love of the once doting mother had turned to something strangely near to hate. No doubt the Prince was much to blame for the Queen's unnatural attitude, in that he had firmly entrenched himself in the enemy's camp with Fox and the Opposition; but that she should determinedly have set herself to revive hostilities between the convalescent monarch and his son is unbelievable. Yet so it was, and all hope of permanent reunion deferred.

The feud between the Queen and the two elder Princes was supported by the partisans of each. When, in the hearing of the Duchess of Gordon, Jack Payne, one of the Prince of Wales' equerries, passed a remark reflecting lewd implication on Her Majesty's friendship with Pitt, the Duchess hurled a breathless tirade at the Captain. 'Why, you insignificant good-for-nothing upstart chattering monkey-how dare you name your Royal master's Royal mother in that fashion!'

Such tales, founded chiefly upon hearsay and scrupulously served to the Queen, were greedily swallowed. Family dissension reached its climax in a duel fought between the Duke of York and a certain Colonel Lennox[1] whom Queen Charlotte greatly favoured. The Duke accused the Colonel of publicly encouraging slanderous talk of him and his elder brother, 'to which no gentleman would have listened without protest'. Lennox's request for an explanation of that statement resulted in an offer from the Duke to waive his royal rank and give him satisfaction.

On the morning of May 26, 1789, the Duke, who was staying at Carlton House, crept out at daybreak wearing his valet's hat-not a particularly adequate disguise. None but his seconds knew of this brave adventure. The Prince was still in bed and soundly sleeping when the parties, armed with pistols, met on Wimbledon Common.

The Colonel, by far the better shot, fired first. His ball, carefully aimed, went whizzing past the Duke's head and singed off, in transit, a curl of his hair. Thereupon the Duke, thankfully declaring he had given Colonel Lennox the desired 'satisfaction', mounted his horse and rode away.

When the news of this encounter was brought to the King, he evinced such alarm for the safety of his 'Hope' that it was feared he would have a

[1] Afterwards Duke of Richmond.

relapse. Not until the Duke had presented himself to his father, little the worse for his outing, was the King assured that his favourite son had not been carried home a corpse.

After that epic duel it was expected that the Queen would refuse to receive the gallant Colonel at her Court. On the contrary, not only did Her Majesty continue to receive him, but insisted on his presence at the King's Birthday Ball. Still suffering from the shock he had sustained on hearing of Frederick's narrow escape, the King kept to his room and knew nothing of the scene that ensued, when the Prince of Wales found himself faced in the same set with Colonel Lennox. Very red, he halted and stared fixedly at him to whom the Queen was wafting kisses from her fan; then, turning to his partner, the timid Princess Royal, he deliberately led her away.

The musicians went on playing; the Colonel went on dancing; the remainder of the guests, not knowing whether to go or to stay, uncomfortably followed his example; and the Queen, stretching her smile to its widest, quacked: 'Sir, do you find it too hot?'

'In such company, Madam,' was the emphatic rejoinder, 'it is impossible *not* to find it too hot.'

The Queen rose; the Princesses, like a flock of startled birds, fluttered to her side. The fiddlers stayed their bows in mid-air; and the room, hushed to silence, heard the Queen answer awfully: 'Then it were best I withdraw'; which she did. And that was the end of the Ball.

It was also the end of the season. In July, the King with his Court retired to Weymouth, and the Prince to his Pavilion at Brighton. Whatever breath of scandal may have drifted after him from London, at Brighton it was wholly disregarded. He had brought wealth, fashion, fame to that once obscure village, where he and 'Mrs. Prince', as old 'Smoaker' used to call her, were fêted, honoured, loved–to adoration.

The birthday of the Prince of Wales on August 12, was ushered in by a ringing of bells; sports were held in a field near the town, sack-races, donkey-races, ladies' races, with an ox roasted whole for the humbler folk and plentiful hogsheads of wine. In the evening when the Prince gave a Ball at the Pavilion, the whole town was illuminated, blazing to the sky.

Such evidence of loyalty was balm to his sore self-esteem. He had suffered much of disillusionment from fickle-hearted Londoners, from his mother's enmity–and cruellest cut of all–from the renunciation of his hopes. More bitter than he cared to own was the loss of his Regency snatched from him as his hand went out to take it.

Perhaps it is his tragedy that he should have been deprived in his first youth of the power which he, then, more fitly might have wielded than in his later years, when over-indulgence had clogged his sensibility. But at Brighton in that summer of 1789 we see him in his heyday, robust, laughter-loving, surrounded by eager disciples ready to follow wherever he led. Their pleasure-mad hunt for new follies was endless. One night, after a particularly tumultuous revel at the Pavilion, young 'Cripplegate' Barry rode a horse up the staircase of Mrs. Fitzherbert's house and into her attic; but once there it refused to come down, and could only be persuaded to descend with the assistance of two blacksmiths fore and aft. Nor was a horse in her attic the lady's sole unwelcome visitor.

After the King's return to health, the Prince, drinking deeper, playing higher than ever before, had played himself into debt again. But Mrs. Fitzherbert, having pooled her jointure with his income for the maintenance of her Pall Mall establishment, was called upon to bear the brunt of it.

No gentlewoman in all Britain could have been in worse case than she, when, one morning, she found the Sheriff's men upon her doorstep come to serve her with a writ. The Prince, who was in the house at the time, but invisible, sent messages at once to all his Hebraic acquaintances, none of whom was willing to oblige. Meanwhile, Mrs. Fitzherbert's attempt to despatch a servant with her jewels to the nearest pawnbroker had been foiled. The bailiffs stood foursquare against the door; not a person must go out while they were in. In vain the lady pleaded—let them take her jewels, her plate, in lieu of payment. They insisted on the cash, and unless it were forthcoming she would have to go to prison. . . . Heaven help her!

It was finally her 'husband', who, still in hiding, helped her. He sent to Carlton House for his own jewels, pawned them, and handed her the proceeds. Then at last was she rid of odious guests. Next day the Prince redeemed his jewels on the loan of an accommodating Jewish gentleman in St. Mary Axe, possibly the only moneylender in London whom he had not approached.

They were always in and out of trouble; they were constantly hard up, but through it all, as she long afterwards admitted, they were 'merry as crickets'. He may have found her merriment something of a strain, if not a trifle elephantine. She was—he had to face it—growing fat. Her features, according to contemporary description, were 'beautiful, except for her mouth which is ugly, having a set of not very good false teeth. . . .' Yet she was still in his heart and his letters, his 'Dear Love', as in the beginning and so until the end.

★   ★   ★

In that mirror by his bed-side at his ornate Pavilion, the Prince at rest, reclining, would have seen reflected there a changeful new procession on the Steine. While the same gaily-coloured shadow-show, diminished to a fairy's size, passed, repassed, and faded like a breath imposed on silver, other figures more sedate and solid came within his range of vision, vanished, reappeared. . . . Dr. Johnson, arm-in-arm with Mrs. Thrale and her brewer husband, a complaisant third, leading his dog a step or two behind them; or Parson Mitchell, Vicar of Brighthelmstone, with his curate Mr. Hudson; and one more conspicuous than these.

An unlovely sight was that *bon viveur,* Égalité, Duc d'Orléans. His mouth had fallen in, his hair had fallen out, and his copper-hued face was a mass of carbuncles. When in 1790 d'Orléans came over from France, then in the throes of Revolution, it is likely he intended to remain in England until the upheaval in his country had subsided, for in the June of that year he rented a house in Brighton and purchased another in London, near Hyde Park. He also brought over with him twenty-eight fallow deer as a gift to his *cher ami,* the Prince of Wales, who kept a kennel of stag-hounds on the outskirts of the town; these were shortly afterwards removed to Kempshott Park in Hampshire. On the arrival of the deer at Brighton an unfortunate incident occurred, due to the misplaced zeal of a Revenue officer. The Frenchman in charge of the stags had omitted to declare them at the Customs; they were seized, confiscated, and only after a great deal of fuss and heated explanation from the minions of the Duc, were the deer permitted to pass.

By what significant bribe Louis-Philippe of Orléans was induced to return to his native land at the height of its regicidal convulsion, is not precisely recorded, but certain it is he was back again in Paris in 1792 to vote for the death of his cousin the King.[1]

Retribution followed swiftly. In November 1793 Walpole was writing to a young friend, Mary Berry: 'of Orleans' exit I know no particulars; nor am I anxious about so foul a wretch.'

To Britain came the backwash of that blood-polluted tidal wave when Whig and Tory disagreements, sunk in mutual loathing of fiendish atrocities enacted in Liberty's name, led to a party split. Fox, for the extremists, was gloatingly exultant. 'How much the greatest event it is that has ever happened to the world . . . and how much the best!'

His iconoclastic doctrine did more than split his party; it split his sagging friendship with the Prince–to Mrs. Fitzherbert's approval. Burke, for whom she had never much cared, won her heart and the Tories'

[1] Louis Seize was executed on January 21, 1793 and the Duc d'Orléans on November 6, the same year.

respect with his fierce denunciation of the Revolutionary movement that found voice in his masterly *Reflections*.

It must have been an anxious time for Britain's future King. Rebellion in France was not confined to the evil passions and hatreds of a persecuted people against seigneurial tyranny. It was a cyclonic phenomenon that threatened the whole of Europe's feudal claims, and, in one mighty thunder-blast, struck at the roots of legislative power. In Britain, on all sides and in all classes, speculation stood divided in upholding or decrying that hydra-headed monster spawned on a bed of destruction from the Devil—or Democracy. And while Burke sounded his clarion-note in a trumpet-blare of indignation to raise those mangled dead rotting in Paris gutters, Thomas Paine, English Quaker, American settler, self-dubbed 'Citizen of the World', brandished his *Rights of Man* in reply to Burke's *Reflections*.

Soon every slum in almost every city could produce its Revolutionary Crusader. Thomas Hardy, with his Corresponding Society; the Unitarian Dissenters, Drs. Price and Priestley with their disciples, Kippis, Towers – these but a few who preached 'Love for their country', 'Liberty bursting its chains', 'Brotherhood'–and all the rest of it. In Birmingham, when Priestley and his party honoured with a dinner the second anniversary of the Fall of the Bastille, their feast was interrupted by a gang of loyal firebrands, yelling for their 'Church and King'. They then rushed off to burn down Priestley's house. A riot resulted that continued for four days, until the red-coats were called out to restore order.

Such assurance of public distaste for seditious propaganda was encouraging enough; but the Prince could not, though his father did, ignore these symptoms of anarchical infection. If Fox had shown his fist, the Prince could show his hand. Henceforth he went out of his way to favour equally both Whig and Tory. To Fox alone he extended no olive branch, no invitation to Carlton House. And in the summer of 1791, he found himself bereft, not only of a counsellor and comrade, but of his brother Frederick's good company.

The Duke of York, who ever since his return from Hanover had blindly followed the Prince's lead, had followed him into debt. Believing that his father could refuse him nothing, he applied to the King for financial help and was offered it on one condition: that he married a Princess of the King's choice–not his. Frederick, whose love-pursuits had been hitherto impermanent and divers, raised no protest to his father's proposition, and accepted in part payment of his debts, Frederica Charlotte Ulrica, daughter of Frederick II of Prussia, and niece of Frederick the Great.

She was no beauty; very small, pock-marked, insignificant, eccentric, and a great animal lover. She turned her house, Oatlands Park, near Weybridge, into a menagerie, adored dogs and kept dozens of all breeds. Puppies sprawled on her bed and piddled on her carpets; parrots screeched in corridors, monkeys leapt about and chattered in her rooms. The Duke was not amused and soon became disgusted at the fleas, the squawks, the yappings, and the smells. There were other reasons also why their marriage went awry. This new Royal Duchess was a haughty little person, fully conscious of her dignity as daughter of a reigning King. While she received Mrs. Fitzherbert out of courtesy to the Heir Apparent, she received her as the Prince's mistress and very decidedly not as his wife. Mrs. Fitzherbert, greatly aggrieved, complained to the Prince of the Duchess's offensive condescension; he, in his turn, complained to the Duke, and much unpleasantness arose. Thus it came about that for the first time in his life the Prince was estranged from his brother.

The Queen, who had never countenanced the presence of Mrs. Fitzherbert at Court, applauded the Duchess's attitude. Her Majesty by this time, must have been heartily sick of illicit affairs in the Family. Her sailor son, William, home from the sea, had now tied himself up with a play-actress. But William had the sense to keep his Mrs. Jordan in her place—far from the sight of the Queen—in a riverside villa at Petersham, where she lived with four children by various fathers, and none as yet by him. Her Majesty might not have been so tolerant of the sailor Prince's latest indiscretion had she known he was destined to be the father of ten—five sons and five daughters by the Jordan. That for the future; for the present the Queen's disapproval was centred on Mrs. Fitzherbert.

A marked exhibition of Royal displeasure had been noted at the interminable Warren Hastings Trial, which it was then the fad of Fashion to attend. When Her Majesty saw that Mrs. Fitzherbert had taken her place in the private enclosure reserved for the Princes, she rose from her seat in the Royal Box, ordered her daughters and ladies to follow, and hustled them out of Westminster Hall.

That same evening the Prince received a chilly letter from his mother requesting that the insult offered her 'by the very unreasonable intrusion of a Certain Lady at the Trial . . . shall not be repeated'.

His love-affairs, his politics, his debts, and his Fitzherbert, were—or so the Queen believed—driving him to ruin. For some years he had been an active member of the Jockey Club, but in October, 1791, his racing interests were brought to a sensational finale. More shock for his poor mother!

His horse, Escape, the favourite for Newmarket, ran third on the first day to a couple of outsiders. In consequence, the odds for the second day's running were dead against him; yet, contrary to expectation, the horse came in an easy first. Both the Prince and his jockey, Sam Chifney, were supposed to have done very well for themselves when the odds on Escape rose from two to one–to five to one against. Immediately after the meeting, a rumour went round that Escape had been pulled on the previous day, and that the Prince had been seen to give his horse a pailful of water to drink before the start, which winded him, lost him the first race, and lessened his odds for the second.

The Stewards at once demanded an inquiry, and Chifney was closely interrogated; but while nothing to his detriment could be definitely proved, the Jockey Club was clearly still suspicious. Sir Charles Bunbury, one of the Stewards, flatly told the Prince that unless he discharged Chifney from his service, no gentleman would run a horse in a race with his again.

Disgusted at the mud slung at his jockey, that also bespattered himself, the Prince, was not, as gossip gave it, 'warned off' the Turf; he resigned. As a last defiant gesture, or maybe because he was deeper than ever in debt, he sold his stud, pensioned off Sam Chifney, closed Carlton House and went once more into retreat. This time, however, his voluntary retrenchment did not meet with any sympathy at all. The public was bored by repetitive economy. His mountebank tricks, his spectacular flamboyance, his lechery, gluttony, and, worst of all, dishonesty–as witness that scandal at Newmarket–were despised and attacked tooth and claw. London had no use now for Prince Charming.

He still retained his hunting-box at Kempshott in Hampshire, for although he had given up racing, he was far too devoted to horses to give up his hunters. He must, besides, consider his weight, that despite all his efforts at reduction, increased. The rest of the year he spent at Brighton; and there, from his windows, he watched for the boats that came in with the tide, bearing fugitives from Terror into safety.

The burning of the Tuileries, the capture and imprisonment of Louis and his Queen, those hellish massacres on a Sunday in September, had roused the better part of Britain to a pitch of indignation that needed but another spark to light the torch of war. It flared–with the murder of Louis Seize. Danton's '*Audace*' was the head of a King, 'hurled as a battle gage at the feet of those who threaten us!'

Refugees were flying for their lives. In one week five hundred émigrés landed at or near Brighton. Among the first batch was a party of nuns. Hounded out of their convent by the Revolutionists, they had escaped from Ostend in fishing-boats and arrived at Shoreham, penniless, starving, soaked to the skin. Huddled together in the last stages of exhaustion, they sat in their drenched robes on the shingle amid a crowd of staring natives. So soon as the Prince heard of their plight he sent conveyances to bring them to Brighton, ordered rooms to be prepared for their reception at the Ship Inn, and more substantial assistance. Between them, he and Mrs. Fitzherbert collected a fund of over one hundred pounds on their behalf, the major part of which was the Prince's contribution.

When he judged them to be sufficiently recovered to receive him, he paid a visit to the Mother Superior. But when she knelt to bless him–'No, no!' he said, and raised her up and made her sit–'I must not keep you standing.' And then: 'After inquiring into the minutest details of every-thing that concerned us,' so one of the community recounted, 'he requested that the Sisters be presented, and received us with a kindness truly royal. We did not know that his protection had extended so far as to defray all our expenses in the town.'

His protection went farther than that. Through his aid and advice the destitute nuns found permanent sanctuary at a convent in Somerset, near Taunton. Nor were they the only victims of Liberty, Equality, and Fraternity, who owed him little less than their lives. The aged Arch-bishop d'Avranches, the Dean of Rouen, the Marquise de Beaule, who crossed from Dieppe in an open boat and was cast up half dead on Brighton beach, were but a handful of those who had fled from unimaginable horrors to find the Heir of Britain waiting with more than lip service in his welcome.

Perhaps the most romantic escape was achieved by the Duchesse de Noailles. Disguised as a boy she slipped the guards at Paris, and after a series of incredible adventures, reached Dieppe, boarded a trawler and stowed herself away under a pile of cable. A day or two later she was discovered by the skipper, and although he might have lost his head for it he landed her at Brighton in a gale. There, in the gusty dawn, they found her lying bruised and bleeding on the sea-lashed shore. Rough fishermen tended her, carried her in and brought her to Mrs. Fitzherbert. She was only twenty-one and very beautiful.

Chaperoned and dressed in woman's clothes borrowed from her benefactress, 'she was received by His Royal Highness', as reported in the *Sussex Weekly Advertiser*, 'with the most polite and cordial hospitality....' For her entertainment the Prince held a cricket-match in the grounds of the Pavilion, invited her to dinner in a marquee on the lawn, and ordered his private orchestra to play for her throughout the meal. Afterwards, with Mrs. Fitzherbert and Miss Pigot, the companion, they strolled in the gardens, 'the better to gratify spectators with the sight of the French lady'.

The sight of her seems also to have gratified the Prince. And if Mrs. Fitzherbert called him to account for the sincerity of his 'polite and cordial intention' towards her pretty protégée, she had been given cause enough, in this case quite unfounded, to misjudge him.

As neither wife nor mistress her position was invidious. Only by wilfully blinding herself to his infidelities, by accepting him for what he was and not as she would have him be, could she have acquiesced to years of insecurity. Financial embarrassment was the least of the indignities to which she was subjected; that she could have gladly faced, but not his indiscriminate inconstancy to shame her. He was 'too much', as she acknowledged, and as Sheridan had put it, 'every lady's man, to be the man of any lady'. She could protest, and she did, with nagging reproaches, with loss to her pride and her temper. They bickered too often for her peace and for his patience. In this submerged hostility she surely must have sensed greater issues at stake than the patching of innumerable quarrels. That all his rapture and her tenderness should be drained away in petty wrangling, or God alone knew what of ultra-critical resentment on his part, and indulgence, strung to breaking-point on hers, was unendurable; yet she endured.

She may have asked herself in what way she had failed; she had never been exacting—perhaps not exacting enough—when she ignored or accepted unquestioned that long list of successors to Perdita, picked from the demi-monde of playhouse or opera. But these were mere will-o'-the-wisps. He had forgotten the name of the one so soon as he followed the next, to sink deeper still in a muck-heap of scandal and debt. On Mrs. Billington, a celebrated singer, he wasted much time and more money. That affair did not last long. If her voice was delicious her habits were not. 'I can only be happy with her', he said, 'when I shut my eyes and open my ears . . .' On Mrs. Crouch, another foot-light favourite, he squandered £10,000 in jewels and trinkets in addition to a settlement of £1,200 a year. He must have been in dire straits to meet the demands of this lady when he sought assistance from another, and with embarrassing result.

In September 1792, a young guest in the house of Mrs. Fitzherbert wrote a letter which her hostess intercepted, and was mortified to read that:

'Miss Paget regrets it is not in her power to comply with the wishes of His Royal Highness, the Prince of Wales *to their fullest extent*, but in a matter of so much delicacy . . . there is not anything Miss Paget would not do to accomplish the purpose which he has in view, and thereby contribute to his personal happiness. As secrecy in a matter of this kind is of the greatest moment, if His Royal Highness will confer on Miss

Paget the honour of meeting her at the faro-table of the Duchess of Cumberland on Tuesday, the business may be arranged to the entire satisfaction of His Royal Highness.'

With laudable restraint Mrs. Fitzherbert hid from Miss Paget her knowledge, and not inexcusable, misinterpretation of this irregular request; but although tormented by suspicion the most vile, she remained as ever gracious and deistically calm.

Together, and on terms of friendliest affection, they drove to the Duchess of Cumberland's house in Pall Mall, where a company, more crowded than distinguished, had been invited to meet the Prince of Wales. He arrived on the stroke of ten o'clock, full of smiles, quizzically observant, shedding grace on this one and that as he passed up the room to bow to the curtsying Duchess. Despite his redundant bulge above the waistline, he was still the epitome of elegance. He now wore his hair cropped *au naturel* and heavily besprinkled with perfumed powder. Revolution in France had wrought its change on fashion. Gone were the brilliant colours and elaborate designs of the early and later years of the century. *Fin de siècle* demanded restraint in hue and texture; broadcloth had ousted brocade; ruffles of lace at throat and wrist had given way to frills of lawn and cambric, forerunner of the shirt-front yet to come; but not until the advent of Brummell and his sartorial dictatorship, did the Prince care to follow any fashion but his own.

The Revolutionary influence on women's clothes was even more apparent. Hoops were out, gathered folds were in. 'Heads' so high that the face of the wearer appeared to be in the middle of her body, belonged to the old régime, The new order demanded *'la victime coiffure'* – with wind-swept locks, carefully tousled; and to complete the illusion, a thin streak of crimson velvet circled the necks of the more daring.

As the company surged round the Prince, eager for a smile, word or look, Mrs. Fitzherbert may have suffered to see his roving glance rest on the brazen Miss Paget. Was a signal exchanged, of eyebrows lifted in an unasked question, or of eyelids lowered to the rounding of pursed lips? . . . The Duchess called the company to cards. They swept through the archway to the faro-table, the Prince leading with Miss Paget, whom he led away, out of sight, 'to accomplish his purpose' – and in secrecy. O, monstrous!

Excusing herself to her hostess the outraged Fitzherbert called for her carriage, leaving Miss Paget to bring herself home.

The next morning 'Miss' was confounded to hear that 'it would be highly agreeable to Mrs. Fitzherbert if she would select another place of residence'. Since no explanation had been offered for this peremptory ejection, the young lady desired an interview that she might know in what way she had offended. When to this artless appeal she received no reply, Miss Paget, with sobs, took her case to the Prince. Incensed at such contumely offered to a guest, he also demanded of his lady explanation.

Unaware that a storm had been brewing all night, the Prince met its full force in a charge of infidelity with the perfidious Paget!

It must have been quite an unique experience to find himself, for once, accused unjustly. He could supply, and he instantly did, a clear defence of Miss Paget's letter which by all the laws of hospitality, good breeding, and good taste, should never have been opened, much less read. To have done so, and to have drawn from it such shameful and erroneous conclusion, was unpardonable. He drove his point home to the hilt. He rammed into Fitzherbert his desperate straits. Gray's, the jewellers, were dunning him for ten thousand pounds; and because he knew Miss Paget's family possessed unlimited resources, he had been driven, much against his will, to approach the young lady with a request for a loan of that sum. She had managed to secure for his 'purpose' seven thousand pounds which she had handed him the night before–'in secrecy'.

But this facile apologia, defence, or what you will, served less to gratify than to infuriate Fitzherbert. She had held herself in; she now let herself out, and poured upon him her impassioned disbelief of Miss Paget's virtue, of the Prince's word, and the whole of his cock-and-bull story. Having then exhausted herself and her vocabulary, she took off her slipper and flung it at his head.

Miss Paget departed, unforgiven.

When shortly after this disturbance Miss Paget was married to a Captain in the Guards, the Prince gave her away at the altar with a present of a diamond necklace. It would be ungenerous to suggest that he paid for the gift from monies advanced by the bride; but there is proof enough that his prospects at this time had never been more gloomy. The perpetual alterations at Carlton House, the treasures he collected–he had lately opened an armoury in the attics which he filled with rare and ancient weapons, gathered from the four quarters of the globe–his bizarre extravaganza by the sea, to say nothing of Mrs. Crouch and her successors, had incurred debts that were soaring to the half a million mark.

Yet he was still to encounter a more costly attraction than any of these; one who with dangerous, dragon-fly brilliance, flashed into his life to his–and Fitzherbert's–undoing.

In June 1794 he wrote from Brighthelmstone to tell his 'Dear Love' that he would be in London for one night returning the next day. They had arranged to meet and dine at Bushey with his brother, William, Duke of Clarence. But the Prince did not appear; instead he sent a note which was handed to his 'Love' at the dinner-table. It contained, in a few brief words, his intention 'never to enter her house again'.

That recurrence, re-enacted, of the Perdita episode, preceded by a letter expressive of deepest regard, is as inexplicable as it was unexpected. No pricking of her thumbs, no premonition, warned the woman he had married that her star was due to set. But her heart received the message before her eyes had read it, to know herself supplanted—and by whom.

*   *   *

Daughter of an Irish bishop, wife of an English peer, Frances, Lady Jersey, born Twysden, was the complete antithesis of Mrs. Fitzherbert. Small in her person, exquisite to the eye, and entirely unscrupulous, she held indisputable right of place as a leader of London society. Women loathed her, men adored her, and Her Majesty graciously accepted her at Court. Such signal favour from the Queen caused some remark in view of Lady Jersey's elasticity of attitude to any moral code. Her regard for the proprieties was light as Fitzherbert's was heavy; but to everyone's amaze not only did the Queen encourage, she directed her son's attention to this ravishing creature who succeeded, where all others had failed, as usurper of Fitzherbert's principality.

Her supple intellect allied to a certain *gamine* impudence which never offended, never encroached on bad taste, enticed, intrigued, alarmed him. That she was several years his senior, and a grandmother to boot, served only to complete his subjugation. He could never love a woman younger than himself, yet he certainly did not love her. While he had pursued, and besought the surrender of Mrs. Fitzherbert to the threat, and the point, of his extinction, from Lady Jersey's approach he retreated. She renewed the attack with the persistence of a midge. She inflamed him, she vexed him, he fled—and she followed. It was all wholly new and exciting to find himself no longer the seducer but seduced.

His capitulation might have ended there; her charm was brittle, her laughter metallic, her energy exhausting. She gave him no peace. She held all the feminine tricks in her hand and she played them with mercurial dexterity. He yearned for the bosom, the comfort, the warmth of his 'Dear Love', discarded, withdrawn into an impenetrable fortress, unapproachable: unkind. He was cruelly hurt that she should have taken in such ponderous, humourless earnest a message sent in a moment of pique—'never to enter her house again!' She should have known it for a whimsy, one of those lightning impulses that came upon him like a

103

summer storm and passed as swiftly, leaving not a cloud and scarce a memory save that of a heavy night's drinking, a headache, a swelling of those troublesome throat glands, or whatever. . . . He had expected tears, the usual volley of reproaches–her temper of late had been awful–a return of his note the next day with an imperious request to explain it, which, had she given him the chance, he would have done. There might have been a scene, he had been prepared for that, but not this arctic, unfathomable silence. She had made a fool of him and everyone was talking! . . . 'A treaty of separation and provision is on foot between His Royal Highness and the late Princess Fitz.'

Separation there was certainly, but of provision none. Not until he could be sure she had left him for ever would he discuss any tiresome terms. He missed her dreadfully. The charms of his grandmotherly enchantress were slowly beginning to pall. The spriteish Lady Jersey looked younger than her daughters, but was older in experience and cunning than the deuce; and not all her subtle tricks, her sensuous abandon, charged with consuming fire that never quite consumed, could pay one half the cost of her. She was mightily expensive, and for ever plaguing him to give her more. He had no more to give, unless he gave himself in marriage. What a prospect! But the King grabbed the chance offered by the exit of Fitzherbert to come forward with a pledge to clear his son of debt, on condition that he take to him a wife.

While he hesitated he was lost.

In December 1793, a marriage between one Mr. Augustus Frederick and a Miss Augusta Murray had taken place, privately, at St. George's, Hanover Square.

The bride, who appeared to be several years older than her scared young bridegroom, and also in a very interesting state, accounted for her condition to the scandalized officiating clergyman by telling him she had married her husband in Italy while he was still a minor. On the attainment of his majority they had decided to re-marry here in England.

When, a month later 'Mrs. Frederick' gave birth to 'a male infant', the affair was all over the town. The King had news of it, and paid a hasty visit to his son, Augustus, who had contracted in Rome–and at St. George's–a clandestine marriage with the Lady Augusta Murray. Prince Augustus Frederick was sent packing, and left his wife behind to weep alone. When the case came before the Courts of Royal Privilege, their brief union was declared null and void, and dissolved in accordance with the Royal Marriage Act.

These proceedings, which created a great stir and brought the King to the edge of lunacy again, dispelled any scruples the Heir to the Throne might have held in respect of Mrs. Fitzherbert. He had now been given all excuse to make the fatal move. If the marriage of a younger brother, sixth in succession to the throne with no likelihood of ever ascending it, had been pronounced invalid, he must accept his cross and know the worst. He was not and never had been married. It was his duty to be married and beget him an heir, which Frederick's wife, the Duchess of York, showed no sign or intention of doing. Moreover, Lady Jersey, for ever at his elbow, had told him–and he could not but agree–that the cause of his present unpopularity was his much-discussed association with a 'Papist'. No objection would have been raised had he kept her in her proper place–the alcove; but to present her to the world as his wife, and to insist she be honoured as such and received into society–surely he must realize how he had made, not only her, but himself ridiculous. That pricked him. So be it! . . . He drove down to Windsor, walked in unannounced on the King, who had just returned from hunting, and without any palaver, said: 'I wish to marry'; then, as suddenly as he came in, he went out.

The King, in high glee, hastened after him with voluble assurance of good-will, promises of debts to be instantly paid, of fabulous settlements and a choice of two brides: his own niece or the Queen's. Which would he have? Either were his for the asking.

The Prince made it plain that he cared not a button which would be his for the asking since–'One damned German Frau was as good as another!' The Queen was urging him to take Louise of Mecklenburg-Strelitz, her brother's daughter, who from all accounts was lovely, accomplished, and in every way suitable to be Princess of Wales, but not to his taste–or Lady Jersey's. If married he must be, she would countenance no rival in her province. Louise was rejected. 'One of *that* family', the Prince flung at his mother, 'is enough.' The Queen was disgusted; the King over-joyed. He had prayed that George would choose his niece, his sister's daughter, Caroline of Brunswick. And, lo! Caroline it was to be. . . . For which he gave thanks unto God; but although he knew it not, the King had more reason to thank Lady Jersey.

For the Prince's delectation she had endowed the Princess Caroline with every beauty, virtue, wit, and all the graces. When a miniature arrived, bearing proof that her plaudits of this Hebe did not exaggerate, he returned his chosen bride a highly flattered portrait of himself.

In a fever of impatience he awaited the arrival of this incomparable being so soon to be his wife. He kept her pictured face before him; he studied every feature: hair of purest gold, eyes of sheer heavenly blue: lips ripe as strawberries and as tempting. No 'damned German Frau' was she, but a sprig of a girl, a laughing *primavera*. . . . And Lord Malmesbury, the former James Harris, had gone over to Brunswick to fetch her away!

If Mrs. Fitzherbert, still in retirement, heard with fainting heart of the betrothal, she gave no sign, uttered no word of complaint. Fiercely determined to let none pity her, she indulged in no pity for herself. She held her head high, 'waived her claim to *Ich Dien*', remarks Walpole, and retired to Margate where daily she was seen to be, 'driving away sorrow in a phaeton and four'.[1]

When it became known that the Prince had made her a settlement of £3,000 a year in compensation for the loss of him, the public ceased to wonder at or query his decision. Mrs. Fitzherbert belonged to his past. All interest now was focused in his future.

[1] Mary Berry to Horace Walpole.

CHAPTER FIVE

1794–1803

LORD MALMESBURY, who had travelled in exceeding discomfort over rough ice-bound roads, lay the night at Peine in 'a decent inn', and completed the three-mile journey to Brunswick on a morning in November.

Met by the Grand Marschal Münchausen, the hymeneal envoy from England was received with a surplusage of fuss. Apartments in the Palace, servants, a carriage immediately placed at his disposal, preceded a pressing invitation from the Duchess to dine.

Not surprisingly, since she was sister to George III, did Malmesbury find her 'garrulous, good-natured and talking incessantly of nothing else but her daughter's marriage'. Her husband, the Duke, was 'civil, reserved –but stiff'. And Caroline . . . Malmesbury is too much the perfect diplomat to disclose, even to the privacy of his journal, that his first impression of England's future Queen was disappointing. For her extenuation he records her 'much embarrassed', concedes her 'a pretty face–not expressive of softness–her figure not graceful–fine eyes–good hand–tolerable teeth, but going–fair hair–good bust–with what the French call *les épaules impertinentes*. Vastly happy with her future expectations.'

He had to make the best of her. Those impertinent shoulders, he hoped, would atone for her saucy impertinent tongue. She had inherited her mother's and her uncle's volubility; was loud in her laughter, but 'quite at her ease–too much so', is Malmesbury's comment. He watched her every movement, was persistently beside her to serve her daily lectures on behaviour and deportment, and to coach her in the part she was to play.

'Sat next to Princess Caroline at supper . . . I advise her to avoid familiarity, to have no *confidentes*: to approve, not to admire excessively –to be perfectly silent on politics and party. To be very attentive *and respectful* to the Queen. . . .'

He ended by reducing her to tears.

He found that she improved upon acquaintance, was pathetically anxious to please, to stand well in the eyes of this fiftyish, fascinating Englishman, with whom she seems to have tumbled head foremost in love; but she soon tumbled out again, when, a week after his arrival, she received that miniature sent from the Prince, depicting him as an ethereal **Adonis**; beautiful beyond imagination.

She was enraptured, awed, and not a little frightened. How could she live up to this miraculous divinity? Of herself she had no conceit at all; she was careless in her dress and not very nice in her person, which fact had already been noted by the eagle eye and sensitive nostril of his lordship. However, he must wait his opportunity to tackle her or her ladies on that most delicate subject. In the meantime it was her mind not her body which engrossed him. She bombarded him with questions concerning her betrothed that taxed even his ingenuity to answer. 'She asked me about Lady ★ ★ ★ ★, appeared to suppose her an *intrigante*, but not to know of any particular connexion between her and the Prince.' Nor on that point was she, seemingly, enlightened.

She wished above all things 'to be popular and feared that I thought her too prone *à se livrer*. I made a bow. She said "Tell me" ' . . . He did. 'Popularity', he warned her, 'was never attained by familiarity. It is only to be acquired by a just mixture of dignity and affability. I quoted the Queen as an example in this respect. The Princess said she was afraid of the Queen. . . .' Which is not surprising, since Malmesbury dinned into her ears the admirable qualities of her future mother-in-law, until Caroline came to regard her as a species of female Cerberus. 'But of this Lady ★ ★ ★ ★, now' – to whom she returned with disconcerting insistence – 'I am determined never to appear jealous. I know the Prince is *léger*. . . .' To which elliptical pronouncement his lordship tactfully replied 'that he did not believe she would have any occasion to exercise this very wise resolution'.

As time was short and she had much to learn before her departure for England, he replenished each moment with advice and correction. At a masquerade held at the Opera House and attended by the Duke, the Duchess, and their daughter, his lordship had 'a very long conversation with the Princess Caroline', whom he found 'inclined to be over cheerful and too *mixing*'.

In order that she should have no chance to be 'too mixing' with insinuating strangers in mask and domino who spoke to her in squeaky falsettos – and to whom it is believed she as squeakingly responded – he led her to a balcony. From that secluded eyrie she could look down on the crowded amphitheatre, unobserved.

She might have envied those who were allowed to 'mix' – as it was *verboten* she should – in every kind of frivolous fancy-dress costume: romping bacchantes, chased in among the revellers by some drunken young Silvanus; a Columbine footing it fleetingly with Harlequin – or any one of that gay company other than a Princess of Brunswick, watching from a balcony with her staid courtly mentor beside her, who preached his English manners in her ear. Dust kicked up from the whirling dance below, pricked her eyes, starry with excitement behind their velvet shield; the music piped its madness into her very toes, while he cleared his throat to tell her: 'He most ardently hoped she would follow the example of the King and Queen, and never on any account miss Divine Service on a Sunday.'

Grave matter this, for a masquerade.

'Does the Prince', she demanded, 'go to church?' Malmesbury's reply was distinctly evasive. 'I have no doubt', hemmed his lordship, 'that you will make him go.'–'But if he doesn't like it?'–'Then your Royal Highness must go with him.'

So daily, nightly, he applied the curb to this unbroken filly. She scarcely chafed against the bit, so expert was his guidance, while he hoped against hope to have her trained before she ran in double harness.

She can scarcely be blamed if she were too prone '*à se livrer*'.

Born of a loveless marriage, brought up in a Court where every woman was fair game for every man, where she had seen her sire's mistress publicly foisted on her mother, small wonder Caroline was uncontrolled and uncontrollable. Although her father claimed that she had been 'élevée sévèrement', Malmesbury saw no sign of it. The Duke enlarged. 'Elle n'est pas bête, mais elle n'a pas de jugement.' Evidently not; nor any dignity and little education. Her French was fluent but her English execrable; and Malmesbury beset with misgivings.

'She has no *fond*, no fixed character, a light and flighty mind, but well-meaning and well-disposed. My eternal theme to her is *to think before she speaks*. . . .'

She never did. On the very day he delivered that lecture she was quizzing him at supper on his supposed *affaire* with her spinster aunt, the Abbesse de Gandersheim; and 'laughed unmercifully' at his discomfiture. The Abbesse, who seemed determined to make trouble, had been at pains to warn her niece that men in general, and the Prince of Wales in particular, 'were not to be trusted', and that her bridegroom elect would be 'certain to deceive her'. Which not improbable conclusion Malmesbury dismissed as mischief on the part of 'an envious and *desiring* old maid'.

It was rather unfortunate that a few days after the aunt had offered her niece this gratuitous preview of her marriage, the Duchess should have received an anonymous letter from England, hot in abuse of the Prince and his connexion with a certain Lady * * * *, who is represented as 'the worst and most profligate of women'. Instead of keeping these revelations to herself, the Duchess immediately showed the letter to her daughter and 'harped on it all day', wails Malmesbury. The Princess, however, had taken more to heart a letter from her uncle, the King, in which he hoped 'que sa nièce n'aura pas trop de vivacité et qu'elle menera une vie sédentaire et retirée'. 'These words', said his greatly vexed lordship, 'shock the Princess, to whom the Duchess very foolishly reads them.'

His last warning before they left Brunswick was a reminder of the English law, to the effect that any man who presumed to love a Princess of Wales would be guilty of high treason and punished by death. 'So also', he ominously added, 'would she.' . . . No wonder he admitted she was 'startled'.

His main purpose now was to expedite the bride's departure before further disclosures from England should arrive.

On December 29, 1794, Caroline, with her suite, her ladies, Lord Malmesbury, and her mother, who was to accompany her as far as Hanover, set out upon the first stage of her journey. The Duke shed tears, but not of grief, to see her go.

It was to be a longer way, a harder way than she, in her blind happiness, could ever have foreseen. War with France thundered before them; the Dutch and English troops pressed in on either side, and the bridal party driven back, and back again, were forced to take cover in roadside hostelries, gingerly proceeding onward by cross-country routes out of the line of fire. The unceasing thud of guns disturbed their nights and terrified the Duchess, who 'complained vulgarly' of the bad food, bad inns, intense cold, foul beds, and Lord Malmesbury's insistence that Her Royal Highness should be more free with her tips to the servants. Caroline, conversely, had to be restrained from 'flinging her money away like a child'.

After leaving Osnabrück, a messenger sent in advance to reconnoitre, brought letters from Lord St. Helens and General Harcourt, in command at British Headquarters, strongly advising their immediate return to Delden. The Duchess, chattering with fright and blue with cold in that severest winter ever experienced within living memory, hankered for the safety of Brunswick far removed from the distant flash and near roar of those guns. At which Malmesbury, unsoftened by her fantods, told her flatly: 'Your Royal Highness *must not* leave your daughter! . . .' But Caroline, all eager to move on, stoutly declared: 'Je n'ai pas peur de canons'. Whatever her faults, lack of courage was not one of them.

During their frequent delays, Malmesbury filled in his time and wasted much ink in minute observation of his charge. He sums her up as 'possessed of a ready conception, no judgment, caught by the first impression, led by the first impulse; loving to talk and prone to confide and make *missish* friendships that last twenty-four hours . . . Great good-humour, much good nature. Fond of gossiping, and this strengthened greatly by the example of her good mother . . .' who regaled him with stories of her nursery days in England, when she shared a bed with her brother, the King. 'As disagreeable a bedfellow as any royal or plebeian infant could be,' tut-tuts Lord Malmesbury. He may have been relieved to hear that His Britannic Majesty's uncomfortable juvenile habit was eventually cured by the insistence of his father–the then Prince of Wales–that he should wear a blue ribbon with a china article attached to it, 'which', cackled the Duchess into Malmesbury's boiling ear, 'was *not* the George!'

After that it is scarcely surprising to find him 'constantly compelled to frown upon the Princess Caroline's disrespect for her mother'–and still more at her disrespect for him . . . 'Nasty and indelicate!' he utters, when one of the Princess's 'going' teeth went, and was sent down to his lordship by her page. He felt himself constrained 'to put a curb upon her desire for amusement . . . Her head', he sighs, 'is very, very, light . . . I make it the daily object of my conversation to urge upon her *never* to stoop to private concerns.' Yet he did not always practise what he preached.

'I endeavour as far as possible to inculcate the necessity of great and nice attention to every part of dress–as well as to what was hid as to what was seen. I knew she wore', he parenthesized, 'coarse petticoats, coarse shifts and thread stockings, and these were never well-washed nor changed often enough . . .' How he came by this knowledge he does not reveal, but it seems her ladies were instructed to supervise her toilet and see to it 'that she be well washed all over'. A 'private concern', surely, that was no concern of his.

At Hanover the Duchess left them, 'much afflicted' at parting from her daughter; and the Princess not at all, whom Malmesbury found 'impossible to be more cheerful, more *accomodante*, more everything that is pleasant'.

No question she had reason to be cheerful. Her tedious apprenticeship was drawing to its close. Her pernickety meddlesome tutor with his scoldings, his croakings and pryings, might lecture a Princess of Brunswick, but never a Princess of Wales.

At the seaport of Stade, the last lap of her journey, came full realization, perhaps with faint panic, of her future exalted position. Flags were flying, crowds on the quayside cheering, guns barking their deep-tongued welcome from the squadron escorting her over the sea, when she stepped aboard H.M.S. *Jupiter*. A rope-ladder was let down; she clambered up. A midshipman, young Mr. Doyle, flushed with the honour, assisted the Royal bride on to the deck; and that same officer was he who, a quarter of a century later, guarded her small coffin in the ship that bore her body home again to rest. . . . Heels clicked; a hand withdrawn smartly sprang to the salute: the sun's gleam on powdered hair, on gold lace and the sword-hilt; then his great moment faded. Hers had only just begun.

It was a marvellous clear evening. The long frozen winter had vanished. Spring danced again in the land-wafted breeze that, like a mischievous urchin, played in the bellying sails, ruffled the water's surface in a million gold-tipped wrinkles, and followed them all the way. But off Yarmouth those fair winds sank in fog, and unable to proceed for fear of running on the flats, *Jupiter* dropped anchor. The ever watchful Malmesbury improved this last unshining hour with a final résumé of injunctions.

'She must be choice in her language – never talk of being *sick*'. . . . Some of the more squeamish, but not Caroline, had succumbed to the North Sea's swell. . . . A further hint to her ladies 'on various subjects'. One might almost believe his *trop de zèle* had set his lordship sniffing at her Highness. 'The Prince was very *delicate*. He would expect a long and careful *toilette de propreté.*' He hoped for the best and expected the worst when, at four in the morning of Good Friday, the fog lifted. On April 3, Caroline took her farewell of *Jupiter's* officers and came aboard the Royal yacht *Augusta*, at Gravesend.

She would have seen, on this her first near sight of England, 'a prospect', that even Malmesbury for all his attention to her '*toilette*', was moved to find 'most beautiful'; a green and golden prospect, unmarred by factory spires or octopus sprawl of docks and wharves and warehouses. Mud in plenty at low tide she would have seen, fringing willowed banks lined with excited spectators come to watch the King's yacht pursue her course up-stream, jostling each other for a glimpse of that small, fair-haired girl in the bows. She would have seen level-lying marshland, casually inter-spersed with ship- and timber-yards where the ring of hammers mingled with the sound of field and farm, of rooks calling, gulls mewing, land and river elbowing the sea; and, as the yacht nosed Londonward, on either side that splendid waterway there would have been lush meadows where pied cows grazed knee-deep in springing grass. For this was an England, three-fourths rural, and an age as vigorous in agriculture and commerce as in war. Those rectangular hedged fields carried the eye upward to softly rolling landscape of pasture set about with oak and beech and elm screen-ing red-roofed villages, squat church towers; here and there a manor-house, coloured like a pomegranate with white-pillared doorway, pompous as its dignified merchant-owner. No Council-planned, jerry-built irruption disfigured that Georgian Arcadia, whose green arms spanned corporeal urbanity even to the verge of London Bridge.

From the river's bend at Greenwich, she who watched – and with what joyful contemplation – would have seen the skyline stencilled in a smoke-wreathed mirage of steeples, belfries, and topaz-pointed light that held suspended high above the city, a vast grey bubble crowning it: St. Paul's.

The yacht edged slowly inward; but from Wren's silvery palace on that sunlit waterside, no greeting came for Caroline; not a coach, not a courtier not a soul was there to meet her.

At the Hospital, where she waited a full hour for the first carriage to arrive, she was 'awkwardly but attentively' entertained by the Governor and his two sisters. All were in the fidgets, his lordship in a state, and the Princess in trouble again. Standing at the window looking down upon the crippled pensioners hobbling on crutches, she made another of her childishly terrible remarks. 'Is every Englishman without an arm or leg?' 'No joking, Madam,' shuddered Malmesbury, 'I beg.'

At last the carriages and their military escort were heard below; but with them no Prince was come for his bride. He had sent, in his stead, Lady Jersey.

Her curtsy was a thing to wonder at; those deep-fringed eyes were quick to note that the Princess, thanks to Malmesbury's untiring insistence, was charmingly dressed for the occasion. Lady Jersey may well have been informed of certain items of that trousseau on which, for once, the bride's father had spared no expense. The choice of her gowns lay not with poor hoydenish Caroline, nor with her mother, the Duchess, but with Mademoiselle de Hertzfeldt, the Duke's mistress, whose good taste was renowned and unerring; but her ladyship had come prepared for that.

With honeyed persuasion Caroline was beguiled to a room in the Governor's house. Her blue quilted petticoat, her muslin, her frills, her black beaver blue-feathered hat, were cast aside in favour of the harsh white satin gown and unbecoming turban Lady Jersey had so thoughtfully provided. Nothing could have been worse suited to the Princess's over-ripe complexion than that close-fitting cap with its high nodding plume, which hid her hair and cruelly emphasized her goggling gooseberry eyes. Nothing could have more effectually concealed 'that good bust', those 'impertinent shoulders', than this shapeless ill-made travesty of a bridal robe. But it delighted Caroline.

Lady Jersey had been much maligned; no angel could have possibly been kinder. All Malmesbury's injunctions against indiscreet confidence and gossip were forgotten; and in the short time those two were alone together, Caroline had rendered up her secret. Though her English might be limited, her rhapsodies were not. She loved–but *how* she loved!–a Prussian officer. 'His one little finger she loved better than the whole of the person of the Prince of Wales!' Who was dutifully apprised of this interesting attachment the next day.

Well pleased with her manoeuvres achieved in half-an-hour, and with a final touch of the hare's foot to Caroline's adorning–a superfluous attention in view of her high colour and the Prince's preference for pallor–her ladyship conducted her willing victim to her coach; but just as the fairy-like Frances was about to follow and take her seat beside her, Lord Malmesbury stepped up to put her down. She must sit with her back to the horses, not facing them with the Princess.

Lady Jersey opened wide her eyes. 'It makes me sick', she protested, 'to sit with my back to the horses.' His lordship bowed. An unfortunate disability for a Lady-of-the-Bedchamber to suffer, since her office demanded that when in attendance she must always sit back to the horses. However, to save her from any likelihood of an occurrence 'as displeasing to herself as it would be highly disagreeable to Her Royal Highness', it were better she sit with him in the following coach. Mrs. Aston, the second Lady-in-Waiting, would drive with the Princess.

Mrs. Aston would do no such thing. Lady Jersey knew her duty and her place–and in she hopped to it. No more was said of sickness.

Led by a detachment of the 10th Hussars, headed by a newly gazetted young Cornet, one George Bryan Brummell, the procession set out upon the King's highway to London.

As the cortège clattered along the wide flat road of Southwark into the city and over its Bridge, Caroline, eagerly observant, ceased to chatter with her new delightful friend. Accustomed to those orderly small Hanoverian towns of her homeland, to clean uncrowded thoroughfares, to narrow cobbled streets and houses unchanged through the centuries, this, her first entry into the world's greatest capital, must have impressed, may have awed her a little.

She would have seen the Port of London with its wherries, tugs and cutters, barges, proud white sails; and the heavy hulks of merchantmen pouring into the metropolis their treasure loads from North, South, East and West: spices, tea, rare porcelain, silks, sugar, tobacco, cotton, wine; animal skins, oil, timber, hides, exotic fruits. Flags of all nations, like so many birds of bright plumage, flew from a forest of masts. A stranger, as was Caroline, would have been half-deafened by the street noises and clamour, the cries of the vendors, the rattle of wheels, the clip-clop of hooves, the seething, incessant hum and bustle. Purposeful business men dodged impatiently for right of way as they hurried to their offices; red-faced podgy men, prosperous and strutting, lean men and pawky men, sickly men with quills behind their ears, their hatless hair unpowdered, dank–the clerks of the city who spent their days perched at their desks totting endless rows of figures. Women mingled with them here and there;

little milliners in mobs and striped pouched petticoats, bent on their various missions; stout farmers' wives from outlying villages, driving their empty gigs homeward from the market. Ragged children there would be with old work-worn faces, stealthy truants loping into foetid alleys from those factories where they laboured through long, dreary sunless days and late into the night; or a black-faced midget chimney-sweep or Master Sweep himself with his stiff-headed brushes, his donkey-cart and sacks; waggoners and hay-wains drawn by shaggy shire horses as were never seen in any other land; a smocked drover with his herd of steers, and beggars by the roadside – blind men, showmen, tumbling dwarfs and whatnot; piemen and news-sheet men yelling through their trumpets; chairmen and hackney-coachmen, pimps and bailiffs, felons, highwaymen, magistrates, gallowsmen, attorneys – all rubbing shoulders one against the other, and none concerned with any business but his own.

It was a city of confusion, of startling sudden beauty, of tawny-bricked houses built upon the sites of those destroyed by the Great Fire, unpretentious, graceful, much of a sameness, with flat high windows and three steps up; a city of smells, odoriferous and acrid, indescribable – of smoke and soot and lay-stalls; of rotting vegetable refuse, of sea-coal, cats and cow-sheds, sewers, grass, manure; a smell of plane-trees, of fields and open spaces, of Hampstead's hills merging blue above a windmill in the distance, for every thoroughfare in this King George's London ended in a glimpse of green. . . . And so into the wide handsome streets of St. James's with their mansions, their gardens, their bow-windowed bottle-paned shops.

But: 'Very little crowd,' is Lord Malmesbury's laconic observation, 'and still less applause on the road.'

Though her drive through the city had occasioned 'little crowd', her arrival at the Palace was met with flattering 'applause' enough from those assembled at the gates to watch the coming of the bride.

Cheer upon cheer rose up to hit the sky when she appeared at the windows of the Duke of Cumberland's suite. Again and again she curtsied, or, as Mr. Walpole gives it 'bowed exceedingly'. . . . She seems somewhat to have overdone her gratified response to all this noisy acclamation, for the curtsies, smiles, bows, hand-wavings, went on till the Prince, impatient of these tributes not directed to himself, intervened, 'made excuses', giggles Walpole, 'of her being fatigued' – and shut the window. 'Everybody speaks most favourably of her face as most pleasing', adds the scribe of Strawberry Hill, who for all his love of royalty cannot withhold a catty rider: 'too much rouge'.

She must, poor girl, have needed reassurance from the people; she had been given none from him whose wife she was so soon to be. With Malmesbury beside her hissing in her ear one last word, 'she must kneel'—so did she, as her bridegroom, stout, florid, and magnificent in his gold-laced Hussar uniform, came hurrying to greet her. His step was buoyant, his hair in perfumed nut-brown curls, his eyes alight and greedy. Then, for one imperceptible second, he paused before he stooped to raise her where she knelt in the trembles, and that pitiful white satin! . . . Was this gauche, highly-coloured, unappetizing, pouter-chested gawk the pictured Hebe of his dreams, his hopes, his future? . . . The very touch of her confirmed revulsion. The throb and surge of senses, flaming with anticipatory excitement, fused and died at his first kiss. He backed, he turned, and without another word or look he walked away.

Malmesbury, watching from his distance the anguish, the despair, the bitter rageful disappointment of that meeting, knew, with conscience-stricken certainty, that the marriage was foredoomed; nor 'was it possible', he afterwards confessed, 'to conceive or foresee any comfort from this connexion, in which I lament very much in having taken a share. . . .'

'Harris!' That high-pitched voice struck through the silence like a whip-lash. 'I am not well, bring me a glass of brandy.'

'Sir!' A glance aside at the staring, small white-satin figure who stood where she was left with her mouth a little open, her jaw a little dropped; and in a careful undertone Malmesbury protested: 'Had you not better have a glass of water?' 'No, by God!' snarled the Prince, 'I will go—directly —to the Queen.' And he went, or rather, bolted from the room.

The Princess, aghast at such churlish behaviour, had received an equal shock. This extolled Prince of Wales, renowned for his beauty, charm, and grace, was as much a disillusionment to her as she to him. She had carried in her heart an image created from his miniature, of a golden youth, a demi-god with classic features and a dimpled chin. True, he had a dimple in his chin, but there resemblance to his portrait ended. Thick-jowled, pendulous, flabby was his face, his nose snoutish, his body bloated and, notwithstanding his corset, swag-bellied—he weighed seventeen stone in his stockings—and his eyes, embedded in fat, were blood-shot with drink or thwarted desire. 'Mon Dieu!' Mortified, scarlet, she turned to the fidgeting Malmesbury. 'Est ce que le Prince est toujours comme cela? Je le trouve très gros et nullement aussi beau que son portrait!'

He who had brought her there—her only friend at Court—came forward with bowing apologies. 'His Royal Highness was naturally a good deal affected and flurried at this first interview, but she would certainly find him different at dinner.'

Indeed she greatly hoped so. She was dubious, and he the more embarrassed at her 'further criticism'–interrupted, opportunely, by a summons from the King.

It did not require the astuteness of a Malmesbury to perceive that His Majesty had already been given an unfavourable report of his niece from the Queen who had listened, with more delight than sympathy, to her son's jeremiad of his wife-to-be. The King asked but one question concerning her: 'Is she good-humoured?' And, on Malmesbury's reply that 'in very trying moments he had never seen her otherwise', her uncle spoke of Prussian politics, and no more of her.

The dinner held that evening in her honour by Lord Stopford, the Vice-Chamberlain, was attended by all who had accompanied the Princess from London to Greenwich. So soon as Caroline saw Lady Jersey and the Prince together, 'I knew how it was', she long afterwards declared, 'and took my *partie*.' But she did not take it well.

Faced with the mistress of her future husband, she shot at her enemy a quiverful of nonsense that made Malmesbury blush for her–and for himself. No credit to him was this flippant, rattling 'missish' persiflage–'these giddy manners, attempts at cleverness and coarse sarcasm', pointedly directed at her ladyship, who sat superiorly mute.

All through that ghastly betrothal celebration, Caroline giggled and chattered, and, in the worst possible taste, quizzed her glaring Prince on his relationship with Lady Jersey. She whispered dirty jokes to him; she breathed her guttural French at him; she thought to charm and utterly disgusted him, and yet she could not see it–did not know.

Later, in the dusk of that warm April evening, the Prince rode at breakneck speed down to Richmond, galloping madly past the house of Mrs. Fitzherbert.

She stood there at her window. The curtain may have trembled in her hand; and, had she raised it, that marriage might have never taken place. But she gave him not a sign; she sent him not a word. She watched him go.

On Wednesday, April 8, 1795, in the Chapel Royal at St. James's the marriage of George Augustus Frederick, Prince of Wales, to Caroline Amelia Elizabeth of Brunswick was duly solemnized.

The bride, in the traditional white satin, pearl-embroidered, appeared to be almost entirely extinguished by her voluminous cloak of crimson velvet. The bridegroom in blue, richly ornamented, wore knee-breeches, high-heeled buckled shoes, 'and looked', so an eyewitness remarked, 'like death and full of confusion'; or, as might have more correctly been reported, full of drink. So unsteady was his gait and stance that he could scarcely be held upright between two Dukes, who, as if they were heraldic symbols, stood supporting. His bride, on the contrary, was in the gayest of high spirits, nodding and smiling right and left, as she pranced up the aisle on the arm of her uncle, the King, to join her swaying bridegroom at the altar. He, having been got upon his knees, stayed there until Dr. Moore, Archbishop of Canterbury, paused to ask the question: 'If there be any impediment why ye may not lawfully be joined together in Holy matrimony?' At which the Prince started up, gazed wildly around, hesitated, made as if to run. The crowded congregation all eyes and ears and murmurs, excitedly awaited the next move.

It came—from the King.

Leaving his seat he crossed to his son who seemed about to burst into tears. Coaxingly, his father laid a hand upon his arm, whispered to him, firmly pressed him down, and the service went on to its end.

The organ pealed, the choristers sang: 'O well is thee! O well is thee! Happy, Happy, *Happy*, HAPPY. . . .'

It was over; and to the ringing of joy-bells, the cheering of Londoners, the waving of flags and the booming of guns, the bride and bridegroom drove to Buckingham House. A splendid banquet had been prepared for their reception, with a wedding-cake so huge that it filled, in transport, one entire coach. Lady Jersey, tacitly accepted by the Queen and the Prince as guest of honour, having previously interviewed the chef, had tinctured the pastry offered to the Princess of Wales with a powerful dose of Epsom salts. This thoughtful act may, or may not, have been prompted by an old midwives' tale that a strong enough purgative ensured conception of a virgin bride.

And when the newly wedded pair had received the congratulations of their guests; when the bridegroom had further soused himself with wine and spirits; when His Majesty had fondly embraced his niece, and Her Majesty had pecked at her cheek, the bride, who seemed to be the only cheerful member of the Royal Family, departed with her husband in their coach for Carlton House.

There can be no doubt, save in the word of Caroline, that he was drunk, if not incapable, that night; for he passed the early hours of next morning in the fender where he fell: and where she left him.

So began his second married life.

The first two days of their honeymoon were spent at Windsor; then, accompanied by a troupe of the Prince's friends and the Princess's Lady-in-Waiting as the only other woman guest, the unhappy pair went on to Kempshott Park.

Whatever discontent the bridegroom may have suffered in the early days of marriage, his companions made the rowdiest use of their time. They drank all night, gamed all day and snored off the result of their festivities on sofas, where, still in their boots and fully dressed, they sprawled with their feet on the cushions.

In this, her disillusionment, Caroline's good humour wilted; drooped. Her blossoming hopes and venturesome spirits were chilled—not to silence; she could never hold her tongue—but to biting sarcastic retort in defence of her pride. The despairing echo of her martyrdom recurs as she recounts it, in her harsh ear-scraping English, throughout the pages of Lady Charlotte's Journal[1] . . . 'If anybody say to me at dis moment – will you pass your life over again or be killed? I would choose death. . . .' Had she a friend, had she a counsellor, a Malmesbury – for all his croakings – there beside her during those few weeks of honeymoon, misnamed, she might even then have saved herself much bitter degradation; but she had now no 'confident', nor any woman to advise her; none but her husband's mistress in supreme command of him, his heart, his body, forsworn before the altar to the worship of his wife.

Constantly humiliated, denied the common courtesies and rights that were her due, she sought to avenge heaped insults by offensive ridicule. When at dinner, Lady Jersey drank with marked deliberation from the Prince's glass, the Princess, seated near to Major Hanger, who had lately inherited the Barony of Coleraine, seized his pipe and boldly puffed a cloud of smoke into her husband's face.

Such kitchenmaid antics served her nothing save to gall him. She had neither the wit nor the tact to perceive how he, epicure and arbiter of elegance, was tormented by her raucous voice, her clumsy insolence, her lack—for him—of physical allure. To stand well in his sight, or heaven only knows from what other confused motive, she 'tossed at him', so she herself admits—and this the day before they married—certain letters from minor Prussian princes and princesses, with the inane remark: 'There! That's to prove I am not an impostor!' And to prove also her tolerance and her understanding, she chaffingly alluded to Mrs. Fitzherbert as 'Fat, fair and forty!'

Her pitiable efforts at ingratiation increased his repugnance for this unfortunate girl until his loathing became a pathological obsession. 'I would rather see toads and vipers crawling over my victuals', he was heard to say, 'than sit with her at table.'

[1] *Diary of a Lady-in-Waiting*: Lady Charlotte Bury, daughter of the fifth Duke of Argyll. In 1796 Lady Charlotte Campell married first, her kinsman, John Campbell, who died in 1809. Some years later she married the Reverend Edward Bury.

The differences between the ill-starred pair were noted with inward glee by Lady Jersey. Not a moment's opportunity did she allow to pass unpoisoned by her venom, and calculated carefully to prick. Every foolish word her lover's wife uttered in her hearing, each complaint of his conduct, each gibe at his person, was whispered to the Prince. One may well believe that Caroline did not spare his *propreté de toilette*; nor his stays.

His taste was revolted, his vanity outraged. That this ill-mannered, coarse-tongued 'German Frau' should have dared to mock at him—First Gentleman of Europe—was utterly intolerable, not to be excused; and the final blow that brought about her fall.

It soon became apparent to those in waiting on the Prince at Carlton House, that his marriage was calamitous. He made no attempt to hide his aversion to her who suffered, not only from his neglect and dislike, but from his mother's malice. The fact that her son had chosen as his future consort the King's niece and not hers, may have accounted, in part, for the Queen's hostility to Caroline. While she knew that this Princess from Brunswick was entirely unsuited to her husband or his state, the Queen made no effort to heal the breach between the two. She continued to endow Lady Jersey with favour, invited her to intimate family gatherings, and sat her at table to play loo with the Princesses.

That gentle 'Sisterhood', cowed by their mother's domination, dared offer no protest nor voice one word of sympathy for the hapless Caroline at whom her ladyship dealt dainty spite with every card she held. In the fulfilment of her triumph the mistress showed no mercy for the wife. Shortly after their homecoming, the bridegroom retrieved from his bride some pearl bracelets he had given her and handed them to Lady Jersey. She wore them unashamed in his wife's presence.

Not all of Malmesbury's coaching had achieved such good result as did this pitiless aggression from her enemy. Caroline was learning how, as he, in his tutelage at Brunswick had advised, 'to *commune* within herself, to question herself, and act up to her situation'.

Her innate courage aided her; and though her heart was bruised it did not break. Nor did she hesitate to speak her mind and let her husband know she would brook no further insult from him or from his mistress. Her protests went unheeded; and when she requested that the woman who had made her life unbearable be dismissed from office, the Prince retaliated by insisting she continue to receive her 'as her friend, to treat her with respect, to entertain her . . .' Finding that her self-assertion had no more effect than to drive him from her bed to Lady Jersey's, she appealed to her uncle, the King.

He who grieved for, and in his fashion loved her, sought by all means in his power to mend the mischief done. He may have felt himself responsible for having urged the marriage, but who could have foretold that it would prove so disastrous a failure? His son's callous treatment of his affectionate, and to King George's taste, pretty young wife, was the more reprehensible in view of her condition, confided to her uncle. And all that was fundamentally good in this rather stupid, conscientious, very respectable King, rose now in Caroline's defence. He patted her, he soothed her, and promised to relieve her of the noxious Lady Jersey. He trotted back and forth between his son and his niece, oozing anxiety and kindliness from every pore. These misunderstandings must be settled, Lady Jersey forced to go—and come no more in waiting upon Caroline.

To his father's peaceable intention the Prince reluctantly agreed. Two factors played their parts in his compliance. The first, and certainly the weightiest consideration, was his debts, which at any cost—even though it be complete renunciation of his charmer—must be paid. The second, scarcely less important to his future, was the trend of public opinion against him. Not only in the Court but out of it, his intimate affairs were openly discussed and his marriage condemned, as 'unwise, unpolitic, ruinous, absurd . . .' To save his face he must appear before the world as a husband well pleased with his wife. None knew what it cost him to make the attempt, and receive guests with her at his side.

When he entertained the Prince of Orange at a dinner, she behaved 'very lightly, even improperly', pronounced Lord Malmesbury. The Prince, who throughout the evening had suffered hideous embarrassment, afterwards asked him, 'how he liked this sort of manners?' Malmesbury admitted that he 'liked' them not at all, and quoted her father, the Duke, who had often told him 'she had been brought up strictly, and if not strictly kept, would, from high spirits and from little thought, emancipate too much'.

'I see it'—indeed the Prince saw it—'too plainly. But why, Harris, did you not tell me so before or write to me from Brunswick?'

In self-extenuation 'Harris' begged him recollect 'he had been sent on the most positive commands to ask the Princess Caroline in marriage . . . Nothing more. Had he discovered any notorious or glaring defects, he would have felt it his bounden duty to have stated them.'

With laudable restraint the Prince forebore to remind his lordship that her defects were glaring and notorious enough to wreck his life and hers; yet—'although the Prince, appeared to acquiesce', confesses Malmesbury, 'I saw it left a *rankle* in his mind'.

Nor, it seems, did he endeavour to rid himself of 'rankle'. He nurtured it, he lived with it, he lay with it, and woke to find it there beside him, a death's-head mockery of all that he had known and loved in shared comradeship of marriage, for ever lost to him.

In June he took her down to Brighthelmstone, to encounter added misery in memories revived. He encountered also Lady Jersey, whose condition occasioned much tattle, and allowed opportunity for wicked Mr. Walpole to offer: '*a bon mot*, though not perfect enough for the Berryana.[1] It seems it has been reported that of the two pregnancies at Brighton,[2] the greatest is a tympany and the biggest a dropsy. "What," said W. Fawkener,[3] "is the Prince still between wind and water? . . ."'

They arrived at Brighton in a downpour of rain that quenched all illuminations in their honour, but not the welcome extended to the royal pair by enthusiastic Brightonians. Every kind of amusement, fête, military reviews, balls, took place daily and nightly; yet the Princess, according to contemporary observation, appears to have preferred her own society to that of any other. Attended only by two ladies and an equerry, she roamed the countryside, sitting under hedges to eat sandwiches and brood upon her wrongs. They were mounting. Her detested rival had managed to secure a packet of letters written by the Princess to her parents at Brunswick. These, entrusted to a certain Dr. Randolph—successively Bishop of Oxford, Bangor, and London—contained a detailed account of every member of the Royal Family; and, with less discretion than veracity, paid particular and unflattering allusion to the Queen.

The fact that these private letters never reached their destination gave rise to the suspicion that they had been intercepted by Lady Jersey. The Bishop, who was responsible for their safe delivery, found himself compelled to vindicate his carelessness in letting them out of his charge. As excuse he gave the illness of his wife that had delayed his visit to Brunswick, and declared he had returned the correspondence by post-coach to Lady Jersey at Brighton. She vowed she had never received it. The Princess insisted she had; and, moreover, accused her of not only reading the letters herself, but of handing them over to the Queen. The Prince, dragged into the fray, was loud in support of his favourite's innocence, and repeatedly asserted that his 'Royal mother would never be a party to any such improper circumstance'. After every possible effort had been made to trace the lost packet, the search was abandoned. Subsequently the letters were found—in the possession of Queen Charlotte.

Thus, from the first, was Caroline subjected to a system of espionage that dogged her to the bitter end of her life.

[1] Agnes and Mary Berry.
[2] The Princess of Wales and Lady Jersey, who gave birth to a son in October, 1795.
[3] William Fawkener: envoy to Russia.

From June until November the Prince and Princess remained at Brighton, during which time the recurrent question of the Heir Apparent's debts was re-introduced to Parliament. In order to secure a settlement appropriate to his marriage, Pitt stated that it would again be necessary to relieve the Prince of Wales from his present liabilities. These, since 1792, when he had owed £200,000, now exceeded more than treble that amount.

It was by no means the most opportune occasion for any such disclosure. The country, weighted with its heavy burden of war-taxation, viewed with little tolerance the fact that in seven years the Prince had squandered more than half a million on his women, his horses, his houses and his drink. But from those who denounced him came no intimation that the greater part of this vast sum had been spent on pictures, furniture, the nucleus of a national treasure-trove which will be remembered to his everlasting credit when all else to his shame is forgotten. The Philistinism of Parliament, however, held no brief for art. Pitt proposed that the Prince's income, exclusive of the revenue derived from his Duchy of Cornwall, should be increased to £125,000 with the proviso that £25,000 a year should be deducted from it until his debts be paid. The Premier offered further, a jointure of £50,000 a year for the Princess, which, with an added Government grant of £27,000 to defray all expenses of the marriage, appeared to be generous enough. The Prince's hopes lightened – and darkened again when he heard that Pitt had no intention of relieving him of his encumbrances until after an accurate investigation had been made.

This was little to his liking. He had rendered his accounts once too often. Fox, ever ready to challenge his Chief, demanded that Pitt make provision, not only for the present, but the future of the Prince. He greatly objected to Mr. Pitt's proposal that £25,000 a year be deducted in settlement of the Prince's debts which, at that rate would take twenty-seven years to pay. Instead, he suggested a deduction of £65,000 a year, plus the sale of the life interest in the Duchy of Cornwall which, Fox estimated, should realize something near upon £300,000, and would effect a speedier discharge of his embarrassments.

The Prince received this intelligence with the uttermost dismay. . . . *Et tu, Brute*! How could Fox expect him to live on £40,000 a year,[1] which was all he would have left to him after so ruthless a reduction of his revenue? Always paranoiac, he felt himself to be the victim of a deep-laid plot on the part of the King, with every man's hand in Parliament against him. On the promise of instant relief from all financial obligations he had been bribed into marriage with a woman he abhorred, and having

[1] By eventual agreement of the Government, the Prince's income was not decreased, but increased by £40,000.

123

married her, his income looked to be razed to a pittance, and he made responsible for the total payment of his liabilities. Nor did William, Duke of Clarence, an eager champion, improve his brother's cause when he delivered to the House of Lords one of those well meant but meandering speeches, with which in later years this Sailor King was wont to electrify his ministers. Red-faced, emphatic, he was on his feet to tell them that the Prince of Wales 'was in the situation of a man who, if he cannot get a particular haunch of venison, will take any other haunch rather than go without'!

This sentiment, that might have been more gracefully expressed, left the Lords with aching sides and the Prince with his 'haunch', for which small mercy he must, perforce, be grateful. He was not: and no longer was he popular. The voice of the people had violently turned in his disfavour. At a time when more than half the men of England were shedding their blood for their country and for his future Throne; when those left behind starved while he battened, this parade of his extravagance brought a tumult of opprobrium upon him—and his father. On his way to open Parliament the King was attacked by a hunger-ravished mob, and the glass of the coach window splintered by a bullet from an air-gun; but on this, as on all such other dangerous occasions, he appeared at his kingly best; cool, unshaken, unruffled. To the Lord Chamberlain who received him on his arrival at Westminster he calmly stated: 'I have been shot at.' No fuss, no agitation. That same night when he attended Covent Garden Playhouse with his wife and daughters, the tale of his courage was in everybody's mouth. As he stood in the Royal box bowing right and left, the house rose to a man and cheered him three times three. All was well with their good old King! . . . But all was not well with the Prince.

For the third time he made an exhibition of his poverty, reduced his Household, refused to entertain, and went into gloomy retreat. Once again he was mistaken in his belief that the public would rally to the side of their Playboy. Not a soul raised a voice in his favour. The people of England had matter of more moment to occupy their interest than the Prince and his spendthrift follies.

News from the fighting front was ominous. War-tormented Britain, smarting under the disgrace of recent defeats, loosed the flood-tide of her humiliation in political meetings all over the country. At the end of June a monster meeting gathered in St. George's Fields; another in October, at Islington, near Copenhagen House. These inflammatory agitations, led by those lately prosecuted, and acquitted radicals, Gale Jones and Thelwell, resounded in yells of: 'Bread! Bread! No King! Peace! Down with Pitt!'

It began to be alarming.

The whinings of the underdog had become a predatory wolf-howl. No longer was Reform a bogey to scare the more timid of Mr. Pitt's Tories; it was a poisonous seed scattered on hurricane winds from Revolutionary France, to bring forth, in that tumultuous period of gestation, a Gargantuan movement destined to father industrial revolt.

And, while the thunder of war shook the skies across the Channel; while the officers and men of His Majesty's Navy held at bay in British waters those French hordes who threatened their island's invasion; while the year closed in darkness for England and her Prince, a new life to both was born.

★   ★   ★

On the night of January 8, 1796, the Prince of Wales, it was said, 'appeared to be much agitated', and conducted himself generally as would any other man under similar conditions. When on the morning of January 7, between nine and ten o'clock, his wife, after a long and difficult labour, was safely delivered of a princess, his relief and excitement knew no bounds. He was free! He had fulfilled his marital obligations and secured his future throne in the direct line of Succession.

So soon as the birth of his daughter had been witnessed and attended by the usual dignitaries and formalities, he hurried in to look at her. One glance sufficed to hurry him out with the unimpassioned observation, 'a fine girl'. No word for her who had brought into the world this lusty, squealing, kicking sprig of Hanover; and with that supreme mark of indifference from her husband, vanished Caroline's last hope to save her marriage.

Not devoid of philosophic humour was her attitude to her unhappy lot. 'After I lay in—je vous jure', thus, in retrospect, she confided to her lady, Charlotte Bury, 'I received a message through Lord Cholmondely to tell me I never was to have de great honour of inhabiting de same room wid my husband again . . . I said very well, but as my memory is short, I begged to have dis polite message in writing. . . .'

And in due course the message came.

'MADAM,

. . . Our inclinations are not in our power, nor should either of us be held answerable to the other because nature has not made us suitable to each other. Tranquil and comfortable society is, however, in our power: let our intercourse, therefore, be restricted to that, and I will distinctly subscribe to the condition which you required . . . that even in the event of an accident happening to my daughter, which

I trust Providence in its mercy will avert, I shall not infringe the terms of the restriction by proposing, at any period, a connexion of a more particular nature. I shall now finally close this disagreeable correspondence, trusting that as we have completely explained ourselves to each other, the rest of our lives will be passed in uninterrupted tranquillity.

I am, Madam,

With great truth,

Very sincerely yours,

GEORGE P.

The Prince, having thus 'completely explained' himself, left his wife no alternative other than:

'. . . to communicate to the King, as my Sovereign and father, both your avowal and my answer. ∴ As I have at this moment no protector but His Majesty I refer myself solely to him upon this subject, and if my conduct meet with his approbation. I shall be, in some degree, at least, consoled. I retain every sentiment of gratitude for the situation in which I find myself, as Princess of Wales, enabled by your means to indulge in the free exercise of a virtue dear to my heart–I mean charity . . . and that of patience and resignation under every trial.

Do me the justice to believe that I shall never cease to pray for your happiness and to be,

Your much devoted,

CAROLINE.[1]

May 6th, 1796.'

So, within a year of their wedding-day these two were disunited. The Prince, whose conscience may have, a little, nagged him, had tacitly given his wife to understand that should she so wish to do she could remain at Carlton House; but her pride would not allow of this concession. If banished she must be from her husband's bed and company, she would, she made it clear, forgo his board.

On the understanding, therefore, that her baby daughter be allowed to visit her, Caroline retired to Charlton, a village near Blackheath. The infant Princess, Charlotte Augusta, remained at Carlton House in the care of Lady Elgin.

---

[1] The above letter is a translation from the French in which it was originally written.

With the same resigned adaptability as one accepts a climate, did Caroline become accustomed to her new life and its surroundings; and though 'everybody blamed me,' she admitted, 'I never repented me of dis step'. Nor did he who, happily rid of his encumbrance, sought consolation in the arms of Lady Jersey. His flagrant disregard for the dictates of society turned once more the tide of popular favour against him. The indulgent British public could forgive him his debts, his liasons, excesses, affectations, because, for all his faults, he was their Prince, entwined into the nation's very heart; but that open relationship with his ageing Circe they could neither forgive nor forget. Her they held to be primarily responsible for the wreck of his marriage and the expulsion of his wife. Even at Brighton, where he reigned as uncrowned King, the loyal townsfolk looked askance at his mistress, with whom, to avoid disagreeable demonstration, he left his seaside palace and retreated to Crichel, the seat of a Mr. Sturt, in Hampshire.

There, throughout the winter months, he rested not contentedly. No woman, however attractive in her spritely middle-age, could comfort, soothe, forbear with him in his unpredictable moods as could his adored, and discarded Fitzherbert. He had exchanged the smooth passage of life with her for a matrimonial squall that had run him on the rocks; and there he stuck. His irregular association he found more difficult to sever than either of his former bonds had been. The limpet-like persuasions of the tenacious Lady Jersey could not so easily be shaken off. She clung.

The news-sheets squirted condemnatory hints at the pair of them. *The Times* (June 2, 1796), remarking on the death of Lady Jersey's infant son,[1] gave this bereavement as a possible cause for the absence of 'a certain High Personage at Court on Saturday last. As there can be no *good* reason assigned,' adds the commentator, 'the above may do as well as any other. . . .'

Such suggestive innuendoes did not pass unheeded. They preyed upon the Prince's mind to rouse in him a growing sense of injury. To be quit of a burden more weighty than his debts was now his sole preoccupation.

The invasion scare of 1798, consequent on naval mutiny at Spithead and the Nore followed by insurrection in Ireland, had roused the fighting blood of every man and boy in Britain. Although sadly lacking in arms, training, and equipment, tens of thousands joined the volunteers to throw their weight against the little Corsican whose military genius and dangerous ambition sought, not only the conquest of 'a race of shop-keepers', but the ultimate possession of all Europe.

At this critical moment, when Bonaparte was preparing to bestride the

[1] Born October 16, 1795; died May 28, 1796.

Near East and, unknowingly, to meet his match and master—a frail, undersized, blind-in-the-eye Admiral—the Prince of Wales seized upon a proffered straw for his release from those silken cords that bound him, more firmly than a felon's chains, to his airy-fairy Frances, Lady Jersey.

To give him his honest due he was as strongly motivated by the frenzy to be up and doing with the rest of them, as to be severed from a mistress of whose well-worn charms he had tired. To show himself eager to enter the lists with his fellow Britons at a time when every man of them was spoiling to defend his country with his blood, would not only, he hazarded, restore his self-esteem and his lost favour with the people of England, but would serve also as excuse to withdraw from his adhesion.

Influenced, moreover, by his love of the spectacular, he may have seen himself a warrior hero, leading his armies into battle as had his gallant forbear, George II. These were visions; reality was sour when he saw his brothers departing one by one, to snatch the glory, of which by reason of his heritage, he must be deprived.

First went Frederick, who in 1794 had met the French at Tourcoing and where he, incidentally, almost met his death. For all his good intentions and long apprenticeship in Germany, Frederick had not, so far, achieved any striking success.

A somewhat smug and highly respectable fourth brother, Edward—soon to be created Duke of Kent—had sailed off on the outbreak of war in command of British troops at Nova Scotia. Then there was Ernest, later Duke of Cumberland, leading the Hanoverian armies in Holland against overwhelming French odds. This un-Guelphlike Ernest, who bore no resemblance to any son of Hanover, had proved himself to be the best soldier of them all. Tall, thin, supercilious, secretive, he had been shockingly disfigured at Tournai, and carried a formidable growth of whisker on his face to hide his scars. Yet at least he had won them, with his spurs, in battle; and ugly though he was the ladies loved him.

King George's youngest son, Adolphus—his father's joy and pride—serving with the Guards in Hanover, had been severely wounded in 1793, during his first campaign in Holland. He returned home to be wept upon and nursed by his adoring sisters and his fond Mamma.

Of them all, two younger brothers only, were, with the Prince of Wales, excluded from taking any active part in warfare. William, Captain Guelph, who two years before and without the Admiralty's leave had sailed his ship home from Halifax, was in consequence granted no commission to serve his King and country.

To Augustus Frederick,[1] however, love was of greater importance than

---

[1] Created Duke of Sussex in 1806.

war. Banished from the Kingdom by his father, after his marriage to Lady Augusta Murray, he lived happily in Berlin with his wife who had fled from England to join him there by means of a faked passport.

But the Prince was not content to lead a *laissez-faire* existence sheltering behind his rank and Lady Jersey's petticoats. Why should he be forbidden the right of every other man to bear arms and risk his life–with six brothers to replace him should he die? And if he should be called upon to make the supreme sacrifice, for whom and for what had he to live? In this exalted mood he sent a note of supplication to the King.

'SIR,
. . . The serious and awful crisis in which the country now stands, calls for the united efforts of every British arm in the defence of all that can be dear to Englishmen. . . . Whatever may have some time back have been Your Majesty's objection to my being in the way of actual service . . . these objections will I humbly trust yield to the pressure of the times. . . .

Death would be preferable to being marked as the only man that was not suffered to come forth on such an occasion. Should it be my fate to fall in so glorious a contest, no injury could arise to the line of succession on account of the number remaining of Your Majesty's children. . . . I presume in no respect to prescribe to Your Majesty the mode of being employed; what I humbly and most earnestly solicit is the certainty of active service in such a character as Your Majesty shall see fit.'

The King's reply to this appeal dashed any hope he might have held of martial self-display, and left him still with Lady Jersey on his hands. She would, or could not see her day was done; that her kitten-playfulness, her tinkling laugh, her exigent demands on his diminished purse, and all those little dainty tricks he once had found enchanting, were no more to him now than an irritant. When looking back upon the first months of his enslave-ment, he remembered how, against his will, she had pursued him. He had not sought, nor had he intended, to be for ever tied to an evanescent whimsy. He knew, despite that she was physically ethereal, her disregard for any calculation save her own was pachydermatous. He itched to have her gone from him; he longed for his Fitzherbert. He took to drink again to drown his memories and narcotize the sting of Lady Jersey. His health became affected; he thought, and half hoped, he would die. He had already made a Will–six months after his marriage–in favour of Mrs. Fitzherbert; and in 1799 he sent a copy of it to his 'Beloved . . . my Wife, my second Self'.

This was followed by a letter enclosing a locket that contained a miniature painting of his right eye. 'How I have ever loved and adored you God only knows', he frantically declared, 'and how I do *now* He also knows. . . .' So it seemed did everyone excepting Lady Jersey.

At last, even to her, was the unwelcome truth revealed. For three years he had laid persistent siege to his 'Love–his only Love–his Wife', imploring her return to him. That she remained deaf to his pleas and his prayers did not entirely distress him. Previous experience had given him to hope that he would win her in the end. He grovelled, entreated, abased himself–but not as before, in her presence. She stayed in her fastness at Ealing, where she had taken a house; nor would she give him entry there. . . . He was content to wait.

When his intention was carried to his second wife, she at once conveyed to one of the Prince's Household that 'she hoped her husband would not feel *her* to be any impediment to the reconciliation which he so much desired'.

This message, duly delivered to the Prince, called forth from him the surprised ejaculation: 'Did she *say* so? . . . Indeed she is very good-natured!'

Having thus gained, and gratefully, Caroline's approval, he renewed his attentions to Mrs. Fitzherbert, ringing the changes on his penitence and sorrow for the pain he had caused his 'Angel', and her hard-heartedness in denying him his rights. Surprising change of front! She was now the breaker of their marriage vows, and he the misused husband at her feet. And still she gave him nothing, no answer to his letters, no admittance to that villa at Ealing. . . . And why Ealing? When if she so desired she could live, at his expense, in a palace in Pall Mall.

As a last resource he threatened her with a public avowal of their marriage. 'Think not,' he wrote, 'that prayer or any advice whatsoever will make me delay my purpose or forswear my oath.'

For her the situation was not without its irony. Time had been when she would have given all she held most sacred to have known him ready to acknowledge her his wife before the world. But to do so now, when the woman to whom he was irrevocably bound had borne him a possible heiress, might well encompass his ruin. The people of England, unanimous in their championship of the maltreated Caroline, would brook no exposition of the Prince's former marriage, sanctioned by the Church of Rome but not by British law.

After much thought and earnest discussion with Father Nassau, her confessor, Mrs. Fitzherbert decided to refer final judgment to the Pope.

Accordingly, the Father set out on a mission to Rome. He returned in December, 1799, with a Papal Brief from the Supreme Pontiff, bearing the Seal of a Fisherman, which stated that His Holiness, having carefully considered the case of Maria Fitzherbert, had pronounced her to be the wife of her third and lawful husband, the Prince of Wales.

Her conscience was salved; since Higher Authority had pronounced her marriage valid, nothing more could hold her back. And with the dawn of the nineteenth century, she and her Prince were reunited.

Their public reconciliation took place in June 1800, and celebrated by a somewhat belated wedding-breakfast. The walls and tables of the reception room at Mrs. Fitzherbert's house in Tilney Street, Park Lane, were decorated with white roses; she carried a bouquet of the same symbolic flower, and the Prince at her side appeared to be almost hysterical with joy. If the wedding guests found it slightly droll to see this adipose middle-aged pair disporting themselves as a youthful bride and bride-groom, the large-minded, displaced Caroline was moved to declare Maria Fitzherbert to be 'the Prince's true wife—an excellent woman. It is a great pity he ever broke wid her'. . . .

But the breakage now was mended; and roses, white, were strewn upon their path from which the obstructive Lady Jersey had removed herself to Margate. There she pursued her latest conquest, John Ponsonby, a very young man, who subsequently married her own daughter. After this defeat her ladyship returned to London and was seen at the Duchess of Devonshire's garden fête. The Prince, '*en polisson*', in a brown suit and a brown wig, had brought with him his own band, and stood by it all the afternoon, choosing the music to be played; while Lady Jersey was amusingly observed to be 'coasting round the Prince . . . who appeared to be annoyed with her and eyed her askance. She is resolved to plague him . . .'[1] Not again, and never more would Lady Jersey 'plague' him. He was guarded.

*   *   *

A great era had passed; one greater still was in its dawning. Yet the birth of the nineteenth century brought to Britain little promise of a future pre-ordained to resound in triumph through the ages. While the Prince of Wales could perceive no cloud on his horizon, the political sky lowered, dark with threatened thunderstorm from Ireland.

Pitt's attempt to secure administrative union between the Parliaments of both islands, and his energetic movement in favour of Catholic Emanci-pation supported by Lords Castlereagh, Cornwallis, and other Irish peers,

[1] Jerningham Letters.

had met with violent opposition from the Protestant contingent and the King.

At the beginning of the year 1801, the coolly professional eye of Dr. Willis again noted symptoms of relapse in his Royal patient. The King's state of mind was clearly betrayed during a levee when he agitatedly demanded of Secretary Dundas: 'What–what! Hey? What's this that young Lord Castlereagh brought over in September? . . . They are going to throw it at my head! The most Jacobinical thing I have ever heard!' –saving those idiot voices that fretted him daily and nightly, to leave him strengthless from lack of sleep or from too vivid waking dreams.

For the last few weeks he had been incoherent, voluble, suspicious of all who came near him, exhibiting those sadly too familiar signs of mental disturbance. His condition had been aggravated, not solely by his 'good Mr. Pitt's' unorthodox exertions on behalf of Catholic Emancipation–the King's anathema–but also by two almost simultaneous attacks upon his life.

The first took place while he was reviewing his troops in Hyde Park when an onlooker received a musket shot in his thigh, obviously intended for His Majesty. Later in the evening when the King, the Queen, and the Princesses attended a performance of Colley Cibber's *She would and she would not*, at Drury Lane, the audience gave him a tremendous ovation.

This was the second time after a narrow escape from death that the King had unconcernedly visited the playhouse the same day. And not a man who called for him but could have failed to be moved by his beaming smiles, his gratified bows, his evident delight at such loyal acclamation. During the last few years his popularity, undermined by internal revolutionary mutterings – the first appearance of dry-rot in the stronghold of monarchical tradition–had ominously waned. And now, with the orchestra playing 'God Save the King', with every voice cheering, every hand clapping, and every foot hammering the boards, he was once more returned to the hearts of his people. . . . Suddenly in the midst of all this massed emotion, a man sprang up from the benches in the pit, levelled a horse-pistol at that stocky, sturdy, nodding white-wigged figure–and fired. The ball missed its mark by a few inches.

In the pandemonium that followed only the King, with his customary indifference to danger, remained undisturbed. The would-be regicide, one James Hadfield, was seized, notified as a dangerous lunatic, and carried off to Bedlam. But such incidents, despite King George's calm exterior, were bound to take their toll of the intrepid old man's strength.

When, on His Majesty's refusal to tolerate admittance of Catholics to

Parliament, Pitt wrote his famous letter and resigned, that poor, sick brain rapidly disintegrated. He had borne enough; too much.

While the next Government, under Addington, was in process of formation, Malmesbury reported the King to be 'still bilious; not better. Fatal consequences of Pitt's hasty resignation. At Carlton House they dance and sing. . . .'

The Prince's hopes had never leapt so high. His longed-for Regency loomed well within his sight. Dr. Willis had pronounced the King to be 'much worse–in the height of a phrenzy fever', and babbling incessantly of his retirement to Hanover–or to his lost colony, America. His son, in no less a 'phrenzy fever', torn between compassion for his father's state and interest in his own, awaited his great day. Although, among his private cronies, he may have laughed and sung at Carlton House, he outwardly maintained a doleful decorum. In the presence of Lady Bessborough, a very private crony whom he had known for twenty years, he burst into tears and called upon Heaven to witness that he loved his father with all his heart. At the same time he loved himself a great deal more, and must first of all consider his own case, as exciting as it seemed to be precarious.

In the event of a new monarchy under that preposterous prig, Henry Addington, his chances of full authority as Regent would appreciably dwindle. Addington, he gauged, would tolerate no increase of any concession to the Regency Bill of 1789. He would still remain a cipher, understudy to his demented father and governed by an inefficient mediocrity. But it soon became apparent that neither his fears nor his hopes were yet to be fulfilled. His indomitable parent was on the way to a rapid recovery; and after a visit to Weymouth in June, 1801, His Majesty's physicians once more pronounced him cured. No festivities attended this second convalescence. Indeed it seemed likely, from the dubious prognosis of his doctors, that his return to norm might be the prelude to an ultimate decline. The Prince, however, had suffered too much of disappointment in the past to dwell on hypothetical illusion.

Again to kill time and discontent, he plunged into exuberant excesses. His conflicting aims and hedonistic friendships, his manifold enthusiasms–music, painting, sculpture, and his architectural anomaly down by the sea, imparted to his life a sensuous intoxication that stimulated, but could never satisfy. He was forty and looked fifty; for despite his juvenile curls, his pearl-powdered cheeks, and his corset, his too solid flesh weighed heavily upon him. His careful stays could not disguise his paunch.

Always in pursuit of new adventure, he returned, notwithstanding repeated infidelities, to the quiescent bosom of Fitzherbert.

His henchman in the chase of fleeting loves was the guardian of his purse-strings, his privacy, his bedchamber, his general factotum, one MacMahon. This individual, the natural son of a butler and a housemaid, both in the service of Lord Leitrim, had begun his meteoric career in a company of strolling players. During the war with America he had abandoned the stage for the army and enlisted in a regiment about to embark overseas. On his return, having obtained a commission, he was introduced by Lord Moira to Carlton House. Although his insignificant appearance gave the lie to his vocation, he was possessed of gab enough to charm the Prince, no less than all the ladies. As his agent in amatory negotiations the Prince found him indispensable. Yet over a period of years, those dainty morsels procured by MacMahon to whet his master's appetite, must surely have lost flavour in the course of repetition.

Scurrilous stories were circulated in connexion with MacMahon's equivocal activities. There is the supposititous incident of a clergyman's young daughters, with whom the Prince's minion scraped acquaintance in a stage-coach bound for Bath.

From 'their apparent simplicity and ignorance of the world', so this indefatigable scout reported to his master, 'they may soon be brought to comply with the wishes of Your Royal Highness. The younger is more of a *languishing* beauty; but from the knowledge I possess of your Royal taste, the elder will be the object of your choice.'

Huish, who cites this letter as an instance of 'cold-blooded systematic destruction of female innocence', may have overlooked the fact that young ladies in the early nineteenth century were no less simple nor ignorant of the ways of the world than are their descendants to-day. But such was the Prince's reputation as a rapacious Lothario, that the mothers of young daughters no less than the husbands of young wives, were rendered uneasy at attentions bestowed on their fluttering charges by the Seigneur of Carlton House.

Even Nelson, in a tempest of jealous rage, sent frantic letters to his Emma when he heard that Sir William Hamilton proposed to invite the Prince of Wales to dinner at his house in Piccadilly.

'Good God, he will be next to you telling you soft things! God strike him blind if he looks at you–' writes the hero of the Nile; then remembers in the midst of his dramatics to add a word of caution. 'This is high treason and you may get me hanged by revealing it. . . .' And again, 'Will you sing to the fellow? Does Sir William want you to be a whore to the rascal? O God, O God, keep my senses! . . .'[1]

And all this storm of emotion had been prompted by the carelessly

[1] Alfred Morrison papers, privately circulated, 1894.

oracular pronouncement of Hugh Elliott, British Minister at Dresden, who declared that 'Lady Hamilton will captivate the Prince of Wales. Her mind is as vulgar as his own.'

Although Emma's answer to her lover's outburst, may have mollified, it called for further warning.

'Your letters have made me happy to-day and never again will I scold until you begin, therefore pray never do. My confidence in you is firm as a rock, and that you direct the ——— to be kicked downstairs if he was to offer to make you a visit. I wonder at Sir William to think of asking such a wretch to dinner. . . .'[1]

The Prince did not dine with Sir William and Emma; nor, when some few years later, the then widowed Lady Hamilton and Nelson were invited to Carlton House, did the Prince, meeting the far-famed beauty for the first time, find her in the least attractive. Both he and she had over-ripened; both were over-fat; and Nelson's agonies allayed.

Yet still the Prince was ravenous for novelty, for someone–or something–refreshingly *different*. He had discovered a tedious sameness in women. Their swooning surrender, their greedy small desires, their calculated platitudes and ineffable simplicity, combined to offer him no more than a soporific to passion. He sought a new interest and believed he had found it in–George Brummell.

According to his own account, Brummell had attracted the notice of the Prince of Wales while he was still at Eton. When he left school at the age of sixteen, he received a cornetcy in the 10th Hussars, but the profession of arms which necessitated some compulsory exertion, was little to the taste of the young beau. Before he attained his majority he had come into a fortune bequeathed him by his father, the son of a confectioner who let lodgings to the Quality in Bury Street, St. James's. The disagreeable consciousness of his undistinguished origin may have inspired this immortal fop to cut his coat according to his cloth–and lead the world of Fashion. A year after his father's death, Brummell resigned his commission and, in excuse, told the Prince that since his regiment had been ordered to Manchester he could not possibly be expected to abide in a dirty smoky manufacturing town. The Prince, amusedly recognizing a fellow epicure in the pretty youth, said he could 'do as he pleased'.

He forthwith did very much as he pleased, to reach the height of his ambition when his portly Royal patron came puffing up the staircase of his house in Chesterfield Street to pay him a morning call.

[1] Phillipps Collection: by permission of the Trustees of the Maritime Museum, Greenwich.

The contents of life's cornucopia were poured at the feet of young Brummell. But not even this bewitching boy, this entirely new plaything, with his impudent expressive face and delicious sense of humour, could offer the Prince more than a transitory interest in an argument on neckcloths to be, or not to be, starched. And although such worthless trivialities may have filled a passing moment, they left him still unsatisfied, completely unproductive; a wasted monumental superfluity.

War with the French Republic had been brought to its indeterminate conclusion by that unsatisfactory Treaty of Amiens in 1802. 'Peace within a week – war again within a year', pronounced Malmesbury, gloomily prophetic.

War again it was – not within a week but well within the year. The British forces, marking time, watched uneasily the shadow of that yellow dwarf, the Corsican First Consul, grown to giant's stature, gradually absorbing all of Europe.

The struggle for supremacy, to which the youth of Britain had returned with renewed vigour, was no longer to be launched against 'French cannibals'; it was launched against the concentrated might of a Napoleon, self-made Master of the land – as Great Britain now was Mistress of the sea.

CHAPTER SIX

1803–1811

'Where O where does this little Boney dwell?
His birthplace is in Corsica but France he loves so well
And it's O the poor French, how they crouch beneath his spell.

Yet still he boldly brags with a consequence full cramm'd
On England's happy island his legions soon will land,
But it's O in my heart if he does—may I be damned!'

THEY sang it in the gutters; they hummed it in the clubs. Young ladies warbled it, with expurgations, at the pianoforte to the tune of 'The Bluebells of Scotland'.

The oft-repeated scare of an invasion had been enormously increased by the massing of Napoleon's armies at Boulogne and a flotilla in the harbours of Dieppe, Dunkirk, Ostend, Le Havre. Once more all over Britain men enlisted by their thousands. The King reviewed the London Volunteer Corps in Hyde Park; and his eldest son sent him another appeal.

'In this contest the lowest and humblest of Your Majesty's servants have been called upon; it would therefore little become me, who am the *First,* to remain a tame, idle and useless spectator . . . Hanover is lost, England is menaced, Ireland is in rebellion, Europe is at the foot of France . . . Ought I not to come forward in a moment of unexampled difficulty and danger? Ought I not to share in the glory of victory when I have everything to lose by defeat? . . .'

And much more in the same strain, which it is suggested was the composition of Sir Philip Francis. However that may be, it strikes a forcible note of sincerity to which the King sent a scathing reply.

'. . . I had flattered myself to have heard no further on the subject'; and then adds an acid compromise, 'should the implacable enemy so far succeed as to land, you will have an opportunity of showing your zeal at the head of your regiment. It will be the duty of every man to stand forward on such an occasion. I shall certainly think it mine to set an example. . . .'

That stung him. Was he expected, then, to do no more, to be no more, to serve no more than in a last bulwark of defence, fighting hand to hand beside his father on the beaches of the Kentish coast or in the streets of Brighton? The notion was fantastical. He would look completely idiotic, plunging in a mêlée of aged Englishmen, young schoolboys, and French soldiers, with the King in his white wig and Windsor uniform waving his sabre and shouting military commands . . . And that jibe at his 'zeal' provoked a furious retort.

'My next brother, the Duke of York, commands the Army; the younger branches of my family are either generals or lieutenant-generals; and I who am Prince of Wales am to remain Colonel of Dragoons. . . . There is something so humiliating in the contrast, that those who are at a distance would suppose that to be my fault which is only my misfortune.'

Finding that his father was entirely unmoved by 'these injuries under which it is in the power of Your Majesty alone to redress', the Prince endeavoured to enlist the aid and sympathy of York. Letters flew back and forth between the two, but Frederick, notwithstanding his professed affection for his 'Dearest Brother', showed him plainly that he refused to be dragged into any more family rows. Meanwhile the Prince had received a cautionary letter from Addington advising him to postpone his return to Brighton in consequence of 'some intelligence received'.

The Prince at once placed his own interpretation on this obscure message: 'By which I apprehend,' he hopefully answered, 'that you expect some immediate attempt from the enemy . . . If there be any reason to imagine that invasion will take place directly, I am bound by the King's precise order and by my honest *zeal* . . . to hasten instantly to my regiment.'

Whereupon, and in defiance of Addington's old-womanish fears, he repaired post-haste to Brighton. But after some weeks he was still kicking his heels in the Pavilion and searching the horizon for a French Armada, vauntingly a-sail up the Channel. No such luck! . . . He then decided on a course of action by which he might convey to the British public, eager enough to condemn him for standing back when every man stood forward, that his inactive part of onlooker in this war against aggression was none of his own fault.

On December 7, 1803, he caused to be published in the *Morning Chronicle* the whole of his correspondence with his father; and drove him to the verge of dementia again. 'He has published *my* letters—*my* letters!' Tearfully, and with maniacal persistence, the King repeated it over and over to his wife, his daughters, his equerries, and his physicians, who shook heads and pulled faces as long as their arms. Could that poor broken mind resist this succession of shocks? In addition to his increasing mental decline the unfortunate King was troubled by cataract and in imminent danger of losing his sight. Yet his unquenchable spirit defied approaching tragedy, defied the ills of flesh, and stayed, a colossus of courage, at the post he refused to desert.

In May 1804, Addington, tardily forced out of office by public opinion, was replaced by Pitt.

The Whigs, who had hoped to form a Coalition for National Defence with Fox, grown grey in long expectancy of leadership as head of the team, were once more frustrated. Thus the terrific weight of war had been flung back upon the frail shoulders of a man whose life was strung upon a thread, and who found himself Prime Minister again to a half-crazy King. With no support from a shuttlecock Cabinet, and with a depleted Exchequer behind him, he faced, virtually single-handed, the might of Napoleon, the Absolute.

Had the Prince of Wales in this crisis been freed from the curb with the chance of a preliminary canter before that day, fast approaching, when he would ride untrammelled and alone, he might have proved his mettle; or, while he waited, also served. But he was baulked, and repeatedly baulked. Even in the charge and education of his daughter he encountered autocratic interference.

The eight-year-old Princess Charlotte, a lively, self-willed, captivating child, had inherited all of her mother's high spirits and much of her father's charm. Perhaps because of his loathing for the woman who had borne her, the Prince's affection for his offspring appeared to be as wanting as his interest in her welfare. True, he saw to her needs, engaged her nurses and instructors, and placed her in a suite of rooms at Carlton House. He would send for her while he sat at his toilet or breakfast, surrounded by his latest purchases, a Rembrandt, a Cuyp—he had lately discovered the Dutch School—a jewelled snuff-box, a Sèvres tea-set, a sample of Chinese wall-paper, or a Chinese panel 'cut in frets very close Green and Red and Shadowed'.

He was just about this time considering an entirely new decorative scheme for his Pavilion at Brighton. And Charlotte, round-eyed, standing at his knee, would watch this large red-faced man, with his bulging calves and profusion of sweet-scented curls, shovelling food into his mouth. . . . She hardly knew him for her father; and he, side-glancing her, must have been relieved to see in this blonde, fair-skinned, sturdy little creature, no likeness to her mother, but a handsome, strong resemblance to himself.

A succession of elderly governesses came and went in the service of Charlotte, some of whom she adored and others she detested. She loved Mrs. Campbell and Lady de Clifford, with whose grandson, George Keppel, she was sometimes permitted to play. 'After all, there are worse people in the world than your snuffy old grandmother,' she told him. There were at least, in Charlotte's small world, two persons worse than the excellent Lady de Clifford; one her tutor, Dr. Fisher, Bishop of Salisbury. This estimable man, whom Charlotte dubbed the great U.P. because of his pedantic pronunciation of the word Bish*up*, was an insufferable bore and his pupil's pet aversion. Scarcely less did she dislike Mrs. Udney, her sub-governess. At the age of ten she seems to have sickened of her life and her attendants–or she may merely have been sickening for one of those feverish colds to which she was subjected; but whatever the cause we find her in the dumps to make her Will.

To Mrs. Campbell she leaves 'my three watches and half my jewels except those that are the most valuable'–which she dutifully bequeaths to 'My Father and Mother, the Prince and Princess of Wales'.

To her Chaplain, the Reverend Mr. Nott, 'I leave all my best books and trust that after I am dead a great deal may be done for Mr. Nott. I hope the King will make him a Bishop. . . . My dogs to Mrs. Anne Hulton, my chambermaid. Nothing to Mrs. Udney *for reasons*'.

So we see her in her childhood, lonely, self-sufficient, controlled, as was her father, by that same pendulum swing of the emotions, from abandoned joy of living to exaggerated gloomy contemplation of her death.

To the ailing King this first grandchild, blood of his blood, future heiress to his Throne, had become suddenly of paramount importance. She must be initiated, and the sooner the better, in those duties which, as a potential Queen Regnant and God's Ordained Anointed, she might, at some distant indefinite date, be called upon to fulfil. And who in his Kingdom more fitted to instruct her than himself?

He would devote his last remaining years to the care of this bud of his dynastic tree, this flower of his old age. While he dismissed his son as a wholly unsuitable guardian for this new delightful treasure, the King acknowledged the child's mother as first claimant to the custody of Charlotte. 'The Princess must have her–must have her!' . . . So would he mutter as if in argument with unseen persons, answering questions unheard by any save that poor fuddled brain, that, even while it wavered on the borderline, was determined to be just. 'The mother must have her child . . . must. . . .'

Those desultory murmurs were carried to the Prince, with the context of a letter from the King to his 'Dearest Daughter-in-law and Niece', in which she is assured that 'no plan for the advantage of the Dear Child', could be contemplated without her 'Authority as Mother'.

The Prince, who hitherto had entertained no serious intention of opposing his father's interest in Charlotte, heard with consternation of the King's approach to Caroline. That she should be considered a fit and proper guardian for their daughter, while he, forsooth, must be excluded from any share in her upbringing, was an outrage to his dignity and an insult to himself. Yet, despite his objections, he was finally persuaded to agree that Charlotte should spend part of the year at Windsor under the King's eye and in his care, on condition that she stay with him at Carlton House whenever he be there in residence.

His choice lay in the lesser of two evils.

Not without good reason was the Prince persuaded to put up a fight for the custody of his own child. Since his separation from Caroline, he had permitted Charlotte to pay weekly visits to her mother. But certain information which he had latterly received concerning Caroline's behaviour in that villa near Blackheath, made the Prince regret he had allowed his irresponsible, scatter-brained wife even that much access to their daughter.

Scandalous reports had been brought to him of those heterogeneous gatherings at Montague House, the residence of the Princess of Wales, which Lady Charlotte Bury describes as 'all glitter and glare and tricks; everything tinsel and trumpery'. There, with indiscriminate impartiality, Caroline entertained courtiers and courtesans, painters and poets, statesmen, peeresses, and all sorts. She played chess with Lord Palmerston and Blind Man's Buff with Canning. She danced Scottish reels with that earnest, shy, young versifier Thomas Campbell, who could never have been more embarrassed. She led Sir Walter Scott into the conservatory and when with native caution he held back, she told him he was 'a false, faint-hearted troubadour'. He followed her then, and she poured into his ear the whole unhappy story of her life. But although Lady Charlotte complained that the Princess 'condescended to talk low nonsense or even gross ribaldry', she enjoyed to read *Candide* aloud to her ladies.

She dressed outlandishly; we know she was not scrupulously clean. She talked to strangers on her outings, to the horror of her gentlewomen; and as a hobby she adopted nine orphans of both sexes and various ages. There was, however, nothing very wrong in that; and until the arrival of a perfectly revolting little boy named William Austin, whom she called 'Willikin', the Prince, for all his secret spying on her movements, could find no possible hope of achieving that for which he yearned even more than for his Regency: an end to his hated marriage by-divorce.

★   ★   ★

It was on a winter's morning in the year 1801, that Caroline had first become acquainted with the wife of Major-General Sir John Douglas.

Attended only by one Lady-in-Waiting, Miss Heyman, the Princess was observed by Lady Douglas to be standing at the gate of her house on the edge of Blackheath, and staring up at the parlour window.

Unseasonably dressed in a gown of lilac satin, with a sable-edged cap of the same on her head, and flimsy yellow 'half-boots' on her feet, the Princess appeared, not surprisingly, to be shivering with cold. Lady Douglas, an inveterate snob and social climber, who had at once recognized this stranger at her gates, left her window and hurried down the garden path dropping curtsies as she came.

The Princess gaily nodded; Lady Douglas repeated her curtsies; the Princess repeated her nods. This interchange of pleasantries went on for quite a while. Then, seizing the golden opportunity of entertaining a Royal Princess, Lady Douglas humbly begged her to walk in 'out of the snow. . . .' Whereupon, followed by the scandalized Miss Heyman, in Caroline walked to her ladyship's parlour.

The friendship that began under such apparently innocuous a circumstance, is something reminiscent of the Spider and the Fly. At last Caroline had found a confidante who loved her, she believed, with a wholly disinterested devotion.

In happy expectation of a future, roseate with promise of reward for her fidelity, Lady Douglas, stoically patient, listened by the hour to Caroline's recital of her woes and of her interests. The boy 'Willikin', whom the Princess had adopted and loved as her own, was her chief topic, at this time, of conversation. To Lady Douglas she talked–and so did others –of how she idolized this awful child. When she entertained her guests to dinner he would be brought in by a footman for dessert and placed in a chair at the table. His manners were appalling. He was utterly spoilt, would scream and kick for everything he wanted, and which was instantly supplied by his fond 'Mamma'. He would make a grab for the dishes, cram his mouth with sweets, pull at the tablecloth, send the glasses flying, and spill wine on the ladies' gowns. The Princess's visitors were expected to laugh at and praise the pretty antics of 'Willikin', who possessed, it seems, not one redeeming grace. 'He was a little nasty, vulgar brat . . .' declares Lady Hester Stanhope. He was also the cause of near catastrophe to Caroline.

The word 'Delicate' is a euphemism, surely, for that 'Investigation' in which the Princess of Wales is accused, not only of having borne an illegitimate son presumed to be the boy William Austin, but also of promiscuous adultery with divers gentlemen, among whom were Sir

Sidney Smith,[1] Captain Manby, and the painter, Lawrence. Caroline had babbled once too often.

It all began when the Princess heard that her 'dear friend', Lady Douglas, was about to become a mother. In strictest confidence, and for reasons that defy conjecture, Caroline divulged that she too was in a similar condition, and offered gratuitous and nauseating symptoms of her pregnancy. There is no possible accounting for these fantasies, unless it were that the poor soul, deprived of her daughter, starved of her conjugal rights, may have found some vicarious pleasure in describing her imaginary state. Who can tell? The fact remains that by her indiscreet and foolish bragging, Caroline had placed herself at the mercy of a wholly unscrupulous woman, who did not hesitate to put the worst interpretation on these entirely fictitious revelations. Very soon was it brought home to the Princess that her beloved friend had publicly declared her to be with or delivered of a child.

Too late did she regret her nonsensical chatter. Too late did she remember Lord Malmesbury's advice 'to think before she spoke . . .' The mischief was done, and augmented by a formal letter from the Princess to Lady Douglas terminating their disastrous acquaintanceship.

From that time forth Lady Douglas conceived a most violent hatred for Caroline. It was generally supposed that the incriminating charges made by this woman against the Princess of Wales, were prompted by jealous resentment of Caroline's intimacy with Sir Sidney Smith. Gossip gave it that Lady Douglas had herself encouraged and enjoyed Sir Sidney's attentions. However that may be, she bludgeoned Caroline's reputation with damnifying evidence enough, in a sworn statement, to secure an inquiry before a Commission appointed by the King.

The Prince's chance of release had come.

Two of his brothers, the Dukes of Kent and Sussex, were brought into the case. To the former, the Princess had appealed for protection from certain libellous imputations cast upon her by the Douglases, who declared they had received an anonymous letter, containing an obscene drawing of Lady Douglas in a compromising posture with Sir Sidney Smith. Both husband and wife claimed to have identified the hand-writing as that of the Princess of Wales.

The Duke of Kent at once sent for Sidney Smith to hear his opinion of the case. Smith's opinion, according to the testimony of the Douglases, endorsed their own belief that Caroline was the author of this curious letter and its pornographic illustration, which Kent, professing to be greatly shocked, lengthily examined and admitted was–'Abominable!

[1] Became Rear Admiral of the Blue in 1805.

143

Foolish, to be sure. But Sir Sidney, if this matter makes a noise, it may distress His Majesty. . . .' He hoped Sir John and Lady Douglas 'would try and forget it'. Needless to say they did not. Soon everyone had news of it and many had a peep at it, and Caroline's name was smudged with the vilest suspicion. Nor did the dirty business end with that.

The boy 'Willikin', to whom Caroline persistently alluded as her 'son', was a more powerful pawn in the game of that brave knight Sir John and his lady than any filthy forgery ascribed to the Princess of Wales could have been. Who and what was William Austin? Why had the Princess chosen to adopt him, whose origin and parentage were so varied and obscure? Some said he was the son of a woman at Deptford; of a sail-maker, or of the man who turned the mangle in the laundry at Montague House. Why should the Princess confess to Lady Douglas she was pregnant, and a few months later 'adopt' this gutter child—unless he were in truth her son? 'Prove it!' She defied her attackers, 'Prove it—and he shall be your King!'

The Duke of Sussex, who had married in haste at St. George's, and whose own legitimate children by Lady Augusta Murray had been pronounced bastards under the King's Royal Marriage Act, bustled in upon the Prince of Wales with a warning. If this alleged son of a docker, a woman at Deptford, a turner of mangles, or what not, should prove to be Caroline's child, it would follow that the Succession must be affected. Why the Hanoverian Succession should be affected by a Brunswickian by-blow, born years after the couple had ceased to cohabit, that imperishable busy-body, Sussex, did not say.

The Prince, however, was delighted to find another weapon in his hand with which to hack at his wife and his marriage.

On the advice of Lord Thurlow, he placed before the King this pleasing evidence, supported by sworn statements of the Douglases and in the presence of his brother, Duke of Sussex.

Notwithstanding the fearful shock the unfortunate monarch must have sustained when he found his niece implicated in a charge, not only of mis-conduct but as the author of a lewd and anonymous letter, the King at once instigated an inquiry. All those concerned in a supposedly adulterous association with the Princess of Wales were separately examined before Commissioners *in camera*.

Throughout the whole of these proceedings Caroline had been fortunate in securing the support of Spencer Perceval, the future Prime Minister and her near neighbour at Charlton. Perceval from the first had believed in her innocence and was determined to establish it. Incredible was the amount of mud raked up against her who, at the end of that 'Delicate

GEORGE AUGUSTUS FREDERICK, PRINCE OF WALES

awn from the life by John Russell, 1794, reproduced by courtesy of the late Sir Robert Witt, C.B.E.

Investigation' could be found guilty of nothing worse than 'unworthy indiscretions'.

Yet although Caroline's name was cleared, the King wrote a letter severely reprimanding her for 'certain circumstances of conduct which His Majesty could never regard but with serious concern'.

The Princess at once demanded a personal interview with her uncle, in the reasonable assumption that she would be given an explanation of those charges which he viewed with 'such serious concern'; a request to which the King did not reply. She had won her case, lost her only friend and nearest relative at Court, and in the losing gained a universal popularity.

The Prince, on the other hand, had never sunk so low. That a man whose flagrant infidelities had, for years, been common knowledge, should so mercilessly seek to victimize his wife while posing as the injured husband, roused a storm of indignation from the fair-minded British people, to which the Prince appeared to be impervious. Indeed he seemed the more determined to pursue his case, and trump up further evidence whereby, at any cost to Caroline, he might obtain his freedom.

When the Princess wrote again to the King complaining of her banishment from his presence and his Court, she was dismayed to learn that the Prince's lawyers had received documents which would necessitate another inquiry. The King thereupon made it clear that he proposed deferring a reconciliation between himself and his niece until the result of this additional 'Investigation' should be known.

But Caroline was not disposed to be returned to the inquisitorial rack.... 'A Princess and no Princess! A married woman and no husband—or worse than none!' she exclaimed, after she had heard the King's dictum. 'Never was there a poor devil in such a plight as I!'

It was Perceval, who in pity for her 'plight', dictated that clever letter to the King in her name which threatened a disclosure to the world of 'my unmerited sufferings and the manner in which they have been conducted'.

As still no reply to this warning was vouchsafed, Perceval prepared his master-stroke—to make public a full report of the recent proceedings against the Princess of Wales. Five thousand copies of *The Book*, by which title it was known, were already in print when a dramatic anti-climax caused them to be withdrawn from circulation. The Coalition group of Foxite Whigs under Grenville's leadership had come to a precipitate end. Its resignation had been forced by the King's refusal to countenance admittance of Roman Catholic officers into the British Army. The return of the Tories under Portland, with Perceval as

Chancellor of the Exchequer, had now secured for the Princess of Wales a politically powerful support. And not until her complete and final vindication had been implicitly pronounced, did Perceval relax his efforts to uphold her.

'Your Majesty's confidential servants concurring in that part of the opinion of your late servants . . . humbly submit to Your Majesty that it is essentially necessary, in justice to Her Royal Highness, that the Princess of Wales be admitted with as little delay as possible into Your Majesty's presence, and that she should be received in a manner due to her rank and station in Your Majesty's Court and Family.'

To that thinly disguised threat–the publication of *The Book*, or His Majesty's acknowledgment of his daughter-in-law's innocence–the King was forced to yield; and the case that had been a nine months' wonder was forgotten in nine days; but not by Caroline.

At a party given in honour of the King's birthday in June of that year, 1807, the Prince and Princess of Wales met and stood, for a moment, face to face. He, coldly disdainful, she, with a smile awry and a shrug of those still impertinent shoulders, exchanged a few words unheard by any.

Then she curtsied; he bowed; and as she rose from the bob he turned and passed on, never to speak with her again.

★   ★   ★

While the Prince of Wales and his followers waged unsuccessful war against his wife, Napoleon, self-crowned Emperor of France, was driving his Grand Army across Europe to meet Austria and Russia, Britain's Allies. But even while these potentially formidable hosts dallied in the rear of their vanguards, and before the British forces could embark to join them, Bonaparte, with a hundred thousand men behind him, had crashed through the Black Forest to bear down upon the Austrians at Ulm.

When the news of this disaster, in October 1805, was brought home to Pitt he refused to believe it. "'Tis a fiction!' he exclaimed to the messenger; and a fiction he insisted it must be until the truth of defeat had been confirmed. Yet, at that very moment, the bitterest in Pitt's all too brief life, Nelson in his *Victory*, with twenty-seven sail of the line, was closing in upon the French and Spanish at Cadiz off Cape Trafalgar.

At sunset, on October 21, Nelson, shot through the spine, lay dying in *Victory's* cockpit; but his mission for all time had been fulfilled. Whatever conquests now might fall to Napoleon's Grand Armies, his fleets had fled the seas, annihilated.

146

The Prince of Wales was at Brighton when he heard of that Battle, and the passing of the sailor who had restored Britain to her ocean throne, and left his name to ring throughout the ages in tune with that of Drake.

He also left a legacy, his Emma, to the nation. He had made his Will the day he died, sitting in his cabin with her portrait on the wall above him; and in his left-handed scrawl he wrote a prayer. He must have expected his death; he may have been sure of his triumph.

The Prince, deeply stirred by the epic of Trafalgar, was equally as shocked at a loss that he and every other Briton regarded as a personal bereavement. According to the sprightly Mrs. Creevey–a constant visitor at the Pavilion and a recent friend of Mrs. Fitzherbert, to whom she blatantly toadied–her 'Dear, foolish, beautiful Prinney' had told her that 'all this bad news made him bilious. . . .' He was certainly subdued; and more sympathetically disposed towards Nelson's Emma than was Mrs. Fitzherbert, who declared that 'hero though he was, Lady Hamilton overpowered and took possession of him quite by force'.

Nelson's dying gesture concerning Lady Hamilton appealed to the Prince's sentimentality, and produced a flux of letters from him to all his friends. 'Did it depend on me,' he wrote to one, 'there would not be a wish or a desire of our ever-to-be-lamented, as well as adored hero, that I would not consider a solemn obligation to fulfil.'

It did not, unfortunately, depend on him, and while the entire country mourned the death of Nelson and with frenzied joy celebrated his great victory, Emma was forgotten.

Yet, Trafalgar notwithstanding, the European prospect was more than ever gloomy. The Austerlitz disaster, in which Napoleon had routed the Allies and brought Austria cringing to his feet with offers of an armistice, together with the total failure of his Continental Coalition, had struck Pitt to his death. The salutary waters of Bath could not restore his vanquished hopes nor remove that 'Austerlitz look', as Fox called it, from his face. On January 23, 1806, he gave up the struggle and sank. His last thought, with his last breath, was 'My country! How I leave my country! . . .'

He left her to that hashed-up Ministry of All-the-Talents under Grenville's nominal leadership, with Fox–who for so long and so vehemently had opposed him–returned to power as Foreign Secretary. He left her to a King half-blind, half-mad, who could still assert Authority in the shadow of his Crown. And he left her, for yet another decade, doomed to war.

And now the Prince of Wales found himself, for the first time in his life, in a position of political importance. But ironically he, once so strong a partisan of Whiggery and who came to the fore with the Whigs behind him and Fox at his elbow urging Peace with France, the abolition of Slavery, and the ever-burning question of Catholic Relief, showed no immediate inclination to take sides. He did, in fact, oppose the measures put forward by Fox on behalf of Catholic Emancipation. The subject, he argued, if broached to the King, would be certain to result in a total derangement. Much as the Prince desired his Regency, he could not have it on his conscience to expedite that for which he had waited so long, and which was now but a matter of time before he attained it.

The reign of the Whigs was also a matter of time–indeed, no less than a matter of months.

With the death of Fox, who followed Pitt to the grave in September, 1806, the country was once again bereft of a leader, and the Prince of a man whom above all others he respected, and had so deeply loved.

By order of the King he was not allowed to attend the funeral, but he dressed himself in trappings of woe, wore black for a year, and wrote Grey a tear-blotted letter.

'From the earliest period of my life, I looked up to no-one but Fox. . . . Having trod that path which he marked out for me, having been guided through it by the support of his hand, I do candidly acknowledge to you that the difference is so prodigious, the loss so immense that my thoughts are quite bewildered. . . .'

From that time forth the Prince refused to be a party-man.

★ ★ ★

It is strangely coincidental that during the years 1803-1807, the two wives of the Prince of Wales should have been involved in law-suits, not fundamentally dissimilar. While the case against Caroline was being fought in private, Mrs. Fitzherbert had become a primary participant in a *cause célèbre*.

Mary Seymour, born in 1798, the youngest child of Lord Hugh and Lady Horatia Seymour, had been placed in the care of Mrs. Fitzherbert during the absence abroad of her parents. When, on their return to England in 1801, the Seymours died within a few months of each other, Mrs. Fitzherbert wished to retain the guardianship of 'Minney', aged three, and to whom she was utterly devoted. The executors of Lord Hugh's will–his brother Henry and Lord Euston–determinedly opposed this suggestion, on the grounds that Mrs. Fitzherbert had no right of kinship to the child, and, in view of her Faith, could not be considered as a possible custodian. Moreover, Minney's aunt, Lady Waldegrave, was equally anxious to undertake the charge of her own niece.

In vain did Mrs. Fitzherbert plead that the child's mother, aware of her impending death, had left Minney to her by adoption. Nor were the inflexible executors at all influenced or mollified by the Prince's offer to settle £10,000 on Minney, providing that Mrs. Fitzherbert were allowed to remain her sole guardian.

These arguments resulted in legal proceedings; and while the Prince flitted back and forth between his lawyers, at that time busily engaged in trying to prove the boy 'Willikin' to be his second wife's son, he was taking an active interest in his first wife's claim to another woman's daughter. The whole Seymour family and in particular Lady Euston, sister of Lady Horatia, furiously resisted Mrs. Fitzherbert's proposed adoption of Minney.

On May 9, 1806, Lady Euston wrote to her nephew, George Seymour, Minney's elder brother, a lieutenant in H.M.S. *Donegal* of the Mediterranean Fleet:

'I find that Mrs. Fitzherbert's friends now complain of Lord Henry's and Lord Euston's cruelty in having left the child with her for this last year unless they intended to give up the cause. If they had taken the poor little soul last year, we should of course have heard of their cruelty in so doing. . . .'

The executors had by then decided to terminate further discussion by bringing the case before the Chancery Division. When a verdict was given against the appointment of Mrs. Fitzherbert as custodian of Mary Seymour, she appealed to the Lord Chancellor, but with no more success. In despair at the thought of losing this little girl, Mrs. Fitzherbert resolved to lodge a further appeal before the House of Lords. It was then that the head of the Seymour family, the Marquis of Hertford, supported by his wife, an intimate friend of Mrs. Fitzherbert, announced his intention of taking to himself the custody of Minney. This decision was, in fact, nothing more than a clever ruse to end a case that had gone on too long and had caused far too much publicity. Hertford had not the least intention of adopting little Minney; and no sooner had the Lord Chancellor accepted his proposal, than he at once promoted Mrs. Fitzherbert to act as his deputy in charge of his niece and ward.

She had won back a daughter, but in the winning lost a husband–to her 'friend'.

He first became acquainted with and fatally attracted to the Marchioness of Hertford, while the Seymour case usurped the attention of his 'wife'.

In her forty-seventh year Isabella Hertford is described by one who knew her as 'of youthful mien and reposeful curves of figure. . . .' The Prince could never have been proof against repose allied to 'curves'. And further to inflame him, if such a spark were needed, Lady Hertford was a grandmother. Irresistible enchantment!

All the usual symptoms were displayed; letters breathing adoration, surgeons in attendance, leeches, blood-letting, hysteria, and so forth. She gave him no encouragement. His advances she repelled. He was in anguish. Creevey declares he had seen the tears run down the Prince's cheeks when he sat at dinner, 'dumb for hours', wrapped in thought of her. But Lady Hertford was not to be won by this exhibition of time-staled tricks. She knew her mind, she knew her place and kept it, at a distance, while her husband and her son, Lord Yarmouth, entertained him –to Britain's advantage. Under the guidance of the Prince that heritage of art, the Wallace Collection, was acquired, and bequeathed to the nation.

Lord Yarmouth, more familiarly known as 'Red Herrings' or 'the Yarmouth Bloater', for the colour of his hair, was a notable Regency buck. After Brummell's decline he became the Prince's adviser on matters of dress, and is supposed to be the prototype of Thackeray's Marquis of Steyne–a doubtful honour–and Disraeli's Marquis of Monmouth.

There is no doubt that the Prince's withdrawal from the Whigs may be attributed to his intimacy with the Hertfords. Both the Marquis and his wife were ardent Tories, and both equally opposed to Catholic Emancipation over which stumbling block the Whigs had fallen, during the recent governmental crisis, never to rise again for near upon a quarter of a century. The Prince, who had not once been referred to or consulted by his former allies, Grey and Grenville, took offence at what he thought to have been a deliberate slight. In a letter to Lord Moira he bitterly complained that his advice on had not been asked; and he ended by repeating his decision 'professed in my own mind upon the death of Fox, to cease to be a party-man'.

Lady Hertford snatched at her chance. She was ambitious. She was also very clever. While she struck with the same weapon that Lady Jersey had used against Mrs. Fitzherbert–her Faith–as a constant and imminent danger to the Prince's popularity, she stayed firmly ensconced in the friendship of his 'wife'. His interest in herself she insisted was platonic; her attraction for him purely intellectual. On that plane and understanding she received him in her salon. Her dominion, esoteric as opposed to the erotic, was possessive: and his infatuation for his aloof Egeria complete.

Daily, for months, the Prince's yellow chariot with its purple blinds had waited outside Hertford House in Manchester Square, before Mrs. Fitzherbert thought of questioning the extramundane quality of this absorbing new relationship. True, she had observed, of late, that the Prince's attitude towards her had noticeably altered. He was less affectionate, a great deal less exacting in his marital demands. Moreover he had made it a condition that she must attend every function at Carlton House or the Pavilion at which Lady Hertford was present: a mortifying situation against which she dared not protest. The Hertfords had been appointed joint guardians of Minney. At any moment Lady Hertford could, if she wished, assert her legal right to remove the child from Mrs. Fitzherbert's custody, as all the Seymour family were urging her to do. Thus Mrs. Fitzherbert had been forced to suffer this humiliation, but not always uncomplainingly. More than once, and even at the risk of losing Minney, she had been on the point of parting from the Prince; yet he seemed determined not to let her go. He thought, maybe, to have the best of both worlds; a wife who was no more to him than mistress, and a mistress who was very much a wife.

This peculiar state of affairs, to which Lord Hertford appeared to have raised no objection, continued unabated for two years. The lampoonists laid their ridicule upon the pair with trowels, and Tom Moore put them into verse.

'Through Manchester Square took a canter just now
Met the old yellow chariot, made a low bow,
This I did, of course, thinking 'twas loyal and civil,
But got such a look, oh, 'twas black as the devil!

Mem:– When next by the old yellow chariot I ride,
To remember there *is* nothing princely inside.'

The Seymours, although dismayed at the notoriety aroused by the Prince's latest love, saw in it the means of restoring Minney to the family fold. Lady Euston, writing to her nephew (May 12, 1807), tells him:

'I know not what Mrs. Fitzherbert does in all these confusions and reconciliations, as the world says it is all owing to Lady Hertford's influence that the Prince is put in a way to become a good Boy. As your poor little sister is doomed to continue for the present with Mrs. Fitzherbert, I should most sincerely rejoice if she should become independent of the Prince . . . Mrs. Fitzherbert looks remarkably well, but she appears in public in an odd situation, having few people to converse with and the Prince not often speaking to her at all, and at other times she appears indignant with him when he does. It is too laughable to see such a parcel of old fat personages playing all the follies and anticks of quarrelling children.'

Not so laughable, however, to one of those 'fat personages'. In 1809 Mrs. Fitzherbert sent the Prince a last appeal.

'What am I to think of the inconsistency of your conduct,when scarcely three weeks ago you voluntarily declared to me that this sad affair was at an end, and in less than a week afterwards the whole business was begun over again.' And she begged for his written answer—'to avoid all unpleasant conversation upon a subject so heartrending to one whose life has been dedicated to you. . . .'

She awaited his reply. It did not come. His silence proclaimed, more than words, his intention; and her pride forbade further approach. Not again would she be seen at Carlton House or the Pavilion as chaperone to Lady Hertford. That was the beginning of their final separation, indirectly expedited by a series of disasters in the Royal Family.

The first of these involved the Duke of York and his former mistress, Mrs. Mary Anne Clarke, in a case that rocked the town.

The charge brought against Mary Anne and the King's son, at the instigation of a certain Colonel Wardle, accused the pair of peddling commissions in the Army on a fifty per cent bonus.

It was a scandal so appalling, so amusing, entertaining, that even the latest war news became of secondary interest to the public. During the whole of the lurid affair which was dragged up before the House of Commons for a full inquiry, the King staunchly upheld his 'Hope's' honour; as also, at first, did the Prince. Any attack on his brother, he said, would be an attack upon him. But when he saw how grave were the allegations lodged against Frederick and Mrs. Clarke, and how extremely awkward it would be to disprove them, the Prince presented to the world a sanctimonious revulsion from, 'such irregularities and such women with whom my brother is connected'.

He had seemingly forgotten Mrs. Crouch and Mrs. Billington, and those others masked, cloaked, smuggled by MacMahon up the backstairs of Carlton House. He, on whom the saintly aura of Egeria had fallen, could remember nothing but 'poor Fred's' disgrace.

Mrs. Clarke, who had practised her profession with such success that she had become the mistress of a Prince and a mansion in Gloucester

Place, played the leading rôle in this popular farce before a crowded House. She was uncommonly pretty, painted with discretion, and exceedingly vivacious. Her pert repartee outwitted the Government speakers, led by Mr. Perceval; and although she brazenly perjured herself a dozen times a day to stand condemned, she conquered. One of the younger and more susceptible members thrust a note into her hand offering her three hundred guineas to sup with him.

Impassioned letters read from the Duke to his 'Darling', together with the evidence of what the butler saw, were seized upon and parodied, lampooned in every news-sheet and quoted, with bawdy, in St. James's clubs. When the case was brought to its disgusting end, and the Duke had been doubtfully acquitted of 'personal corruption and connivance at the infamous practices disclosed by Mrs. Clarke', he promptly resigned his command in the Army. It was the least he could do. His reputation had been irremediably damaged. Urchins tossing pennies in slum-alleys cried instead of 'Heads or Tails'–'Duke or Darling'! He could never live down those letters to his love read before six hundred tittering members of Parliament.

The King's health, slowly breaking under the shame and degradation wrought upon him by this, his favourite son, suffered further strain from the news of the Walcheren disaster. That expeditionary force which had set out with such high hopes to capture Antwerp under Sir David Dundas, York's successor as Commander-in-Chief, had lamentably failed. Inefficient Generalship, crass stupidity and disease–men died by their thousands in those pestilential swamps edging the dykes–were the main causes of that miserable fiasco. The King took it hardly, 'in a prodigious degree of the fidgets', that greatly increased on his Jubilee Day in the fiftieth year of his reign.

He could not see, and could scarcely hear–for he was going deaf as well as blind–the roars of rejoicing, the flags, frenzy, and illuminations in his honour. Tottering, white-haired, red-faced, goggle-eyed, he was still their 'good old King' to the people of Britain; he could still enjoy the scent of new-mown hay drifting up from his fields as he walked on the terrace at Windsor, could still faintly hear the muted strings of his fiddlers playing the music that he loved; could still thank them–'his good gentlemen', with a courtesy jerk of his head and a raising of his hat when they had done. The tumult in his mind was hushed in a curtained tranquillity where he rested, bemused, untroubled, for a few peaceful months. Then, once more the trumpet-blare of scandal beat its devil's tattoo around the name of another–his fourth son.

On May 31, 1810, in St. James's Palace, in the middle of the night,

Ernest, the 'Dreary Duke' of Cumberland, had been all but murdered by his valet!

Like fire spread the news till London blazed with it. Sellis, an Italian, had been blackmailing his master, threatening exposure of some murky secret known only to this highly trusted, confidential man. The Duke, it was said, had paid vast sums of money for his silence; but he had not paid enough. This primary account gathered flavour in retelling. Sellis, rumour gave it, had been cuckolded by the Duke. He had come upon his wife in the Duke's arms, and in his bed. Motive enough, surely, for him to kill his master – unless his master had killed him.

The Duke's version of the case, spiced with melodrama, turned full suspicion upon Sellis. The Duke had spent the evening, innocently, at a concert, had returned to his apartment in the Palace and retired to his bed. He was in a sound sleep by midnight; and about one in the morning had been violently awakened by a blow on the head. He started up and received two more blows accompanied by a hissing noise. In the dim lamp-light he peered about him, believing a bat had flown into the room through the window. He saw no bat, got out of bed, called for Sellis, and was again attacked – this time by the thrust of steel in his thigh. His second valet, Neale, on hearing the Duke's shrieks, rushed in, armed with a poker, and tripped over something on the floor – the Duke's sword, freshly stained with blood. Then, after having placed his groaning master in a chair, he roused the household and went in search of Sellis.

He was found in the privy leading from the Duke's bedroom, with his throat cut and a razor in his hand.

At the inquest the jury listened unimpressed to this dramatic history. It seemed that Sellis had hidden himself in the closet in order to attack the Duke when he was in bed and asleep. His first attempt had been almost, but not quite, successful, although medical evidence insisted that the Duke's skull had been hacked open to lay bare the brains. Thereupon, the would-be assassin had apparently hoped to finish off the Duke with his own sabre. No one had seen a bat in the room, nor was it possible that any creature so small and inoffensive could strike with such force as to cleave a man's head in twain. . . . And do bats hiss?

All this hodge-podge of evidence considered, the jury brought in a tactful verdict against Sellis of suicide.

The public was disappointed; and the question rose on every lip – had Sellis been murdered by the Duke or had he not? None credited the word of any witness. All were convinced that the Duke had raped the valet's wife, killed his valet, and, if justice had been done, deserved to hang.

The King, shambling up and down his terrace, tapping with his stick, stared blindly at the faces of his daughters as they guided his feeble steps. They wept. . . . Why did they weep? He whispered the name of one he missed among them. . . . Amelia, his youngest, his most loved Amelia.

And when he asked for her they told him she had died.

With her passing fled his courage, his spirit, and his will; and the curtain of his darkness fell upon him. Into a phantom world, empty of sorrow, empty of reason and sight, he retreated—a world wherein the past became the present, and all of life a clouded memory.

The King was incurably insane.

CHAPTER SEVEN

1811–1814

IT HAD come–that day so long desired and for so long deferred. The curtain, which had fallen on a bewildered lonely figure, talking with the dead, mouthing, hymning, praying in its hoarse cracked voice, rose again upon the Transformation Scene.

The First Gentleman, who for more than twenty years had been standing by as understudy to the leading part, was now called upon to play it. There was, however, some delay in the process of production. Perceval, who had succeeded Lord Portland as Tory Prime Minister, intended to present the chief player in the same restrictive rôle for which he had been cast by Pitt in 1789. But when Perceval, with the Queen and Parliament to back him, drew up a facsimile of Pitt's former programme depriving the Regent Elect of the power to grant pensions, create peers, or to deal with the King's property and person, the Prince called his brothers to a conference.

All six of them signed and sent to the Premier their protest against 'measures we consider to be perfectly unconstitutional and subversive of those principles which seated our Family on the Throne'. Whereupon, and prior to the passing of the Bill, Perceval arrived at Carlton House with a deputation from the Lords and Commons to offer the Prince an Address.

No concessions had been made in the Premier's reply to the protest of the Royal Dukes. The Address made it emphatically clear that His Royal Highness would assume authority 'subject to such limitations and restrictions as shall be provided . . . so soon as an Act of Parliament shall have been passed for carrying the said resolutions into effect'.

The Prince received the deputation with remarkable restraint. He gave no inkling, save to those who knew him, that his genial acceptance of these 'said resolutions' was merely a blind to furious resentment.

At the beginning of January, 1811, he sent for Grey and Grenville, and ordered them to draft a reply to the Address. They did. It was not to his liking; too tepid, and a tantamount agreement to those limitations which would dispossess him of his rights as Impresario. The draft must be revised, and by one more compliant to his will and to his interests than these two pragmatical Whigs.

In due course his answer was presented, with careful amendments, much to the chagrin of Grenville and Grey, who, in a pompous rebuke, expressed to the Prince their 'deep concern that their humble endeavours in His Royal Highness's service had been submitted to the judgment of another person'. Since the other person happened to be Sheridan, nothing could have been more ill-advised. Not only had they mortally offended the Prince by their dictatorial attitude, they had laid themselves open to Sheridan's satire and found themselves pinioned in print.

> 'In all humility we crave,
> Our Regent may become our slave
> And being so we trust that he
> Will thank us for our loyalty
> Then, if he'll help us to pull down
> His father's dignity and Crown
> We'll make him in some time to come
> The greatest Prince in Christendom.'

The excitement of the Whigs was tremendous. All the lesser fry were jockeying for places in the new Government. Not the least doubt dimmed their joyful expectation that the Prince would send the King's men out and bring his own men in. The Tories, glum as the Whigs were gay, felt equally certain of their fall. And while the fate of both parties hung in the balance, the Prince sent for Mrs. Fitzherbert.

She came in hopeful wonder. Why on the eve of his Regency should he call her to his side? Was he about to fulfil his promise so long ago pledged—of strawberry leaves—when he should come to unrestricted power? Was this the decline and fall of Lady Hertford's Empire, and was hers about to rise again? Or what exactly did he want of her?

He wanted nothing more than her advice, or so he said, on his choice of a new Administration. Which should it be—Whig or Tory?

She must have been greatly astonished. In common with everyone else she believed his Ministry had already been decided in favour of the Whigs. True, Grey and Grenville had offended him again by refusing to reinstate the Duke of York as Commander-in-Chief, but he would surely never penalize his party for their blunders? She advised him, 'Retain them in power, Sir, if only for six weeks.'

He agreed it were better to do so; and on that coolly impersonal note he bowed her from his presence.

No sooner was she gone than he hurried to Manchester Square. To Lady Hertford he put the same question—Whig or Tory? Let her advise him, and by her decision would he stand. . . . Not six weeks, but six days later the Whigs were out and the Tories in, with Perceval to lead them.

When on February 5, 1811, the Prince of Wales took his formal oath as Regent, the Tory Ministers were mortified to see a bust of Fox brought from the Prince's sitting-room to accupy a prominent position in the Council Chamber. There, ghostly reminder of his master's predilections, it stood on its pedestal throughout the whole proceedings.

The Tories, put completely out of countenance by those marbled features glaring at them above the Prince's shoulder, were by no means assured that, although retained in office, they would stay. The Whigs, on the other hand, who had suffered considerable shock at their dismissal, were by this same pallid token encouraged to believe that they would be recalled so soon as the Regency restrictions, imposed for one year, should expire. The Prince, however, seemed determined to maintain an attitude of strict impartiality to either side. So soon as he had been sworn in as Regent, he made himself a Field Marshal, and handed round appointments right and left to all his intimates.

The first to benefit was the Duke of York, reinstated Commander-in-Chief of the Army. Then came the greatest sensation of the year, a Grand Ball and Banquet given by the Regent, ostensibly in honour of the Bourbons, but actually in honour of himself.

The King, meanwhile had, throughout that summer, shown signs of returning lucidity. In May he had been well enough to take a ride in Windsor Park and to walk upon the terrace. From time to time his doctors issued hopeful bulletins. The Prince therefore decided that to celebrate his Regency if there were to *be* no Regency, would make of him a laughing-stock and how the Whigs would crow! So, the Bourbons were invited with two thousand other guests of the very highest French and English *ton*.

June 17 was the date fixed for this glorification at an expenditure of fifteen thousand pounds. The whole of Carlton House, from attics to basement, was thrown open as reception rooms, and then failed to accommodate the company. Horse Guards stationed in Pall Mall, St. James's Street, Piccadilly, and St. James's Square, strove to direct the crawling mass of coaches, carriages and chairs that blocked the routes along the way from nine that evening till past midnight.

In his Field Marshal's uniform, scarlet and gold-laced, with the ribbon of the Garter and its Star ablaze upon his chest, the Regent, garish, florid, fat, was mightily imposing, none the less.

He had spent so long in dressing up and making-up for this performance that his entrance was, perforce, a trifle flurried. His arrival at his post in the reception room simultaneously clashed with that of his most important guest, the Comte de Lille.[1] He could scarcely have recovered breath enough to bow—that famous bow extolled by a contemporary Irishman as 'the concentration of all grace, elegance and easy pliability. . . . Never was such a bow! I could swear he was born bowing, and never did anything but bow from his birth to the present time. . . . Powers of Heaven! It is wonderful! . . .' The Bourbon may have found it so when he was greeted by the Regent, nose to knees.

Blue drapery, embroidered in golden fleur-de-lys, served its dual purpose as a graceful compliment to his Royal guest and a decorative backcloth for the host. Magnificent beyond belief were the State apartments, revealed for the first time to the majority of those who thronged the Prince's palace. Tall pier-glasses, carefully placed, reflected interminable vistas of room after room, each more ornate than the other. The Throne Room, hung with crimson velvet, gold-fringed and gold-tasselled, was supported by fluted pilasters, solidly gilt. Four pelmets of pure gold surmounted by white ostrich plumes, crowned the canopy. Rose-tinted light, sprayed from crystal chandeliers, burnished the two lions couchant guarding the Grand State Chair. The adjoining Ante-Room was panelled in blue with a white and gold cornice and a frieze of sphinxes encircling a bust of Minerva. In the Rose-Satin Drawing-Room, festooned with carven flowers, a series of august emperors in cameo—Constantine, Pericles, Pompey, and Alexander the Great—may have suggested, to the more discerning, a faint austere resemblance to the Master of the House.

Ecstatic women in high-waisted pastel-hued gowns of satin, gauze, or muslin damped, regardless of chill, to cling, sank to the curtsy before him, a multi-coloured rosary, blush-white or full blooming. Then, their lily-tall feathers proudly a-nod, they passed with their attendant cavaliers into the Blue-Velvet Closet. This was the shrine of Dutch Masters, beloved of the Prince: Vanderheyden, Wouvermans, Cuyp, and Rembrandt's 'Christ Restoring the Paralytic'. . . . On again down the Grand Staircase where a bronze Atlas carried the world on his shoulders, the awe-struck throng clustered and crowded and pushed themselves into the Vestibule with its twin rows of Corinthian columns endlessly amplified in mirrors; its bronze griffins, urns, and doors of ebony, gilded and bordered in scarlet; its niches ornamented in *basso-relievo* holding busts of Discobalus, Antinous, Muses; so, through the Gold Drawing-Room into the Conservatory.

[1] The dethroned Louis XVIII of France, brother of the decapitated King.

This, the Regent's pride, the crux of his whole Exhibition, was built in the pseudo-Gothic manner of a diminutive cathedral with a nave and two aisles.

From pillared arches a glazed trellis spread upward and fanwise to the perforated roof. The walls were gilt-moulded, the curtains of crimson, the windows emblazoned with heraldic arms. An arched doorway gave access to the garden, where by day the Regent's peacocks preened and strutted on plush-smooth lawns, and where on any other evening the nightingales thrilled the air with song; but not this gala night. Those grassy spaces were enclosed in canvas walls, lit by fairy-lamps and Chinese lanterns. At the upper end of the Conservatory stood a circular buffet creaking under its load of gold plate, and overhung by a medallion draped in pink and silver bearing the initials G.P.R.

The supper-tables stretched the whole length of the Conservatory out into the garden and under the marquees. Immediately in front of the Regent's seat had been erected a toy temple whence a miniature fountain flung a sparkling cascade that flowed between banks of moss in a continuous stream spanned by four fantastic little bridges. Gold and silver fish flashed in those bubbling waters to charm the Regent's guests, but not to cool them. The heat was excessive. The noise of the bands, four of them blaring at once, the babble, the laughter, the popping of corks, the eating and drinking, went on until cock-crow. And still they stayed.

More than half the male members of the company were in heavily laced uniforms, the remainder in Court dress; but all of them dripped sweat from lack of ventilation. The women, although half-naked, were for the most part in the vapours; yet, when supper was done, they danced with the utmost vivacity in the ballroom. There was talk of the new Waltz, considered very shocking, which had just been introduced; none ventured to attempt it. A year later it became the craze of the Byron Season.

Among those ladies—and so many disappointed—praying to be partnered by the Regent, whispers tinged with malice fluttered round their fans. 'Why were his two wives sitting at home?' . . . Neither was present; the first because she had refused to sit where the Regent intended to place her—below the Salt and not at his table; the second because she had not been invited to sit at a table at all.

The Princess of Wales, for almost fifteen years excluded from her part in any royal function, was resigned to insult heaped upon her by the 'Great Mahomet', as she was pleased to call him. When her ladies, all of whom with exception of one, Miss Berry, drove off that night to Carlton House—some of them in gowns lent by the Princess—she good-

CAROLINE, PRINCESS OF WALES

From a mezzotint after J. Stothard, R.A., by I. Murphy, by courtesy of Brighton Art
Gallery and Museum

humouredly remarked: 'I am like de wife of an Archbishop, who does not partake of her husband's honours.'

But Mrs. Fitzherbert was not disposed to forfeit any honour which as wife of the Regent, and by Papal jurisdiction, she regarded as her due. On receiving her invitation she had presumed she would be placed with the Highest at her husband's table. Hitherto, on any similar occasion, the Prince had accorded her precedence above all others. She then heard from official quarters that she would be expected to join the general company in the marquees, and that Lady Hertford would occupy the favoured position, which, on tacit understanding, had been hers. And she was wrath. She drove to Carlton House, broke in upon the Regent and demanded audience to ask where he had placed her.

'Madam,' he replied, as cool as she was hot, 'you know you have no place.'

'None, Sir,' cut to the quick, she retorted, 'save such as you choose to give me.' And with that she left him.

The next day he received from her a letter.

'June 7, 1811.

Sir,
      After the conversation Your Royal Highness held with me yesterday I am sure you will not be surprised that I have sent my excuses for not obeying your commands for Wednesday next. . . . You, Sir, are not aware, in your anxiety to fill your table with persons only of the highest rank, that, by excluding her who now addresses you merely for want of those titles that others possess, you are excluding the person who is not unjustly suspected by the world of possessing in silence unassumed and unsustained a Rank given her by yourself above that of any other person present. . . . And for which reason I can never submit to appear in your house in any situation but in that where you yourself first placed me many years ago. Yesterday I was too much surprised when you informed me that from my want of rank I would not be admitted to your table, to be able to express my feelings in due bounds . . . but on reflection I think it more candid and open to lay my reasons before you.'

And, 'upon reflection', she made it clear that if he refused her a place at his table she would hold henceforth no place in his life.

It was the end.

Soon after their formal separation she retired to a villa on the Thames at Battersea. There, with her adopted daughter Minney and a handsome Royal pension to console her, she entertained discreetly. The Regent's

161

brothers were her constant visitors. She went often to Brighton, but never again to the Pavilion. Although she received formal invitations to the Regent's parties, she declined each one and sent Minney in her stead. At Sherwood Lodge, her riverside house, she made gardening her hobby and became, so the *Morning Post* reported, 'one of the most scientific botanists in the Kingdom'.

She was in her middle fifties when she ceased to be the Regent's wife. Thereafter, if unavoidably they met, they greeted each other as strangers; but when William, Duke of Clarence, came to the Throne he insisted she should wear widow's weeds for his brother and offered to make her a duchess. She declined. She had borne the name Fitzherbert for almost half a century, she told him, and did not wish to change it at her time of life. She was then seventy-four. She died in 1837 at the age of eighty-one, outliving George the Fourth by seven years.

★   ★   ★

In those darkened rooms at Windsor, enshrined within a world of mysterious dimensions that can neither dismay nor delight, dwelled an old man, blind and deaf. At his window, huddled in his purple dressing-gown, day in day out, he sat up-gazing at the sun he could not see, ears strained for sounds he could not hear above the pitying voices of angels with whom those about him believed he conversed. The ebb and flow of reason, like cloud-drifts in a starless night, came and went and fled for ever. That lost confused identity which once had been a King and had for so long troubled him, would trouble him no more.

His son had now become the unrestricted tenant of his father's House; but, when in February 1812, he entered into full possession of his Regency, he was heralded by no fanfaronade. While dissension ran riot at home, Wellington, abroad, was raiding the Peninsula, Napoleon marching on to Moscow, and the Americans preparing for another war with Britain: not the most propitious time to play the Regent's part on the political stage.

His health, too, was causing him anxiety. He had grown considerably fatter, and suffered from a peculiar numbed ache in his right arm which gave him greatly to fear he would lose the use of it. Nor was his condition improved by an accident he had sustained in the previous November at Oatlands, when the Duchess of York gave a ball for his sixteen-year old daughter. All of a sudden, in the middle of a dance, he had heaved his huge bulk up from his couch and called for a Highland Fling. Charlotte must be taught the steps and he himself would teach her.

A space was cleared in the centre of the room for the Regent to take the

162

floor. With the Princess dutifully following his capers, he pointed the toe, he flung out his arms, he jigged and he hopped emitting Gaelic shrieks, until one more hop sent him sprawling.

Charlotte, choking back her giggles, flew to his assistance. His gentlemen, preternaturally solemn, hoisted him up and bore him away to his bed.

For two weeks he lay there groaning, rolled over on his stomach and taking laudanum every three hours to deaden the pain caused by a twist– a very slight twist–of his ankle. There were those unkind enough to say that his agonies and posture, since he preferred to lie face downward than face upward, were not due to a sprain at all, but to a thrashing given him by Lord Yarmouth who had resented the Regent's attentions to his wife.

That tale went the round of St. James's; and when in January, 1812, he returned for the reopening of Parliament, sadly debilitated from over doses of narcotic, he was in a highly nervous condition, anticipating grins on every face.

Now that the Regency was firmly established, the Whigs, eagerly awaiting their recall, had become apprehensive of the Regent's vacillation. He dallied; he toyed with the fancy for a Coalition Government composed of Sheridan and Moira and other of his favoured Whig associates, with those two 'Honour and Duty' Lords, Grey and Grenville, thrown in as appeal to the popular taste; and, by way of Tory flavour, he intended to spice his Cabinet pudding with the brilliance of a Canning and the caution of a Wellesley.[1] He should have known better. His attempt to serve both parties with the same dish failed to satisfy any.

While Grey and Grenville frigidly refused to join the Government unless the question of Catholic claims were considered, Perceval and his Tories stood aloof and unperturbed, secure in the support of Lady Hertford. The Regent found himself wedged in what appeared to be an inextricable position. He had no love for Perceval since he had drafted him a letter to send to the Whigs, which the Regent described as 'written in a style that would disgrace a washerwoman'. Nor was he anxious to retain the Tories. At the same time he realized that a strong Whig factor favoured peace with Napoleon, and, come what may, he would have none of that. A pacifist Government founded on ideological theories of Reform could only lead the country to a patched-up truce and so to war again, depleted of an army. . . . What to do? Wouldn't anybody tell him what to do?

Lady Hertford told him, gently, what to do. Perceval and his Tories must stay.

The Whigs never forgave him for their downfall. Ever since the King's rapid decline and the chance of a permanent Regency, they had seen them-

[1] Marquis of Wellesley, elder brother of Lord Wellington.

selves cosily ensconced in snug offices, with heads as swollen as their incomes, endowed with dukedoms, earldoms, baronetcies, pensions on retirement; and now nothing–but inglorious defeat.

When on May 11, 1812, the Tory chief was shot dead in the lobby of Westminster Hall by a maniac with some imaginary grievance, the Whigs were heartened to hope that all was not yet lost. They were mistaken. The Regent cruelly dangled them upon his baited line, and sent for Wellesley. 'Form your own administration', he told him, 'take your time–although not a shilling', he plaintively lamented, 'is left in the Exchequer.' And little more in the Regent's Privy Purse, of which MacMahon was now appointed Keeper.

Wellesley, aware of breakers ahead, advised co-operation with the Whigs. The Regent, in a pitiable state of indecision, shilly-shallied. His chief concern was to choose the most accommodating party, in the event of that avalanche of debts, unforeseen by the Marquis but about to fall on him. The Whigs might not be so eager to come to his assistance, since once already he had sent them to the deuce. They and their would-be electors had only too plainly shown him their fangs when they booed and hissed him in the streets, while their cartoonists and pamphleteers made his life hell with their jests at his figure, his corsets, his Lady in Manchester Square.

He gravitated from Wellesley to Grenville and Grey, courted them warily, then turned to call them 'a couple of scoundrels'. For Grey he conceived the most violent hate since he had heard the report of his speech in the Lords referring to Lady Hertford as 'a pestilential secret behind the Throne'. And Wellesley did not improve the situation when he announced to the peers that, owing to these 'dreadful animosities', he must refuse to undertake the leadership of a new Government.

The Whigs were hilarious, and Creevey, their gossip, spurted malice in ink-blotted scrawls.

'Prinney must be stark staring mad, by God! . . . Late last night he sent for Moira and flung himself upon his mercy. Such a scene I never heard of; the young monarch *cried* loud and long. . . . He is playing, I have no doubt he thinks, some devilish deep game.'

He was far from playing any game, devilish or otherwise, and had almost ceased to play his part; yet even as he stood prepared for a dramatic exit by offering to abdicate his Regency, he saw his way made clear; not by retreat, but by action. As always, when flung back upon his own resources, his impulsive intuition, streaked with common-sense, served him fairly.

Lord Liverpool, that most exclusive of Tories, answered the summons to Carlton House.

The crisis was over; the Tories were in to stay–for the next fifteen years.

The Whigs, flung overboard, were left to flounder in the mud. They, who once had fawned upon their Prince, greedy for his favours, snapped in snarling fury at the hand they had so fondly licked. They had a stealthy following behind them, picked from those famished hordes, stirred to revolt, not secretly in back rooms, but in the dark backways of towns and cities.

The tidal wave of change swept down upon the nineteenth century fanned by the winds of Reform, whose pioneer leaders, Fox and Burke, had issued gale warnings long ago. And now the storm in onward flight gathered impetus to hurl itself upon the battlements of Georgian security; while above the rolling thunder of unrest could be heard the fevered throb and whir of wheels. The new age had brought with it the–Machine!

More formidable a menace than Napoleon's invincibility was this iron-girded monster that reared its ugly head in the homes of honest weavers. Men, who from time's beginning had earned their bread by the work of their hands, were now thrown aside to starve while their masters battened.

Hunger-stricken mobs whose only crime was poverty, whose only means of sustenance for their children was food stolen by their mothers from pig-troughs, flung themselves upon the stocking-frames at Nottingham to wreck that Christ-defying Thing which deprived them of their sole means of existence. All over the country in those districts where machinery replaced hand-power in the spinning-mills, the Luddite insurrectionists pillaged and burned for their rights–they who had no rights.

Soon after the Nottingham riots, an eccentric, comparatively unknown young peer with a beautiful, turbulent face limped into the House of Lords to take up the cause of the workless. . . . 'Never in the most oppressed provinces of Turkey did I behold such squalor as I have seen in the very heart of a Christian country.'

A few days later the whole of London buzzed with his name–not because he had made a daring speech, but because he had published the first two cantos of a daring poem. In *Childe Harold*, Byron, the new Poet, had voiced the New Creed.

Shelley, expelled from Oxford for hurling his New Moral Code in the teeth of bigotry, created at the feet of Godwin a New World, based on 'Political Justice'. Side by side with these ardent young enthusiasts, a Welshman, Robert Owen, was building his New Model factory, north of the Tweed, and teaching children to read and write in the first infants' school known in the land. All this was excellent, but also it was ominous.

What did it portend, and where would this New Progression lead? To irremediable rivalry and hatred between the 'Haves and Have-nots'? To group grievances and discontents that crept like vermin to penetrate the crevasses, walls, and hearths of every Englishman's castle–his home?

The Regent in his Castle, although besmeared with Whig slime, stayed untouched and undisturbed by any prophecies that threatened destruction to the soul of man. He had no reason to fear his world would shake or that his skies would fall beneath the Iron Yoke.

When, in 1812, he had struggled through the ordeal of political fire, he was left much in need of relaxation; yet scarcely had he come to himself after his pains and his strains, than he encountered further trouble–not from those sullen crowds who hooted him as he passed in his yellow coach, shrinking disgustedly behind his purple curtains from the sight and stink of them; and not from rebellious Whigs spewing petty spite at him–but from a rebellious young daughter.

In that same summer of 1812, Charlotte, who had hitherto been permitted to see her mother once a week, heard that in future she would not be allowed to visit the Princess of Wales more than once a fortnight. Her father had his own good reasons for this edict. Since the 'Delicate Investigation', Caroline had continued to live alternately at Blackheath and Kensington Palace.[1] Ostracized by the Royal Family, debarred from any of those privileges to which she was entitled, she continued to keep open house to casual acquaintances. Discarding social barriers she sought distraction from her isolated, and somewhat dreary existence in any doubtful company likely to amuse her.

In 1810 she had formed an injudicious friendship with the Sapios, father and son–a couple of Italian musicians. Enraptured with the music and song of these swarthy signors, Caroline insisted on their constant attendance in her salon–'frightening the air', complains Lady Charlotte, 'with horrible sounds until one in the morning'. And so that she should have at her command a perpetual cantata, the Princess rented a cottage in Bayswater near to the home of the Sapio family.

Impervious to the effect upon the jarred ears of her ladies, she delighted to join in a duet with the 'Ourang-Outang' and 'Chanticleer', as the Princess respectively dubbed her serenaders. 'Squall-Squall', moans Lady Charlotte. 'The music-mania is at its highest pitch. In short nobody is to come into the house but Squallinis'–until the fall of the Opposition. Then

[1] When the Princess of Wales was requested by the Regent to vacate these apartments, she acquired Connaught House on the north side of Hyde Park as her London residence.

Caroline discovered a new interest in the flattering attentions of a lawyer and a brewer.

Brougham, that forceful personality who, at the start of his amazing parliamentary career, had suffered in common with his fellow Whigs the Tantalus-pangs of fruitful promotion denied him, saw in Caroline the means of sweeter vengeance. Political capital might be made in the cause of the Princess of Wales. So, with Sam Whitbread as his Sancho Panza, Broughman set out on his quixotic campaign.

He began by persuading Caroline, to whom in his letters he refers as 'Mother P' or 'Mrs. Prinney', that she had a right to insist her daughter be permitted to visit her more often than once in two weeks. On October 4, 1812, acting on the advice of her kind friend, Mr. Brougham, Caroline drove down to Cumberland Lodge, Windsor, and demanded to see the Princess. She was politely refused admittance. Having come prepared for a battle royal, Caroline, nothing daunted, called at the Castle and forced an interview upon the Queen–with no more satisfactory result. To her query why her daughter's visits should be so strictly limited, the Queen gave an icily evasive answer, offered her no refreshment after her journey, and dismissed her with the doubtful hope that 'they would continue to be friendly.'

A few days later Caroline received a message from her husband, delivered through the medium of Lord Liverpool, stating that the Regent had heard she had been to Windsor, and forbade her to go there again. Caroline returned him reply to the effect that if she were allowed to see her daughter once a week she would obey–'if not she thought her duty to her child was paramount to all others'.

When this request was entirely ignored, Caroline, prompted by Brougham and Whitbread, announced her intention of appealing to Parliament for the right of access to her daughter. But before taking drastic action her advisers drafted her a letter to send to the Regent. With caustic sarcasm and one eye on the gallery Brougham presented her case in a document, skilfully worded.

'It is with greatest reluctance that I presume to obtrude myself upon Your Royal Highness . . . and to interrupt the more weighty occupations of Your Royal Highness's time. . . . I presume, Sir, to represent to Your Royal Highness that the separation of the mother and daughter, which every succeeding month is making wider, is equally injurious to my character and to her education. I say nothing of the deep wounds which so cruel an arrangement inflicts upon my feelings. . . . To see myself cut off from one of the few domestic enjoyments left me, the

167

society of my own child, involves me in such misery as I well know Your Royal Highness could never inflict upon me if you were aware of its bitterness. . . .'

Then, after appealing to the Regent's 'excellent sense and liberality of mind'—one can almost hear Brougham chuckling into his immaculately tailored sleeve as he wrote that—she begs him to remember that their daughter 'has never yet enjoyed the benefit of confirmation. May I earnestly conjure you, Sir, to hear my entreaties upon this serious matter?' A gentle reproach from the afflicted mother, whose high principles and devotion to the spiritual welfare of her child could not fail to draw tears from an audience. And it ends on a sobbing note of 'profound respect and an attachment that nothing can alter'.

The next day it came back to Caroline unopened, with Lord Liverpool's compliments, and the reminder that some years ago the Regent had declared he would never receive any letter or paper from the Princess of Wales, by which determination he intended to abide.

Back again went the letter to Lord Liverpool, and was returned with its seal unbroken as before.

The Regent was now becoming restive. Bitterly did he complain to his mother of 'this most mischievous intriguing Infernale . . .' and her irrepressible persistence. Brougham, perceiving that nothing could be gained by further correspondence, held a consultation with Whitbread and Creevey and decided that the time had come to act.

On January 28, 1813, the *Morning Chronicle* astonished the world by publishing in its entirety that letter of the Princess of Wales to the Regent.

Meanwhile, Charlotte, primary cause of these disturbances, had been kept strictly in the background at Windsor; or, when in London, at Warwick House, adjacent to her father's palace in Pall Mall.

Self-willed, capricious, with an aggressive bust, a skin like a flower, and an unruly mop of fawn-gold hair, she had the makings of a beauty and the manners of a ploughboy. When she laughed she showed every tooth in her head; when she argued she would stand with her chin out-thrust and her hands behind her back. She was proud of her hands—they were small for her size—prouder still of her ankles and legs; she had inherited her father's shapely calves, and his slightly hesitant speech, more pronounced in his daughter and not the least of her attractions.

Her greatest pleasure in life was to ride at the gallop cross-country, jumping hedges, ditches, challenging her shocked groom to a race. She was utterly fearless, arrogant, adorable, and—she was seventeen.

168

Into that grim gynocracy over which her shrivelled old grandmother presided, burst this coltish madcap of a girl who polluted the ears of her maiden aunts with 'something near to swear-words'. She called the Queen 'that Merry Wife of Windsor', and said that the King 'was mad as a puss'.

How those ageing vestals, her aunts, must have shuddered to see her lolling in a chair with her legs stretched out, admiring her ankles and the frills on her pantalettes—an attitude deplored by her governess, Lady de Clifford.

'My dear Princess, you are showing your drawers!'

'I der-don't care if I do.'

'Your drawers are too long.'

'I don't think so—the Der-Duchess of Bedford's are longer.'

The Princesses at their tatting—that interminable tatting—clicked tongues as fast as their needles, as, heads together, they sat in a ring darting daggers at their niece.

Sulky-mouthed and youthfully intolerant of acidulous virginity, she listened, ears alert, for sibilant whispers. *She said, He said, We said. . . .*

'The Queen said the Prince had accepted Lady Clifford's resignation with regret, but upon Lady de Clifford stating she thought she had lossed Charlotte's *confidence* it was impossible to ask Lady de Clifford to stay & she was hurt to find Charlotte *appear to feel* her going so little considering Lady de Clifford had been 9 years with her & given up so much of her time to her. Charlotte said she would have liked Lady de Clifford as a lady. The Queen ran over Charlotte's manners in general as not what would please in the long run in the world and her want of civility some days to people and over civility at other times. . . The Queen hopes that as she has completely paved the way for you, *you* will lose no time in haveing a conversation with Charlotte, but I think it right to state the Queen has got a very bad cold & is quite unequal to comeing up to town and coughs a great deal. . . Therefore if you *will* speak to Charlotte you must come down to Windsor. . . .

P.S. The Queen hopes you will be *very very* firm.'

So! Aunt Mary had been writing to the Regent, making mischief. It was true that Lady de Clifford had resigned her post of governess, to Charlotte's sorrow but not through Charlotte's fault—as Aunt Mary was perfectly aware. They were trying to force on her, in place of Lady de Clifford, the Duchess of Leeds and Miss Knight—Miss Cornelia Knight—a prim and proper person who had been in waiting on the Queen for several years and was sorely in need of a change. Charlotte, however, had told her Aunt Mary, who had promptly repeated it in writing to the Regent, that 'she would not have the Duchess of Leeds put about her as a Governess nor would she obey anybody in the capacity of Governess. . . .' What Charlotte now demanded and what she meant to have, was a Lady of the Bedchamber and her own establishment.

On the same day that Mary wrote her letter to the Regent, Charlotte wrote a letter to him too.

'*Sunday Mng.* (10, *Jan.* 1813)

I throw myself on your indulgence most respectfully to assure you that I am most ready & willing on all occasions to meet your will, wishes and pleasure . . . Allow me then to say that I felt very much hurt at never having been informed of the resignation of Ly de Clifford & consequent alteration. That I was the last to know of it & not till everyone talked of it & it reached my ears by hearsay, & more particularly as the once kind & grateful promise you gave me of there never being a third person between us gave me hopes. . . . I trust my dear father will pardon the freedom and the candor with which I have addressed him. . . . I feel the difference of my age. I cannot help judging from the view of other young people of my own age who cease to have Governesses at 17. I think it my duty also to state, before any final arrangements are made with the Duchess of Leeds that I have no *personal objections* to her, none therefore to her being appointed as *my lady*, but that under the name of Governess as such either her or anyone else I never can and never will accept or submit to. . . .'

It was the stone of defiance slung in the face of Goliath. And as he received the full impact of that impertinence, the Regent's whole majestic edifice rocked to its jellified foundations.

He ordered his carriage; he summoned Lord Eldon and drove down to Windsor non-stop.

In the Queen's room and in the presence of her lizard-faced grandmother, her triumphant Aunt Mary, and a trembling Lady de Clifford, Charlotte stood to meet her father's wrath.

He began by asking, in a voice to raise the ceiling, what she meant by her refusal to be governed by a governess, and by writing such a letter –to Him?

She answered not a word; she moved not a muscle. We can fancy how, exasperated by her silence, his eyes bulged, his massive chest inflated, and the sweat of his fury bedewed the powder on his face. He was the Regent, and this chit, this midget, this insufferable child with her chin stuck out, defied him!

He hurled abuse at her; he shouted. She was 'stiff-necked, stubborn'–
'And', croakingly chimed in the Queen, 'obstinate, perverse.'

'You're a fool–a silly fool!' roared her father. 'I know all that has
passed and you may depend on it that as long as I live you shall never have
your own establishment until you marry.'

It is possible that even as he uttered that immense admission he may have
heard an echo from its source, who sat in muffled solitude conversing with
the spirits of the past. And now this spirit of the present had arisen, re-
created in the image of himself. But what to do with her? ... Overheated,
scarlet, he turned to his Lord Chancellor whose vast fortune derived from
coal. 'What would *you* do with her?'

'Do with her?' echoed Lord Eldon. 'If she were mine I'd lock her up!'
A remark that horrified Lady de Clifford.

'Rather violent language from a coal-heaver's son to the future Queen
of England', she reported to the mother of this future Queen.

The Regent did not lock her up. With Lord Eldon he departed, in a
thunder-cloud; and the victory–a very minor victory–was Charlotte's.

On her next fortnightly visit to Kensington, she gave her mother her
own version of that scene. 'She could not *bear* her situation any longer, and
as soon as Parliament met she would go to Warwick House and remain
there.'

'The Princess of Wales', recounts Lady Charlotte, 'was in a great bustle
–enchanted at such character determination, firmness'. . . . Since that
royal row in the Queen's room at Windsor, the Regent had issued a
mandate forbidding his two Princesses to be left one moment alone together. Caroline, however, overcame that difficulty by stuffing a large pair
of shoes full of papers which she told Charlotte to take home with her
and read. 'We must *frighten* the man into doing something,' she said darkly,
'and if gentle means will not avail, then–' she left her threat unfinished,
'but looked', adds Lady Charlotte, 'quite fearful as she spoke. . . .'

It was shortly after this that the Princess of Wales publicized her letter
to the Regent. She had not frightened, she had goaded him to swift
retaliation. He called a meeting of his Privy Councillors and insisted that
a further inquiry must be made into the conduct of his wife. All the stale
garbage of the previous 'Investigation' was now to be raked up again.
If by this Augean repetition he hoped to find more grimy evidence against
her which might at last secure him a divorce, he was disappointed. When
twenty-three members of the Council and two bishops had re-examined
all the scum relating to the case of 1806, they decided that the Regent had
been amply justified in restraining his daughter's visits to her mother.
This ambiguous verdict, though it stabbed at his wife's reputation could

not kill it; and since no positive proof of misconduct had been offered, the case was reluctantly withdrawn.

The effect upon the public, as Brougham and his party had foreseen, was instantaneous, and aroused the chivalry of all men-in-the street on behalf of the Princess of Wales. Every mother wept with her, poor persecuted lady, deprived of her daughter kept captive at Windsor. Cruel! Cruel! . . . What a beast was this Regent, and what a saint his wife.

Brougham, writing to Creevey at Brighton, tells him: 'Come to Town to-morrow for Mr. Prinney. Let me console you. . . . The fellow was hissed to-day going to Court and hooted loudly. . . .'

Caroline had the Whigs behind her with a nation-wide support. In Parliament Whitbread presented her cause in a series of heart-rending speeches that drew tears from the Opposition benches. One Whig member was so overcome that he broke into audible sobs. Whitbread, wet-eyed, piped his variations on the fool-proof theme of mother and daughter torn apart till the whole country cried 'Shame!' on the Regent. While letters of sympathy were showered upon Caroline, he underwent a fusillade of scorn. Every time he made a public appearance he was hissed. When he attended at St. George's Chapel, Windsor, the disinterment of the martyred Charles I, whose remains rested beside the coffin of Henry VIII, Byron offensively spat at him:

'Famed for contemptuous breach of sacred ties,
By headless Charles see heartless Henry lies;
Between them stands another sceptred thing,
It moves, it reigns in all but name a King.

Ah, what can tombs avail! Since these disgorge
The blood and dust of both to mould—a George.'

Yet Byron was proud enough to be presented to the Regent and to receive his graceful tribute to *Childe Harold*; prouder still to learn from Scott that His Royal Highness had spoken of Byron and Homer in one breath.

Leigh Hunt, editor of *The Examiner,* got himself two years' imprisonment in Surrey Gaol for publishing a libel on the Prince Regent whom he described as a 'corpulent Adonis of fifty . . . a libertine, head and ears over in debt and disgrace, a despiser of domestic ties, the companion of gamblers and demireps'.

His Regency had brought him little joy. He suffered, and more deeply than his revilers believed, when they made of him, Prince Florizel, an overblown Silenus. There he stands, eternally accused of greed, lust, persistent cruelty to his virtuous unhappy wife, and jealous persecution of his daughter. Yet sift to the dregs the truth of his sinning and what can be found? That he drank to excess? So did others; that he whored? So did they. He deserted his friends – but only when they failed him. He threw over Brummell, and why? Because he had dared to utter the unutterable.... He *was* fat, but he would rather that Brummell had shot him than said it. He wore stays to hold in his belly – and what fun they all had out of *that*! The First Gentleman so tightly laced that his stomach rolled up to his chins! He had three, and to hide them wore stocks to his ears. So did half a thousand other men who followed Brummell and his starch.

As for his wife, he had found her unlovely to look at, unpleasing to touch, and incredibly stupid – no bedmate for him who worshipped beauty. He was faithless, had jilted Fitzherbert, and, while still Lady Hertford's acknowledged adorer, was laying siege to Lady Bessborough – another old flame – blubbering beside her on a couch, begging like a spaniel for favours, and rolling off the sofa to flounder at her feet. We have only her word for it.

And what of his daughter? It must have sickened him to know that as she drove out in her carriage his people shouted after her, 'God bless you! Love your mother!' She did love her mother and she did not love him, as he was too unhappily aware. When in January, 1813, she was to have been formally presented to the Queen, Charlotte heard at the last minute that the Duchess of York and not the Princess of Wales would present her.

'My mother or ner-no-one!' she stuttered. It was a cannon fired from a bed of roses. Her ladies entreated her, scolded, despaired. The befeathered debutante stuck to her guns. . . . There was no presentation that day. And another instance of bare-faced indocility was carried to her father, to his disgust and the Whigs' delight.

On a morning in March, when driving round the Park, Charlotte overtook her mother's equipage on Constitution Hill. She bade the coachman stop, and there in full sight of a cheering crowd, the Regent's wife and daughter leaned from their carriage windows and lovingly embraced. This affecting incident resulted in a demonstration from a Whig-incited mob hooting insults at the Regent outside Carlton House.

It was clear to him now that if this girl of his could not be moulded to his will she would have to be removed. Lord Eldon had advised him 'lock her up'. He wished he could; but with half the country at her heels he dared not run the risk. He had been brought into contact with an unsuspected personality; whose crowning – and how bitterly he knew it – all Britain awaited as once they had waited for his. Youth, crude, stumbling, egotistical, supremely self-confident, usurper of his dignity, heiress of his future Throne, had robbed him of his absolute faith in himself. To be rid of her, as he longed to be rid of her mother, was now his sole obsession. If she could not be cowed she must be eliminated – married to some princeling who would take her off his hands. That should not be difficult. He must admit her comely, crocus-limbed, enchanting – and mated she must be before she committed some immitigable folly. He had been told of meetings with a certain Captain Hesse when she rode in Windsor Park; of notes exchanged – love letters more than likely – and heaven only knew what else, encouraged by that 'Infernale', her mother. Charlotte had the fellow's portrait, in full uniform of the 18th Hussars, hanging on her bedroom wall. He soon had put a stop to that, but not to her flirtations; first this one, then another – and now it was the Duke of Devonshire. 'It signifies nothing how they go . . .' wrote Brougham to his gossip, Mr. Creevey. 'In the long run quarrel they must.'

Quarrel they did. The Regent changed his tactics, turned his charm upon her, gave her presents; a sapphire from the Stuart Crown and – more to her taste – 'a beautiful white greyhound with cropt ears', that had belonged to the Empress Josephine. She accepted them unmoved. He invited her to an open-air fête at Carlton House, held in celebration of the Battle of Vittoria. At this, her first public appearance, she was much admired. She danced on the lawn with the young Duke of Devonshire, then wickedly called for the Highland Fling, in which her father could this time, be persuaded to take part.

Soon after these joyful proceedings the Regent heard that she had been seen driving to and from Chiswick on the very day that the Duke of Devonshire was entertaining his friends to a 'great breakfast'. He immediately sent for Miss Knight and demanded an explanation. Miss Knight threw all the blame upon herself. Her Royal Highness had of late been so dispirited that 'I was anxious to do anything to cheer her.' It had been her suggestion that they take a drive to Chiswick 'to see the carriages'. The Regent received this lame excuse in silence; but when, on August 12, he celebrated his birthday in the grounds of the new Military School at Sandhurst, he markedly did not speak to his daughter nor to either of her 'Lady Companions'. The timid hare's eyes of the Duchess of Leeds were quite red-rimmed with weeping. Miss Knight, who had borne the brunt of the Regent's displeasure, was made ill, she confessed, with the shock of it. And to the Queen the Regent told his tales of that boy and girl affair between young Devonshire and Charlotte.

That distant feud between mother and son had long since been healed. Now, more than ever in his life, did he need her unstinted devotion, her sympathy, and her experienced advice in the handling of his terrible young daughter.

'What a kind, Oh! what a kind kind, very kind dear letter I have been favour'd with from you; never no never never, can I find words sufficiently strong or powerful, to express to you the full tide of all my gratitude for your affection, kindness, goodness and attention to me and to my wishes. . . . As to the subject which gave rise to this most amiable & delightful of letters. . . . One cannot disguise in whichever way one views it but that it arises from a sort of natural & intuitive spirit of restlessness & premeditated systematick kind of dissatisfaction. . . . With regard to the intimacy itself (it really is such complete stuff & nonsense) . . . never till now did I know that it existed as I have been kept in total ignorance that that particular person[1] who I believe to be perfectly harmless by the bye in themselves had ever had an opportunity of conversing with the other young person & much less had I any idea that they had been in the habit of visiting. . . . All this is to be ascrib'd to the infamous treatment I have experienced from those in whom I had so sadly misplaced my confidence . . . & whose sole & only object & principle has been & was as I am now convinced from the very first & the last to deceive me systematically. . . .'

But within a few days the Regent's concern in this, or 'the other young person', was completely forgotten in:

'Great Events   *Great Events*   *Great Events*

I am delighted at having it in my power to be once again able (under the blessing of a divine Providence) to be the channel of communicating to you the most satisfactory & important intelligence. In primus Mecklenborg is entirely free'd from the French; & Swedish Bulletins have been this instant receiv'd to the 8th and 9th inst. stating the Prince Royal of Sweden has after a long and well contested action taken 18,000 prisoners & 60 pieces of cannon. . . . I am too much elated at this moment to be able to make any comment, but my first impulse was & is, before I can allow myself to collect my ideas, to communicate to you best & dearest of mothers, these most joyful tidings. . . .

P.S. I shall fly and embrace you the first moment I am able. If you receive this as I hope you will whilst you are at supper, pray drink a bumper all round . . . to the health of the Prince Royal of Sweden & do not forget poor me, who have I think some little merit at having been the first to set them all at work.'

[1] Duke of Devonshire.

He honestly believed it; and as victory succeeded victory so did he take upon himself all the honours of war. Under his Godsent guidance, the European struggle that for almost twenty years had torn the hearts out of his people, was drawing to its close. Yet even while disasters thickened round Napoleon, while the glacial roads from Moscow lay piled with frozen dead, while Russia, reinforced by Austrian and Swedish alliance massed her columns to confront him, Bonaparte gathered his ragged army of two hundred thousand men and boys—and strode out again to meet them, still unconquered.

He surely must have known his end was near. In the first week of November, Caroline's brother, the Duke of Brunswick, whose father had lost his life in the Battle of Jena, was returned to his patrimonial domain. The streets of London, lighted by the leaping flames of bonfires, re-sounded to a tumult of rejoicing at the news of Leipzig's fall. A few days later, German troops, weeping with joy, re-entered their Rhineland and knelt to give thanks at the sight of it. In Holland, the Dutch, from whom for nineteen years the Corsican had squeezed, as from a sponge, their trade, their mercantile resources, their very life and soul, turned to harry the last of the French under whose lordly occupation they had been reduced to serfs. In December, 1813, the exiled Prince of Orange returned to Amsterdam as Holland's restored King. And in that same month Prince William, his Hereditary Heir, came to London.

In this sickly-faced weak-chinned youth, the Regent saw his saviour—a husband for Charlotte, and one who, as future sovereign of Holland, would take his too popular daughter out of the country for six months in every year. The Dutch Prince was flattered to receive an invitation to dine at Carlton House and meet the Princess Charlotte.

She had naughtily chosen her most unbecoming gown for the occasion. 'Violet satin trimmed with black lace . . . a toilet by no means recherchée,' complains Miss Cornelia Knight.

The Princess was pale; the Hollander nervous. They had nothing to say to each other. The Regent exerted his charm, shed smiles, drank health to the Prince, and despairingly drew his 'young person' aside. It may well be imagined he was hard put to restrain himself from violence, seeing her so surly and dressed as for a funeral. 'Well', he demanded, 'I suppose it will not do?'

'I don't say that,' she hedged. 'I like his manner very well—as much as I have seen of it.' But she told her mother quite a different story. 'Marry I will—but not the Prince of Orange. . . . He's so ugly.'

She was keeping in reserve another William, her father's cousin the Duke of Gloucester, twenty years her senior. More intimately known as

'Silly Billy', he had a face like a cheese and was as little to her fancy as the Dutchman; yet the fact that he was regarded by her Family as her spinster Aunt Mary's last hope may have added something to his favour. Charlotte had a quiet score to settle with Aunt Mary. The Regent, however, knew nothing of that and cared less; nor did he feel disposed to wait while she made her choice. He made it for her.

When a day or two after that doleful dinner at Carlton House, the Prince of Orange called upon the Regent, he was significantly left alone with Charlotte. Her father, accompanied by a tremulous Miss Knight, retired to an ante-room adjoining. There, by the fire, he sat affably chatting with the 'Lady Companion', to whom he confided that 'the Princess Charlotte was engaged to the young Prince of Orange', but that on no account must anybody know. . . . Miss Knight was in the highest degree flattered that the Regent should have chosen to entrust her with this romantic secret; and still more at his desire–possibly attended by happy winks and nods–'that Miss Knight should give her royal charge some good advice–particularly against flirtation'.

Nothing could have been more amicable than the Regent in this confidential mood, sprawling on a sofa with his hands on his knees, one eye on the door, and all ears for the voices beyond it.

Presently the low guttural murmurs of Charlotte's betrothed were interrupted by loud distressful sobs. Starting up, the Regent strode across the room, flung open the door, and found Charlotte, crumpled in her chair, the picture of Niobe. The Orange Prince stood over her, obviously scared and dreadfully embarrassed. 'What!' with roguish tact exclaimed the Regent, 'is he taking his leave?' For only the sweet sorrow of his going–so his heartiness implied–could have caused her such unmitigated woe. 'Ner-not yet!' blubbered Charlotte; and without another word she dashed from the room, banging the door behind her.

While waves of shocked vibration beat upon Cornelia, the Regent's winning grace remained unruffled. Turning to the pallid Prince he invited his attendance at a City dinner to be held at the Guildhall that same night.

After they had gone Charlotte confided to Cornelia the reason for her outburst. 'The Prince', indignantly records the faithful Knight, or 'Notti' as Charlotte more familiarly called her, had given her to understand that she was expected to reside every year for two or three months in Holland, 'and even when necessary follow him to the army'. He had furthermore impressed upon her that 'he was quite an Englishman himself and hoped she would invite what friends she liked . . .' And Charlotte boiled; but was wise enough to know who had prompted her invertebrate Dutch suitor's condescension. 'I have no manner of doubt that it is decidedly the object of *more than one* to get rid of me,' she said. She found herself between the devil and the Zuyder Zee, and miserably chose to take the plunge.

Her engagement to Prince William, Heir to the House of Orange, was publicly announced in the New Year.

★   ★   ★

It was the year of the Great Frost, when snow-drifts higher than the coaches blocked the King's highways; the year when a Fair was held on the Thames, and the cost of coal went up to fifteen shillings a sack. All water traffic was suspended. Wherry-men led their fares across a footpath that ran from bank to bank, threading a way through crowds packed about the hastily erected stalls of cheap-jack tradesmen, peddlars, pie-men. Chilled old folk sipping hot grog, warm ale or raw gin, sat around the fire-glow of braziers that, no matter how fiercely they burnt, could not melt the solid ice. There were fur-capped skaters, showily performing, swings, roundabouts, minstrel bands, and fiddlers to set the boys and girls footing it madly.

The Regent, just recovered from the influenza, remained in his hot-house rooms at Windsor writing letters almost daily to the Queen. 'You cannot conceive how mortally I hate this weather.' He was in continuous complaint about his health – 'disagreeable pains, a sore throat and symptoms of lowness' – possibly due to lack of news from the fighting front. The last he had heard was that the Allies had invaded France and were marching on to Paris. Brussels was taken: Antwerp besieged. How much longer could Napoleon hold out? Wondrous rumours filtered through to Britain. Boney had been slaughtered by the Cossacks at the very gates of Paris. . . . No! He had turned in his tracks to cut through Blucher's lines at Vauchamps. Scarcely stopping to lick at his wounds, he went limping on with his war-weary pack behind him. But when Spring struggled free of that winter's iron grip, when the swollen Thames, whipped with the tides of March, rose up to overflow its greening banks; when in English cottage gardens the snowdrops and the crocus fled before the trumpet-peal of daffodils, Wellington swept in upon Toulouse.

On April 9, 1814, Paris surrendered to the Allies. The French, sickened of blood, destitute, famished, laid down their arms. At Fontainebleau the Emperor heard from Ney's lips, 'The Army will not march.' He heard – and did not hear.

'The Army will obey *me*!'

'No, Sire, the Army will obey its Generals. . . .'

Napoleon's abdication set the joy-bells pealing throughout the land.

178

Every house in every street blazed with coloured candles, fairy-lights, transparencies. The Regent's palace in Pall Mall proclaimed his rejoicing in letters of fire and very bad French, 'VIVE LES BOURBONS'; and to the Queen excitedly he wrote, 'I trust, my dearest mother, that you will think I have fulfilled and done my duty at least, and perhaps I may be vain enough to hope that you may feel a little *proud* of your son.'

His unshakable naïve conceit in himself was nothing lessened by the fact that while these momentous triumphs were scored across the face of history, he had been sunk in his chair with a gouty foot and had scarcely stirred out of it since the last snows melted. But now he must pay to the Allies and the exiled French King all honours due to those victories for which he, the moving spirit behind Wellington and his Generals, was primarily responsible.

Louis XVIII of France, who kept his Court in impoverished imitation of Versailles at a house near Aylesbury, was the first on whom the Regent let the light of his countenance shine. The very day that Napoleon with a guard and a small fleet set out for the island of Elba, the Regent drove in state to meet the Bourbon.

His chariot, drawn by eight cream-coloured horses and escorted by a body-guard of Blues, was attended by heralds, outriders, and postilions in white liveries—a compliment to the emblem of French monarchy. Through the leafy lanes of Middlesex the procession wound its way, followed by excited crowds of villagers, who likely thought the show to be a circus. Outside the Abercorn Arms at Stanmore these two fat men embraced; and there the Regent, who had sent his head chef in advance to prepare a meal, right royally entertained his guest. Then, when both had feasted to capacity and Louis something more than to his fill, he was hoisted into the Regent's carriage where he sat with his niece, the Duchesse d'Angoulême, facing his host and the horses. As they clattered through Edgeware village and out on to the high road again, the crowds were lined up four deep against the bursting green of hawthorn, blossom-starred. Orchards, heavy-laden, white with bloom, offered nature's token to the King of France. He may have known nothing, seen nothing of that, as he bowed and alternately belched in response to the cheering. But as they neared London and the crowds grew more dense and more noisy, swarming in the gutters, holding up the horses, so did the Regent grow more nervous. He never knew when the mob would turn ugly at the sight of him. He summoned his most devastating smile, bowed this way and that to the clamour, and heard not a hoot; nor did he hear one God-blessing.

At Tyburn Hill women leaned from their windows waving aprons.

white sheets, pillow-cases, bolster-slips, to welcome the French King. In Piccadilly, ladies in new white gowns fluttered new white scarves and ribbons at the Bourbon–a ghostly if uproarious reception. At Grillon's Hotel in Albemarle Street, where Louis was to stay for two nights before he crossed the Channel, he was fêted 'with all the pomp and rabblement of royalty', sneered Byron.

After they had feasted, the paunchy pair exchanged congratulatory addresses; although to be sure the tearfully grateful speech of King Louis was a trifle marred by his inability to stand upright, which the more sympathetic onlookers ascribed to the gout, and others to the Regent's hospitality.

Nor did it end at that. On April 23, when Louis departed for his capital, his host, in full Olympian rig, went with him to Dover and stood on the end of the pier to bow him God-speed as he sailed by in the Royal yacht. It was perhaps unfortunate that this last gesture of grace was lost upon Louis, who, as the ship shook herself free of her moorings, had retired below, greenly pale. But the Regent still stood there hatless and bowing in the breeze, while the yacht, like a white swan, skimmed over the sea to give back to France her King.

CHAPTER EIGHT

1814–1817

IN that victory summer of 1814, the Regency attained its highest pinnacle of splendour with the visit of the Allied Sovereigns to England. From the first week in June until the end of the month, when the Royal guests departed, the citizens of London gave vent in massed hysteria to their joy at deliverance from twenty years of war. Never had been seen or heard such a tramping of feet, such a flying of pennons and flags, such display of bunting and dazzle of lights, coiled like a glowing serpent round the city.

The cynical Czar Alexander of Russia, unstirred by all this multitudinous emotion, managed to slip the crowds that since dawn had lined the streets in anticipation of his coming. Unattended, he took his Ambassador's coach, made a circuit of the pre-arranged route, and arrived unrecognized at the Pulteney Hotel in Piccadilly. He was met by his sister, the lively, attractive, widowed Grand Duchess Catherine of Oldenburg, who had been in residence there for some weeks.

The Grand Duchess of Oldenburg had much to tell this adored brother who had hoped to see her married to one of these despicable but eligible Guelphs. The Prince Regent was out of the question since he had not yet obtained his divorce, but there were other sons of the mad King of Britain who should be honoured at the prospect of an alliance with the sister of the Czar. ... She soon disabused his mind on that score, laying much emphatic stress on his host's unpopularity which the Russian Emperor, god of a servile people who loved because they feared him, had no wish at all to share. And although State apartments in St. James's Palace had been prepared for his reception, he found the hotel better to his liking. For the Regent's disappointment the Czar cared not a rouble; nor for the military bands and Officers of State waiting with his British Ally to receive him.

From his balcony at the Pulteney, facing the Park where cows grazed beneath the trees in delightfully rural surroundings, the Czar could look down upon those hordes of excited, foolish Britons bellowing with one vast cavernous mouth every time that he appeared.

There were seemingly only two types of Englishmen; the one typically

John Bullian, short, stout, bovine, his face shining red as the sun in a fog; the other lean, pale, long in the tooth and chinless; and both bore a ludicrous resemblance to a Rowlandson caricature. As for the women—one glance sufficed for the Emperor to purse his wry little lips in repugnant opinion of *them*. He had come prepared to scoff, and he did—at these barbarians, and also at their Regent whom his sister contemptuously described as 'un voluptueux'. The Regent's brother, the Duke of Clarence, who had hurried down to Dover to meet the noble Czar, was disdainfully dismissed as a clumsy buffoon with a pineapple head, and an inelegant habit of wiping his nose on his finger.

If the Regent observed, in this hullabaloo of rejoicing offered to a parcel of foreigners, a marked contrast to the gloomy silence that was his portion when he drove out in public, he showed no sign of rancour. He threw open his house to the potentates in a sybaritic pageantry of balls, dinners, gala fêtes. But to Blücher was given the greatest ovation of all when he rolled up in his carriage to Carlton House and stood on the seat to salute the colours of the Horse Guards as he passed. And because he looked such a jolly, white-whiskered, red-in-the gills old rip, the crowd went mad and yelled for him. They stormed the gates, knocked down two sentries, had a fight with the porter, and when at last the gates were shut against them, they clambered up and over the walls, while a few even gained a foothold on the roof of the porter's lodge.

Inside Carlton House, the Regent, encircled by his Court, graciously conferred upon the kneeling Blücher a medallion of himself set round with diamonds. After that, in response to the clamour outside, he led the veteran Field Marshal to the window; yet, for all that he bowed himself stiff, not a voice raised one cheer for the Regent.

A few days later the Czar and his sister visited Oxford. The Duchess of Oldenburg wore 'a plain travelling dress', and the latest thing from Paris, 'a large straw bonnet shaded by a broad pendant feather', vastly unbecoming to its wearer but speedily copied by ladies of fashion and known as 'the Oldenburg Poke'.

Followed by a cheering mob of undergraduates, brother and sister drove to Merton College, while the King of Prussia and his sons, the next arrivals, went to Corpus Christi. In the afternoon they called upon the Regent, who had got up before six that morning and driven post-haste all the way to be there in time to receive his guests. He received them—to the wonder of the Cossacks attendant on the Czar—in cap and gown; and still in that scholastic garb he conducted them round the city, striding ahead, pausing to point out the architectural beauties of the colleges, and to dilate in a knowledgeable manner on their history. His lecture unfortunately, was lost upon his party and their respective suites, since none save the Grand Duchess spoke English enough to understand him, and she did not listen. She was flirting with a don who had never been more flattered. In the evening a grand banquet was held in Radcliffe Library, watched from the gallery above by those not privileged to attend. There were speeches and toasts; and when the Regent, in merriest mood, lifted his glass to the undergraduates clustered on the balcony, the uproar exceeded belief. Caps, hats, shoes, flew in all directions. Gowns and coats were wrenched off their wearers, and not until the military had been called in to quell the noise could anyone hear himself speak.

Before they left Oxford the Regent solemnly invested the Czar, the King of Prussia, Prince Metternich, Count Lieven, the Russian Ambassador, and–to his profound amaze, the grizzled old Blücher, also–with honorary degrees. The next morning the Royal visitors returned in state to London. The Czar, determined to see all he could cram into his allotted space of time, rode in the parks before breakfast, drove to Westminster through Southwark to the City, visited the Docks, the Bank, the Royal Exchange, and Ascot races. Wherever he went he was mobbed. Never could those rowdy, clattering, cheering, perspiring Londoners have enough of that wondrous procession which daily delighted their streets with its uniforms, banners and Cossacks, its heralds and trumpeters, cymbals and bands–all a-glitter. Never had the city seen the like of it.

On June 18, a banquet was held at the Guildhall for the Royal guests. They were met at Temple Bar by the Lord Mayor, Sheriffs, and Aldermen mounted on horses, robed and bedizened, arrayed in gold lace and cocked hats. The Czar was welcomed as usual with jubilant yells; the Regent with groans and shouts of–'Your wife! Where's your wife! . . .' Most unpleasant.

Under a canopy of crimson velvet, fringed and roped with gold, over which hovered a white dove bearing an olive branch in its mouth, he sat in brooding silence, the two Kings either side of him. The Czar made no effort to disguise his yawns; he drank little, loathed English food, and found his host's charm over-rated. The Regent spoke not a word to him throughout the lengthy dinner. He was in bad temper because he had been forced to give up his seat to the Duchess of Oldenburg, who had insisted on inviting herself to every function held in honour of her brother. The Regent was well aware that current gossip coupled her name with his as a possible Consort if he should ever be rid of his wife. But better the devil he knew than this Muscovite devil whom he heartily wished he never had known, with her airs and her flirtatious graces. She had been particularly difficult that night when, on plea of a headache, she covered her ears and protested to the playing of 'Rule Britannia' by the band. If that noise did not stop, she declared, she would be sick. To oblige her the Regent stopped the 'noise', and greatly disobliged his civic hosts, who took such immediate offence that he begged her, in an earnest aside, to allow the National Anthem to be played; and although to this appeal she unwillingly consented she sat with her eyes closed, grimacing till the end. . . . 'All agree that Prinney will die or go mad,' was Creevey's report of these doings. 'He is worn out with fuss, fatigue and *rage*.'

The discourteous behaviour of his Russian guests did certainly not improve his temper. Yet tirelessly still he entertained them. And when at night the windows of Carlton House glowed like fiery planets beneath a star-studded sky, and a cavalcade of carriages and coaches lined the Mall, those insatiable herds who watched there would have seen, against the dim tangled foliage of trees, women in high-waisted gowns, their plumed heads glorified in gauzy jewelled turbans, drive up to the Regent's house. From dusk till dawn they came and went attended by their menfolk in uniform or full court dress of pastel-coloured kerseymeres, knee-breeched and white-stockinged, chins hidden in their high cravats, and orders glinting. Yet this gaiety and jollity brought no pleasure to the Regent. 'Prinney is exactly in the state one would wish', chuckles Creevey. 'He lives only by protection of his visitors. If he is caught alone nothing can equal the execrations of the people. . . .'

He had none but himself–and the Whigs–to blame for that.

During the whole of this festive season the Princess of Wales had been excluded from her share in the rejoicing; she had long since been banished from the Court.

This succession of slights was nothing lessened by the fact that Caroline's mother, the Duchess of Brunswick, resident in England since the death of her husband, received invitations to Carlton House and frequent visits from the Queen.

A dingy uncomfortable lodging had been found for this tiresome old woman in New Street, Spring Gardens, which Lady Charlotte describes as 'the dirtiest room I ever beheld, empty and devoid of comfort. . . .' Equally devoid of comfort, indeed a further trial to Caroline, was this 'melancholy spectacle of decayed royalty'. The Duchess seemed to take delight in hurtfully boasting of the attentions bestowed upon her by the Regent–in striking contrast to the insults he heaped upon her daughter.

When it became known that the Queen had refused to admit the Princess of Wales to the two Drawing-rooms held in honour of the potentates, public indignation at this added injury brought into harsher evidence the scandalous relationship between the Regent and his wife. But with more than half the country and all the Opposition on her side, Caroline was emboldened to announce in a letter to the Queen her determination to appear at one or other of the Drawing-rooms. The Queen at once replied that since the Regent had expressed his unalterable decision not to meet the Princess of Wales upon any occasion, either public or private, it was clearly impossible to accede to her request.

Popular sympathy for Caroline had now reached such a pitch that not only the Regent but his mother was hissed when she drove out. Nothing daunted, the wizened old matriarch let down the window of her carriage and, with guttural dignity, addressed the snarling rabble that surrounded her. 'Look you! I am above seventy years of age. I have been for more than half a century a Queen and never before have I been shpit upon! . . .' That silenced them. They fell back and let her pass.

All such indications of support, even though it emanated from the lowest most criminal classes, encouraged Caroline to show herself on every possible occasion, and to capitalize her injuries fourfold. She was frantic for a sight of the handsome Czar of whom she had heard such glowing accounts; and when it came to her knowledge that the Regent had commanded a box at the Opera, she determined that she too would grace with her presence the Theatre Royal on the same night that her husband and his guests were due to attend the performance.

She took considerable pains with her toilet that evening, and finally decided in favour of black velvet, a black wig, and a diamond tiara from which sprang a towering black plume. Her face, smothered in white lead, looked like a clown's, and her mouth was a crimson gash. When she waddled into her box followed by her apprehensive ladies–who only with the greatest difficulty had dissuaded her from bringing 'Willikin' –she found the house on its feet and the orchestra playing the National Anthem.

The Regent, seated between the smiling Czar and the round-eyed King of Prussia, glanced neither to right nor left but gazed fixedly before him as she entered and stood till the end of God Save the King. The pit was the first to recognize and raise a cheer for the Princess of Wales. Then from the gallery above to the thronged tiers below, came such a storm of applause that she to whom it was directed shrank back in her seat overcome; and though her ladies begged her to rise she refused. 'No, my dears,' she told them. 'Punch's wife is nowhere when Punch is present here.'

The amused Czar put up his quizzing-glass and was staring at her through it; men were grinning; heads were dodging, women buzzing, and the Regent, gulping his mortification, made his exquisite *beau geste*. Rising from his seat he bowed to his wife for her and the world to see.

It must have cost him every ounce of his pride to give her that which she, in her confusion, unfortunately missed. But when the curtain fell on the last act the warmth of her reception was prodigious. While the Regent and his guests retired to a modicum of temperate applause, the house roared for the Princess of Wales. Bewildered, flushed beneath her paint, she jerked at them three curtsies in response and hurried off. Her exit created a furore. As she stepped into her carriage she was hailed with cries of 'God bless you! Long life to you! Long live the innocent! . . .' The poor soul, with every kind of slander to her name, believed they mocked her. And when a few of the more daring dragged open the coach door and offered to burn down Carlton House—'No, no, good people,' she implored them, half laughing, half in tears, 'let me pass—go you home to your beds.'

She went home to hers, dejected; but a few days later Lady Charlotte found her in a great state of excitement—'big with news'. The Czar of Russia, who had side-glassed her with such flattering attention at the opera, had been so taken with her charms that he had sent word to say he would call upon the Princess of Wales at her residence. What a conquest! 'My ears are very ugly,' she admitted to her lady, 'yet I would give them *both* to persuade the Emperor to come to me.'

She anticipated he would not require much persuasion. Arrayed in her finest, bewigged and berouged to the eyebrows, she waited, poor soul—and she waited. From noon until sundown she sat; and when at tapertime no Emperor appeared, she gave up hope and called for her fiddlers, the Sapios, to cheer her.

'It is not the loss of amusement I regret,' she complained, 'but being treated as a child and made the puppet of a party.' She was shrewd enough to see that Brougham, Whitbread, and all those who professed to be her friends were using her—'not for my gratification but for theirs—and that's how things will always be until I can leave this vile country'.

She had long been debating in her mind whether to go or to stay. Her detestation of her husband was now as great as his for her. She alternately teased and terrified her ladies with her curious tales and threats. One day she went out for a walk unattended, and was followed by two gypsies who insisted on telling her fortune. 'And what do you think they told me?' Lady Charlotte, to whom this adventure was imparted, uneasily replied she could not guess.

'They told me,' said the Princess, rolling her eyes in a most alarming fashion, 'that I was a married woman but will not be married long . . . and that I should go abroad and there marry the man I love and be very rich and happy . . . !'

On that delphic utterance, and to Lady Charlotte's consternation, she dwelled, declaring 'she would *kill* the Regent, sell her plate, her jewels, everything that she possessed,' and on which she could raise money, and so tour the Continent, presumably in search of this nebulous rich lover. Or she would sit, like some pantomime witch, mumbling curses over a wax image she had modelled of her husband into which she had stuck pins–with the amiable addition of a pair of horns–and would then leave it to roast in front of the fire.

Her exclusion from the Court and Carlton House during the visit of the Allies, finally decided her to write to Lord Liverpool announcing her intention to travel abroad–'for persecuted as I am, life has become a burden to me'.

When Liverpool conveyed this pleasing intelligence to the Regent, his relief at such good riddance was implied in his answer, 'she could go if she wished'. But having obtained his permission she seemed in no hurry to go. She would delay her departure until after her daughter's marriage –if the marriage should ever take place. Caroline had received certain knowledge that gave her to think it would not. Charlotte, from the first, had shown herself unwilling to accept the clammy hand of her Dutch suitor. She could not love him, she did not even like him, and she sought by every means to let him know it. This engagement had been forced on her against her will and inclination, and though to all intent she was officially betrothed, her heart–she made it clear–was disengaged. When her future husband suggested she should accompany him to Holland and be presented to his family, she would not hear of it. He persisted. She opposed him; and they quarrelled.

The Regent was greatly put about. Not only had he to contend with the devilish works of the Whigs, who sought at every turn to exploit his hateful wife, but he needs must exert himself all day and half the night to provide entertainment for a pack of foreigners who yawned through his banquets, derided his music, and sneered at the glories of his palace. And while the populace bawled Hallelujah to the Czar, he was treated to groans and demands for the Princess of Wales! She, prinked out like a harlot, was followed wherever she went by shouts of 'God bless you! We'll make the Prince love you before we are done with him.'

'Done with him!' . . . Ill-omened words. And in addition to these trials, here was his daughter threatening to break off her engagement! The Regent had been given some account of those almost daily squabbles between Charlotte and her flaccid affianced. Since all the apartments at Carlton House were occupied by more important visitors, the Prince of Orange had found a lodging with his tailor in Clifford Street; at which

Charlotte took fierce umbrage. If the future Consort of England's future Queen could, without a word of protest, allow himself to be so unceremoniously shifted to make room for petty royalties and their respective suites, what an inconsiderable prince – in the Regent's estimation – must this Prince of Orange be! It was evident to Charlotte that her father had determined to marry her off, never mind how or to whom, so long as he be quit of her. Very well, then! She would show the Regent and all of Britain that she would never be married save to the man of her choice, which William of Orange decidedly was not.

There had come in the train of the Czar a pauper Prince of no account, third son of a ruling Duke. To be sure he bore a distinguished record for war service, and looked exceedingly well in his uniform, but his income was barely two hundred a year and as for his status and rank – he had not even been offered so much as an attic in the Harley Street house of the Russian Ambassador. He was poked away over a greengrocer's shop in the High Street of Mary-le-bone.

Prince Leopold of Saxe-Coburg had been presented to Charlotte by her latest, dearest, and most delightful friend, the Duchess of Oldenburg. The Duchess encouraged girlish confidences in her salon at the Pulteney Hotel. The Duchess had a sister – an old maid elder sister – for whom her brother, the Czar, cherished the hope of a diplomatic alliance. The Hereditary Heir to the House of Orange, would, he decided, be a suitable match for the Grand Duchess Anna.

Neither Charlotte nor her mother was proof against the fascinating Oldenburg's beguilements. 'She is a very clever woman and knows the world and mankind well', wrote the Princess of Wales in a confidential letter, 'my daughter could not be in better hands. They are a great deal together which makes the Regent look outrageous.'

He had reason enough to look 'outrageous'. Fearing any moment a combustion, he had made all haste to expedite the marriage. The trousseau was ordered, invitations were issued, and a list of the guests was sent to Charlotte. When she saw that her mother's name had been omitted, she took up her pen, scratched out the name of Prince William of Orange, and returned the list, with that deletion, to her father.

The Whigs cracked their sides laughing; the Regent was frantic, and Creevey wrote in high glee to his wife.

'*June 21, 1814.*

We have now a new game for Master Prinny . . . Whitbread has formal authority from young Prinny to state that the marriage is broken off, and that the reasons are – first, her attachment to this country which she cannot and will not leave; and, above all, her attachment to her mother, whom in her present distressed situation she likewise cannot leave. . . . By God! It is capital. And now what do you suppose has produced this sudden attachment to her mother? It arises from the profound resources of old Brougham, and is, in truth, one of the most brilliant movements in his campaign. He tells me he has had direct intercourse with the young one; that he has impressed upon her this fact that, if her mother goes away from England, as she is always threatening to do from her ill-usage in the country, that then a divorce will inevitably take place, a second marriage follow, and thus the young Princess's title to the throne be gone. This has had an effect upon the young one almost magical.'

But more magical effect upon the 'young one' might perhaps have been traced to the *beaux yeux* of that penniless prince who rode out each morning from his greengrocer's shop to meet a certain carriage in Hyde Park.

★   ★   ★

The Hereditary Heir to the House of Orange took his dismissal with customary phlegm, and expressed in a few brief lines the hope that his late betrothed 'would never have any cause to repent of the step she had taken'.

Charlotte made a copy of his letter, sent it to her father, and with some trepidation, awaited the result.

Nothing happened; no word from the Regent other than a scribbled note coldly stating his concern at her decision; no visit from her aunts, nor her uncles, nor the Queen. The Duchess of Leeds, scared out of her wits by this sinister silence, sent in her resignation. The staunch Miss Knight stuck to her post, and Prince Leopold of Saxe-Coburg came to tea.

Another Prince, a Prussian Prince,[1] had arrived in London with the Allies and was first presented to Charlotte by her father at a dinner at Carlton House.

Poor Prince Leopold was nowhere in the running against the persuasions of this very experienced youth, who laid successful siege to Charlotte's heart.

He sent her books, he gave her a ring; and Miss Knight, cherishing, it

---

[1] Greville, in his memoirs, erroneously names this Prince, Augustus, and has thus given rise to some confusion. Frederick was the nineteen-year-old son of Frederica, widow of Prince Louis of Prussia, killed at the Battle of Jena. Princess Frederica was the daughter of the Duke of Mecklenburg-Strelitz and niece of Queen Charlotte. After the death of her second husband, the Prince of Solms, she became the wife of Ernest, Duke of Cumberland.

seems, a *tendresse* for Prince Leopold – 'a handsome young man', admits her Princess now to be 'by no means partial' to him. Poor disgruntled Leopold was left to kick his heels among the vegetable boxes in his dingy room at Mary'bone.

Frederick, at this time, is the burning theme of Charlotte's letters to the friend of her bosom, Mercer Elphinstone.

'A man *must mean something* by writing as he does – and how he does!' thus she distractedly unburdens to Miss Mercer.

Mercer and Miss Knight were infinitely bothered. What if the Regent should hear that this Prince Frederick was so constant and so welcome a visitor at Warwick House? And then those rings and things! They had entertained the highest hopes of Leopold. Too sad that he should be outrivalled by a Prussian princeling! But was he outrivalled, after all? Cornelia and Mercer may have been intrigued to hear that 'the two Princes to the end of time would always be sparring, and why and what made them jealous', Charlotte, with disarming innocence declares, 'she does not know!'

Then three weeks after she had dismissed her sickly Orange, fell the thunderbolt.

With the Great U.P., Charlotte's tutelary Bishop, and four dour-visaged ladies in his wake, the Regent, on an evening in July, swept down upon the fold at Warwick House, hustled his daughter into a room, and raged at her for near upon an hour.

Presently, pale and tearful, she came out to tell the quaking Miss Knight that her dear, kind, too-indulgent 'Notti' was to be dismissed at a moment's notice and all the household with her; that Charlotte was to be removed to Cranbourne Lodge in Windsor Forest, and in that gloomy habitation, guarded by her four lady-wardresses, she would stay, pending the Regent's displeasure. Whereupon Cornelia begged the Princess to be calm, and herself promptly fell into hysterics. 'God Almighty!' appealed Charlotte, grant me patience!' – and with that she was out of the room like a rocket.

Mercer Elphinstone, who happened to be staying with her in the house, occupied a bed-chamber adjoining that of the Princess. Miss Mercer was in the hands of her maid, preparing for dinner, when Charlotte rushed past her into her dressing-room, snatched up a bonnet and cloak, and before anyone could stop her she was gone. Down the back stairs an astonished footman saw her running – into the courtyard and out at the gates. At Charing Cross she found a hackney-coach, clambered in, flung the man a guinea and told him to drive to Connaught House.

Here was a fine to do! The Princess had fled – and none knew where, and the Regent looked to have an apoplexy. He sent for her ladies and questioned each in turn. Miss Elphinstone said she believed the Princess was at her mother's. Mrs. Lewis, Charlotte's dresser, thought she had gone to Carlton House. To which the bursting Regent replied that 'everyone would know his daughter *now* for what she was. Her escapade would be talked of all over the continent and no man would ever want to marry her.' Mercer knew of one at least who wanted much to marry her, but she held her tongue and cried–a very little–and hoped His Royal Highness would not think *she* was to blame. . . . What he thought of Miss Mercer and her tears and her connivance in this deplorable affair is not recorded, but he accepted her offer to go with the Bishop in search of the truant Princess.

She, meanwhile, had arrived at Connaught House to hear that her mother had gone for the day to Blackheath. So in she went and despatched a page with a message for Mr. Brougham, and a footman with a note to her Mamma. Then she rang the bell and ordered dinner. Before very long her pursuers drove up. Mercer and the Bishop in a hackney; Brougham in his carriage, Lord Eldon, her uncles–the Dukes of York and Sussex–in such a commotion as never was seen. Charlotte enjoyed herself hugely. For the first time in her life she was the centre of attraction. If a national revolt had been sprung upon the company it could not have occasioned more concern. Brougham, who had been engaged on a legal case almost all the night before, and was, he says, 'in consequence exceedingly fatigued', had left his dinner to attend her summons and tried to persuade her to return to Warwick House. She laughed and shook her head at him. 'But', she said, 'I've just run off!' and asked him to sit down with her at table. He refused. And still the Regent's envoys thronged the house. Her mother was the last to come, and, to Charlotte's vexation, loudly supported Brougham's attempt to get her home. When Lord Chancellor Eldon put in his word, 'she kicked and bounced', he relates, 'but would not go! I told her I was sorry–for until she went she would be obliged to entertain us.'

She raised no objection to that. Dinner was served and she called upon everyone to eat it. To humour her they sat while she played hostess, drank wine with her bald-headed uncles, chattered, cracked jokes, and had never been so happy. 'She was like a bird set loose from a cage,' remarked Brougham. Her spirits soared with the spread of her wings and sank, panic-bound, when her kindly, cautious Uncle Sussex was moved to take Counsel's opinion. 'Did Mr. Brougham consider they would be legally entitled to resist if the Prince Regent should carry her off by force?'

'Certainly not,' was the comfortless reply.

'Then, my dear, you have heard,' said her uncle in a fuss, 'and I can only advise you to return with as much speed and as little noise as possible.'

In the end it was Brougham who succeeded where her mother, her uncles, and Mercer, Lord Eldon and 'Notti', and all the rest of them had failed.

Dawn was in the sky when Brougham led Charlotte to the window. 'Look there, Madam. In a few hours the streets and the park, now empty, will be filled with tens of thousands. I have only to show you to the crowd and tell them your grievances, and they will rise in your behalf.'

That ruffled her again. 'Why should they not?' He proceeded to prophesy why they should not. 'Carlton House will be attacked, perhaps pulled down, the soldiers called out; blood will be shed, and if Your Royal Highness were to live a hundred years it would never be forgotten that your running away was the cause of the mischief.'

But even Brougham, the cynical hard-headed man of law, watching the colour drain from that young startled face, was shocked at the effect of his words. If she cared nothing for her duty to her father, she cared much for her duty to the State . . . 'I have told many a client that he was to be committed,' confessed Brougham, 'but I never saw anything like her stupefaction . . . She was lost.'

They granted her one last appeal before they took her: that a formal declaration of her refusal to marry Prince William of Orange, should be drawn up and signed in the presence of witnesses; and that if ever there should be an announcement of any such marriage, it must be understood it was against her will.

When this had been done she told them to send for her carriage; and, still with that 'lost' look about her, she went down to it.

* * *

The story of Princess Charlotte's flight and the consequent penalty, enforced by her father and not altogether undeserved, was in everybody's mouth. 'The thing is buzzed over Town, of course . . . and all are against the Prince', commented Brougham.

Well might the Regent believe himself to be the victim of bedevilment. Throughout that sorry season he had been dogged by some ill-fated circumstance or other. Those jubilations, on which with unbounded good intent he had laid his Midas touch, had been turned not to gold, but to dust. He, once the nation's darling, had become the nation's fool. The more bitter was the knowledge that his incalculable daughter had brought him to this final, most humiliating pass. Her crowning folly–that unprecedented act–had made of him an ogreish Caligula whose cruelty to his helpless child had driven her to seek protection from her equally tormented mother. Who could tell, with the Whigs to brand him monster, of what unspeakable brutalities he stood accused? But though his last hope of popularity be sacrificed upon the public altar, Charlotte would not go unpunished.

After a few days' solitary confinement in Carlton House, he sent her to Cranbourne Lodge in the charge of those four grim ladies who had replaced her own attendants. Charlotte, however, had still some fight left in her. Nothing would induce her to submit with lamblike meekness to her father's disposal of her person. The whole world should know of her unnatural parent's tyranny; of how, by his direction, her odious women watched her day and night; how her desk had been rifled, her letters intercepted, none permitted to be written, and, what was worse, no friend allowed to visit her. She had to steal the sheet of paper on which she scrawled a pencilled message to her simple Uncle Sussex, full of piteous complaints of her ill-treatment. The Duke, poor gentleman, walked straight into the trap. Wrung with compassion for his niece's plight, he hastened to the House of Lords with burning indignation in his heart, and a list of questions in his hand.

Did the Princess see her friends as usual? Did she write and receive letters? Was she under the restraint of actual imprisonment? Had her physicians ordered her sea air? And if so, why had this medical advice been ignored? But to the Duke's well-intentioned inquisition Lord Liverpool crushingly replied that the questions raised bore 'disagreeable implication, as unwarranted as it was unnecessary'.

A few days later the news-sheets were full of the Princess Charlotte's daily rides in Windsor Park. 'The case in appearance is much altered,' Grey wrote regretfully to Brougham. '*Miss Mercer* was at Cranbourne....' Moreover, the Bishop of Salisbury was prepared to offer statements of the Prince's kindness to his daughter and of '*des scènes larmoyantes* between them—quite touching!'

Since it was clear no purpose could be gained by pursuing a case of cruelty to a child against a father whose care for her well-being had been so sadly misconstrued, Sussex, persuaded by the Whigs, withdrew his motion.

Then the Regent, of long suffering, turned to castigate the Duke for his entirely redundant interference. High words flew; the gentle Duke retaliated. Never in his life, he vowed, would he cross the Regent's threshold or speak to him again. Nor did he until, in an invalid chair, he was trundled to his brother's death-bed.

This unfortunate publicity decided the Regent that at any cost must he regain his hold upon the people. Thankful indeed was he that the Allies had departed before his daughter's flight. He could believe the Czar would never have done laughing. He had seen the last of *them*, he hoped; but not the last of the season's festivities. With the return of Wellington, now honoured with a Dukedom, Carlton House once more became a scene of jubilation.

Considerable forethought and expense had been lavished on this entertainment, which exceeded in originality if not in magnificence all previous productions. White was the *motif* for the décor; white muslin draperies swathed the walls of a brick-built structure erected in the garden to seat two thousand guests. From behind banks and temples of flowers, hidden bands played stirring military airs. Curtains of virginal white gauze, caught back by silken cords, displayed mirrors and busts of the national hero. And if there were some who believed this chaste effect to be more appropriate as welcome to the Regent's absent daughter, than to the rugged Field Marshal with his stupendous nose and his Goddammes, none doubted the evening's success.

The festival season closed on August 1 with a Grand Jubilee in which the Chinese influence was markedly predominant. The Canal in St. James's Park had been spanned by a Chinese Bridge of Nash's design. In its centre stood an immense seven-storied pagoda, painted blue and yellow with attendant temples and columns either side of it; and all these to be illuminated with the latest marvel of the century – gas-lighting!

In the Green Park had suddenly appeared a mysterious castle with a round tower and ramparts a hundred feet square. This martello-type fortress, that excited much conjecture, was made to revolve so that it could be viewed from every angle. And in addition to all these phenomena, Sadler, the famous aeronautist, had agreed to make a balloon ascent, after which event the battle of the Nile was to be re-enacted by a miniature fleet on the Serpentine.

The thin drizzle of rain that fell during the morning of their long anticipated treat, did not damp the holiday spirit of those thousands who flocked to the parks; and when at noon the sun shone through the lifting clouds, the whole exultant populace ran riot in dancing and song, in picnicking, strolling, and playing and sprawling all over the grass while they waited for Sadler's balloon to go up. It had taken all day to inflate itself.

At twenty minutes to six he climbed into the car. The ropes were cut. The great meshed ball, rising slowly at first, gained speed as it mounted to a chorus of cheers from the gentlemen, and timorous shrieks from the ladies. With a gesture of gallant reassurance, Mr. Sadler, plaything of the elements, leaned over the side of his swinging car, waved his cap to those upturned terrestrial faces—and floated away into illimitable space.

It was a perilous voyage, for no sooner had he vanished out of sight than the network of the balloon became entangled, and when he decided to come down he found the valve was frozen to block the escape of gas. By this time he had drifted over the Thames Estuary and would likely have been carried out to sea and lost for ever, had he not, with exemplary presence of mind, cut a hole in the balloon and landed himself in Mucking Marshes.

But a worse mishap than Mr. Sadler's hair-raising adventure brought to a dramatic finale the joys of that Jubilee day. Until darkness overcame the dusk all had gone joyously well. The Battle of the Nile had been presented with much realistic banging of guns to the complete annihilation of the enemy; then, so soon as the roar of cannon had ceased, a necklace of jewels was strung among the trees: Chinese lanterns, silver crescents, golden moons; while, from everyone of the Pagoda's seven storeys, light poured a reflected sheet of flame upon the water. That was the signal for the Grand Firework Display. Curving snakes of colour whizzed heavenward to break in fountains of falling stars—and set ablaze four ships of the Serpentine Fleet! . . . The terrific flare-up that resulted was hailed as part of the fun by all save the scared swans that fluttered screeching to the safety of the banks, and one itinerant pseudo-Pindar pressman who fired his own imitative squib:

> 'The R — — — thinks to make us stare,
> By raising rockets in the air;
> His scheme to please will fail, he'll find,
> Since we for it must raise the *wind*.'[1]

Yet despite the ridicule and disasters that rounded off the Jubilee, the Regent's 'scheme to please' did not fail. When at midnight the Fortress, emblem of War, revolving on its axis, exploded in an ear-splitting combustion and stood transformed as a Temple of Concord, symbol of Peace, the applause that greeted this miracle must have gladdened the heart of him who had worked it, and watched from his stand outside Buckingham House. But before the crowds could raise another cheer, the Chinese Pagoda on the bridge began to sway, and belching forth smoke, catastrophically caught fire and fell with a deafening crash into the lake. Two men were killed and five seriously injured, but the Regent knew nothing of that. The success of his efforts was assured. He had brought joy to the people of London, and though they sneered at him, jeered at him,

[1] Attributed to Lawler.

mocked his endeavours, he was one with them now in their triumph. . . .
And as for the 'wind', the Exchequer and Lord Liverpool must raise it.

The Exchequer and Lord Liverpool were very loath to raise it. With the price of bread soaring to a shilling a loaf, and the under-paid wage-earners threatening revolt, this was no time to exploit the Regent's reckless waste of the national funds. Moreover, the Princess of Wales, now determined to go into voluntary exile, had demanded and been granted by Parliament an income of fifty thousand pounds. 'C'est mon droit', she stated calmly; then astounded the Commons by begging them to reconsider their decision and give her not more, but fifteen thousand a year less than the sum agreed.

After such generosity on the part of his wife, the Regent could scarcely have expected the Exchequer to provide him with a Fortunatus purse to relieve his obligations, even though they were incurred in the cause of diplomatic hospitality. Since, therefore, he could not bring himself to press for immediate disbursement, he and his creditors must wait.

The day after the Jubilee, August 2, the Princess of Wales left England for the Continent. Attended by a motley retinue and the fourteen-year old William Austin, she drove down to Worthing, thence in a pony-chaise to Lancing. From there, in the frigate *Jason*, she embarked. Conspicuous among her luggage was a large tin case, bearing the device painted in bold white letters: 'Her Royal Highness, the Princess of Wales, to be always with her.' She travelled in a costume of dark cloth, reminiscent of a Prussian Hussar's uniform, and adorned with massive gold clasps. Her cap of violet and green satin was much admired by the yokels assembled on the beach to watch her go, and to whom from her barge she blew rapturous kisses of farewell.

That night, at table, her husband drank a toast – 'To the damnation of the Princess of Wales – and may she never come back!'

★   ★   ★

'London is just as dull and stupid and deserted as can be imagined; no event, not even the least bit of scandal stirring,' wrote the Regent to his brother York at the end of that strenuous summer. The excitement and feasting had told on his health. He was gouty and 'ill of the bladder', said Brougham. 'God make him worse!' prayed Sam Whitbread. But God – or sea air – made him better.

He was at Brighton in October to superintend a metamorphosis of the Pavilion. It must have been somewhere about the year 1807 when the Regent first visited Sezincote, the Gloucestershire seat of Sir Charles

Cockerell, a retired Nabob. The startling orientalism of this remarkable house, fashioned by Repton after the Indian style, so enthralled the Prince that he decided he too must have a Rajah's palace that would put to shame the marbled mosques and temples of Kashmir. He commissioned Repton to draw him the plans.

Year after year the process of reconstruction under a series of architects continued, but his Indian palace, from lack of funds, failed to materialize. Instead, a fantasy, in principle Chinese yet vaguely suggestive of the Taj Mahal and the Kremlin, emerged from Holland's classic villa on the Steine.

'You can see it for sixpence,' jibed Thackeray. You can still see it for sixpence.

There, in courageous defiance of shrieking modernity, with its onion-shaped dome and its minarets, pinnacles, arches and columns, it stands as it stood, upon that border-line between life lived and life envisioned. The greatest of Corinthians, for once oblivious to ridicule, had achieved the impossible – the capture and retention of a dream; or, as was said of it, a nightmare. The spirit of his youth, impaled on the lance-head of patriarchal restraint, flaunts its delighted release in each overgrown schoolboy precocity; all are there. The five-clawed Imperial dragon – surely symbolic – struggles eternally in the coils of a fearsome serpent; mythical birds and beasts, insects and flying fish, mandarins, dolphins, trees, rocks, foliage, and flowers plucked from the mists of a Thousand and One Nights; ancient Chinamen with long white beards; warriors and winged lions stalking in the golden grass of panels painted the colour of dried blood – and these, for his keeping, in perpetuity imprisoned on the walls of an imaginative wonderland, hung with chimeless bells and glowing lanterns.

In the Music-Room a giant lotus-flower swings from the great domed ceiling. The upper leaves of this exquisite lily-lamp are of white frosted glass edged with gold and pearls, the outer petals tipped with vermilion; and in its base is found a golden nest to rifle – of young snakes.

To this Aladdin's cave he brought his treasures of ormolu and porcelain, of lacquer, of ivory, bronze; his wonderful K'ang Hsi clock, his Sèvres and his Chinese Pagodas – 'Enamelled with Butterflies, Kylins and various other devices'. And there in sheer exuberant zest, forgetful of gout, he would dance or call on his band for more music, slapping time to the tune on his white buck-skinned hams; or he would sing a duet in his sonorous bass, 'Ritornereno a Closi'.

As he grew older he was given to talk at interminable length of his more or less illusory adventures. One of his favourite anecdotes was of his famous fight with a butcher, 'a great big fellow, fifteen stone, six feet two . . .' whom the Regent met out hunting one day with his harriers, and who 'over-rode my hounds, ma'am, several times. I spoke to him to hold hard–in vain. At last, Goddamme, ma'am, he rode slap over my favourite bitch, Ruby. I could stand it no longer, but jumping off my horse said, "Get *down*, you rascal! Pull off your coat!" . . . By God, ma'am, he did, and we fought for an hour and twenty minutes. . . . At the end of it the big bully butcher of Brighton was carried off senseless–whilst I had hardly a scratch!'

It was in the autumn of 1814 that Queen Charlotte paid her first visit to the Pavilion. The day after her arrival the inhabitants of Brighton were greatly touched to see the decrepit old lady go tottering along the Steine on the arm of her corpulent son. He was now utterly dependent on her whence he had come, and to whom, as his second childhood approached, he had returned. In her dotage she reclaimed him, refilled the empty niche left by that lost mother-image which all his life he had sought in the loves of his women. He gave her his entire confidence, poured out in voluminous letters his woes, his fears, and his anxieties. Charlotte was causing him more trouble. The Whigs had launched a request before the House of Commons that she should be given her own establishment and a proportionate allowance. To which the Chancellor of the Exchequer succinctly replied, 'No command from His Royal Highness had been received upon the subject.'

This attack from the Whigs, which again reflected on his unwarrantable treatment of his daughter, decided him to stage an affecting reunion at Windsor on Christmas Day.

In the presence of her aunt, Princess Mary, who made a full note of that interview and sent a copy of it to the Regent, Charlotte was led to her father. She came sullen and scowling, was melted to tears, ready to fling herself at his feet when she found him so lovingkind, full of forgiveness. Nothing could exceed the godlike clemency of him whose 'first object in life', he solemnly adjured her, 'was her interest'. After that, of his grace, it was easy to answer all questions. Firstly, concerning the boy William Austin who had gone with her mother abroad. What of him?

'The boy had always been greatly preferred before her', acknowledged Charlotte; and she went on to describe him as a 'sickly looking child with fair hair and blue eyes. . . . He always slept in the same bed with her mother until he became too old, then he slept in a cot in her room. . . . This led to the society which Princess Charlotte used to meet at her mother's house', recounts Mary with relish. Too shocking! The Regent was 'horror-struck' when Charlotte admitted to a former 'partiality' for Captain Hesse. Gradually her father drew from her the whole unhappy story, of how her mother would contrive to lure Charlotte and the Captain to her bedroom and turn the key upon them saying, 'À présent je vous laisse. Amusez-vous' . . . 'God knows,' Charlotte piously added, 'what would have become of me if he had not behaved with so much respect.'

What already *had* become of her?—was the more likely question that prompted her father's unctuous reply: 'My dear child, it is Providence alone that has saved you'. . . . But had Providence, Charlotte wondered, saved her from the Orange Prince? Although peace between herself and the Regent was now happily restored, he had made no allusion to her broken engagement; nor had he officially agreed to her rejection of his choice. So, determined to know the worst, she braced herself to write:

'I hate all concealments and still more with you, yet the subject I felt so delicate, that tho' I had fully intended to have spoken most fairly to you on it, I had not courage when it came to the point. . . . I have understood from my family, it is still your wish to secure my marriage with the Prince of Orange. Pardon me if I say *that* information greatly pained me. . . . I am fully aware that in our situation we cannot marry as the rest of the world do, but still I feel that esteem and regard are absolute requisites. . . . It is feeling this that makes me thus resume a subject which I hope may now be for ever dropped, as I am aware it has already been too much a source of misery to us both.'

'Whatever my family has known from me,' came the Regent's prompt answer, 'I have never given them any specifick authority to impart to you what my private opinions are on the subject to which your letter of the 20th refers. . . .

'I can assure you that however near my heart it is to have you settled in marriage, & however I may prefer that alliance for reasons most obvious as they respect your happiness & tranquillity . . . yet I had determined after what had already passed upon it, never to be the person first to move in it. . . . You earnestly say that you are aware that in our situation we cannot marry as the rest of the world do . . . In all this I agree, but you have no reason to apprehend in a union with the Prince of Orange the grievous calamity which I alas! my dearest child, have experienced from a marriage with a person whose character we have had occasion so recently, so fully & so freely to gather. . . .

'Such being the situation in which your letter has placed me, every sense of public duty, my parental love for you . . . compel me to state without reserve that I see no matrimonial alliance so desireable [*sic*] in any respect as this.'

Which left her little wiser than before; but having dared thus far she dared farther, to retort:

'No one can feel the delicacy and the peculiar awkwardness of their situation more keenly and bitterly than I do . . . notwithstanding this, I *cannot* indeed comply with your wishes for marrying the Prince of Orange.'

And the Regent accepted her decision. He accepted it because the experience of fathering an unsuspected revolutionary had proved too much for him. In his day fathers had been autocrats, and now the picture was too dreadfully reversed. He had only this to say, and 'with no inconsiderable degree of pain', he said it. 'I have the satisfaction which must always follow upon the conscientious discharge of my duty. . . .' A duty so conscientiously discharged that, having pumped his daughter dry of more than he had ever hoped to know, he was encouraged to pursue his case against his wife.

Eagerly he devoured reports brought to him of her misbehaviour abroad. She and her discreditable entourage, composed for the most part of vagabond Italians, were attracting censorious attention. At Genoa, that beautiful gateway to Italy, the shrill gesticulating natives must have greatly wondered to see a phaeton of gilt and pearl in the shape of a shell, drawn by seven piebald ponies and driven by a child dressed like an operatic Cupid in pink bespangled tights, go clattering along their sun-baked streets. Past proud palaces of marble, and shadowy sideways joyous with brown laughing urchins, past shouting muleteers prodding their patient over-loaded beasts to and from the harbour; past gardens full of orange-trees, pomegranates, citrons, where fountains played and every wall splashed colour from all kinds of flowers, this remarkable equipage went lumbering down to the *Porto*. Inside sat a plump, smiling, highly-painted lady. Her hat gaily sprouted pink feathers, her skirt was pulled up to her knees displaying fat stumpy legs in top-boots. And this edifying spectacle was Caroline, Princess of Wales.

But a greater shock than any tale carried to the Regent concerning that extraordinary caravanserai, explosively descended to obliterate all thought of it.

Napoleon had slipped his guards at Elba and escaped!

What now of that glorious premature Peace and the million nameless graves of them who had given their lives in its cause? Gone – in the hurricane dawn of the first of those Hundred Days. Yet, even while the messengers of Rothschild in Paris were bringing him the secret news which he turned to his own good account, a convulsive mob was storming round the gates of Carlton House.

The recent Corn Laws, passed in the Commons by a large majority, had placed an embargo on the import of foreign wheat till the home market price stood above eighty shillings a quarter. And the endurance of those tattered hordes who had fought Britain's wars for her, toiled, and starved for her, broke in demonstrative protest. The mansions of Mayfair, the Bloomsbury houses of rich city magnates and members of Parliament, were set upon and ravaged. The windows of the house in old Burlington Street, where dwelled Robinson, proposer of the Corn Bill, were shattered, doors torn off their hinges, his servants man-handled; and not until the soldiers had been called out to quell them by firing at random in their midst, were the maddened rioters dispersed, but not appeased. The Regent was their target, and 'Bread—or his head!' their battle-cry when they stuck a loaf, steeped in blood, on the spiked wall of Carlton House. He took it coolly, and wrote at once to assure his mother that the 'depredations of last night were not as great as might have been expected. . . . At present there is an immense crowd all the way from the Horse Guards to and about the two Houses of Parliament but as to what they may intend in particular to do, or to attempt, it is impossible to calculate. . . .'

Still more impossible to calculate were the movements of him who had landed in Cannes, and on his mountain march northward had vowed that 'when he set foot on French soil the Eagle would fly from spire to spire until it alit on the tower of Notre Dame.' And he had done it! Three weeks after he had disembarked on the Mediterranean coast, he was there with all Paris at his feet crying: 'Vive l'Empereur!' Then they lifted shoulder high and carried that pale-faced, grey-coated figure into the Tuileries, whence had fled, at his coming, the panic-stricken Bourbon.

The peace of the world was at an end.

When on April 5, Wellington arrived in Brussels to take command of the Allied Forces, he had counted on the promise of seven hundred thousand troops to support him on the French frontier. He was still waiting for the fulfilment of that promise in June, by which time he had mustered a bare total of ninety three thousand. Blücher, at Namur, had a hundred and ten thousand Prussians behind him; but Napoleon had the spirit of France and his sixty-three thousand behind him, hot with the flame of their pride in this greatest of adventures—their Emperor's last throw.

Not a man of them wavered nor doubted the issue.

Creevey, who in the previous autumn had taken his wife and his two pretty step-daughters, the Misses Ord, to Brussels, found the city full of London Guards. Two weeks before the battle he met Wellington out for a stroll in the park. 'Do you calculate', inquired the loquacious Mr. Creevey, 'upon any deserters in Bonaparte's army?'–'We may pick up a Marshal or two perhaps,' was the Duke's dubious answer, 'but not worth a damn.' And pointing his stick at a British soldier gaping about him at the statues he added: 'It all depends upon *that* article whether we do the business or not. Give me enough of it, and I am sure.'

He did the 'business'–as all history knows–even though he had not nearly enough of 'that article'. And when it was finished and Creevey had swallowed the glorious news, he hurried off to the Duke's house in the park and was tremendously flattered to see Wellington beckoning him in from his window. 'The first thing I did of course', chatters Creevey, 'was to put out my hand and congratulate him on his victory. . . . "It has been a damned nice thing–the nearest run thing you ever saw in your life . . ." admitted Wellington. "Blücher lost fourteen thousand on Friday night and got so damnably licked I could not find him on Saturday morning . . ." Then, as he walked about,' continued Creevey, 'he praised greatly those guards who kept the farm at Hugomont, uttering repeated expressions of astonishment at our men's courage . . . I asked him if the French had fought better than he had ever seen them do before.–"No," he said, "they have always fought the same since I first saw them at Vimeira. . . ." '

★   ★   ★

At a quarter past eleven on the night of June 21, a Major Percy, still in his battle-grimed uniform, presented himself to Lord Bathurst, Secretary of State for War. He carried despatches from Wellington. So soon as he had read them, Bathurst drove with young Percy to the house of Mrs. Boehm in St. James's Square, where the Regent was attending a banquet. It must have been a sensational moment for that lively assemblage seated at dinner to see, in the doorway of the dining-room, a dishevelled blood-splashed figure bearing aloft the Eagle and the tattered colours of France. A silence like a cloud fell upon the room to steal the gaiety and laughter from those around the table. Then the Regent asked the ladies to withdraw, and as the door was closed upon them he called upon Lord Liverpool to read aloud Wellington's message, and the list of the wounded and killed. When this was done he turned to him who had hastened across Belgium and France and over the sea to bring him the news. 'I congratulate you, *Colonel* Percy,' said the Regent; and, with that token of his gratitude, the tears splashed down those pendulous cheeks. 'It is a glorious victory, but . . . I have lost many friends.'

Early the next morning the guns of the Tower thundered forth their salute to the City of London. Once more the lamps of rejoicing sprang into blossoms of fire that glowed through the heat-laden nights; yet, though the weight of war was lifted, Britain grieved for those thousands of unforgotten dead who lay slaughtered on the field of Waterloo.

Three weeks later, and for the first time since the Battle of Agincourt, a British Army marched into Paris followed by the leaders of fashion from London and Brussels to welcome the return of Louis, the Bourbon. Described by his people as 'partly old woman, partly a capon, and partly a son of France', he was restored in triumph to the Tuileries by his fickle-hearted subjects who yelled at him 'Vive le Roi!'–they, who a few months before, had cried to that other, 'Vive l'Empereur!'

Trapped in the frigate *Bellerophon*, Napoleon sent his grandiloquent plea to the Regent . . . 'I come like Themistocles to throw myself on the hospitality of the British people. I put myself under the protection of their laws, which I claim from Your Royal Highness as the most powerful and constant and most generous of my enemies.'

To which there could be no possible reply. The episode of Elba must never be repeated; but there were still some eager enough to abuse the British Government for rendering to Caesar nothing save that gaunt rock-bound, mid-Atlantic island. Byron hotly complained how Captain Maitland, who took the fallen Emperor aboard the *Bellerophon,* curtly addressed him as 'General'. And, when on August 7, a multitude crowded on the beach at Plymouth and in boats about the harbour to see the end of him whose audacity had shaken the world, they cheered him well and truly on that last voyage to his lonely grave.

★ ★ ★

The year 1816 brought with it a revival of the Luddite insurrections. While the industrial centres of the Midland and the North renewed their attacks on engine-controlled factories, the agricultural counties rose up to destroy the new threshing-machines. All over the country flaring hayricks marked the approach of ragged scarecrow processions, spreading panic as they tramped through peaceable villages carrying banners inscribed 'Bread–or Blood!'

From the ashes of Napoleonic aggression had risen the phoenix of Reform, shrieking murder at the Regent.

A disclosure of his reckless expenditure at Carlton House and the Pavilion; the rebuilding to Nash's design of a thatched cottage in

Windsor Great Park[1] together with the rumour that on his assumption of the Regency he had misappropriated, for some other purpose than its original use, a Government grant of a hundred thousand pounds, had inflamed the antagonism of a people driven desperate by post-war unemployment. No consolation to them was it to hear him declare in his opening speech to Parliament how 'happy he was to inform the House of Commons that the manufacture, commerce, revenue, no less than the art and science of the Kingdom were in flourishing condition'.

So flourishing indeed that those who had fought and won his battles by land and on sea, must fall upon and pick bare with green ravenous teeth any maggot-crawling hank of bone flung out to rot in the gutters. Not entirely unjustified were the grievances of those homeless survivors of that bitter war-struggle, when they turned to rend the Regent while their new-born died for want of milk from starving breasts. They could not forecast the future he would hand to their descendants in a legacy of taste and culture comparable only to that of Elizabeth's time. He who had beautified Brighton and had given to London the street that still stands to his name, although its superb Nash crescent was unforgivably demolished less than a hundred years after his death, is not now remembered as Thackeray's 'fribble, dancing in lace and spangles', but as the Colossus of Elegance, whose reign is lit by an almost unlimited galaxy of genius; John Keats, the ostler's son dissecting pickled limbs in Guy's Hospital by day, and star-gazing on Hampstead Heath by night; Shelley, Byron, Coleridge, Lamb, Wordsworth, Jane Austen, Blake, Hazlitt, De Quincey; and some still at school or in petticoats: Dickens, the Brownings, Disraeli, Macaulay, Tennyson—a host of them dawning in the sunrise of their day. But Jane Austen's sun was setting. Two years before she died, she published *Emma*, her last book, and sent a copy 'most respectfully dedicated to His Royal Highness the Prince Regent', which he was charmed to receive.

One by one those he had loved were dying or dead. Sheridan, whose debts he had paid to the tune of three thousand pounds, was destitute again. 'All he looked for in the company he kept', the Regent told Croker long afterward, 'was brandy and water.' And he went on to describe his last glimpse of this devoted companion of his youth, whom he accidentally encountered when driving from his brother's house at Oatlands back to Brighton. . . . 'In the road near Leatherhead I saw old Sheridan coming along the pathway. I see him now in the black stockings and blue coat with the metal buttons. . . .' But when he caught sight of the Royal carriage, 'Sherry' turned sharply down a side-path and walked away.

So, alone and comradeless, in deepest poverty, with the bailiffs in the

[1] Now Royal Lodge.

house, passed that master of wit and oration. Yet, all who had shunned him in the latter years of his life, attended his grand funeral in Westminster Abbey.

Not only the friends of the Regent were going, but some of his enemies too. In 1815, the year before Sheridan's death, Sam Whitbread committed suicide; a loss much lamented by the Whigs, and serenely recorded in her journal by Miss Knight: 'Mr. Whitbread cut his throat the other morning.'

With death all about him, the Whig-bitten Regent, afraid to be seen driving through the streets lest he be assaulted, and whose last attack of gout had laid him low, was disposed to look more kindly upon Charlotte. He believed he had not long to live. At his doctors' advice, and much against his will, he had renounced his stays. He could not walk without a stick; and when he rode, which he still enjoyed to do, he had to be mounted from a chair run on rollers up an inclined plane to a platform and let down into the saddle with much heaving and pushing from his attendants. And even though he soon regained his health and equilibrium he had it firmly fixed, that, come what may, Charlotte must be married to secure the Succession.

His brother York was childless. William, who had now discarded Mrs. Jordan, retained the custody of his ten illegitimate Fitzclarences whom he adored. Edward, Duke of Kent, had a mistress, Madame St. Laurent, whom he also adored. The Duke of Cumberland's wife had as yet begotten him no heir. The marriage of Augustus Frederick, Duke of Sussex, to Lady Augusta Murray, had long since been dissolved in accordance with the Royal Marriage Act. The Regent, who had by this time gleaned some knowledge of Charlotte's fleeting passion for her Prussian prince, was relieved to learn that she had now come to her senses. He may have been still more relieved to hear of a prim little secret she confided to her favourite Uncle York; a secret which she surely must have hoped would not be kept. 'I have never seen a prince who prepossesses me as much as does Leopold of Saxe-Coburg. . . .'

No royal marriage before or since could have been received with more widespread delight by the people of Britain than that of their idolized young Princess Charlotte to Leopold, the man of her choice.

All London stood to watch her pass in her bridal coach on that green and golden evening of May 2, 1816.

She dressed at the Queen's House[1] and was married at her father's palace in Pall Mall. The ceremony took place a little after eight o'clock, and the

[1] Buckingham House.

Regent, splendid in full regimentals, his chest plated with orders, gave her away at the altar.

The moment the blessing had been pronounced she turned to her father, flung an arm round his neck, and there for the sour old Queen, the Primate, her bald beaming uncles, her whispering aunts, and the whole of the peerage to see, she kissed him for her joy. Then, later, amid the cheers of the boisterous well-wishers who lined her wedding route, she drove off with her happy young bridegroom into the lavender night.

*   *   *

But at Windsor, that old man, forgotten, knew nothing of marriage nor giving in marriage and nothing of life nor of death. While the deep-throated guns roared their welcome to his granddaughter, and Britain's bride, the King of England, groping in his darkness, heard no sound save the voices of the ghosts with whom he talked. 'Lord North, my good Lord North, I am exceedingly desirous of seeing you. . . .' Sometimes he sang, and sometimes he went hunting with his visionary hounds while his unresponsive keepers played at dice. And sometimes he remembered, 'when I lived upon the earth. . . .'

And the bulletins reported: 'His Majesty's disorder has undergone no change.'

Yet beyond those walls where he sat islanded in solitude, the inexorable march of change surged on, setting its milestones of progress along Macadam's highways. Speed was the tempo of the age, beating the measure to the ring of hoof and horn as the brightly painted coaches, drawn by four spanking blood-horses, dashed without a halt through village streets where their clumsy predecessors once had jogged. Across the border, Telford, the son of a Dumfriesshire shepherd, was intercepting Scotland from Caithness to Carlisle with his canals and aqueducts. Waterloo Bridge, that stupendous feat of engineering, begun in 1811 by John Rennie, a millwright's apprentice, was completed in 1817. And George Stephenson, another shepherd's son, who had left his flocks ten years before to tramp across the Cheviots and down into Northumbria's collieries, watched his first steam-propelled engine go jerking and groaning along its metalled lines carrying coal to save man-labour; and as he watched he dreamed of the day, not far distant, when his iron horse, 'the Rocket', would replace the horse of the flesh. In the Channel, and up and down the River Thames, experimental little boats with slender funnels vomited black noisome smoke; and, in 1812, the first passenger 'steamer' was launched on her maiden voyage up the Clyde.

The Regent had launched a boat too; his pleasure yacht, the *Royal*

206

George, hauled up from Deptford Dockyard and refitted at a cost of sixty thousand pounds. In this gorgeous vessel so richly gilded that it looked, with the sun upon it, to be made of solid gold, he cruised the coast.

His mania for alteration had, during the last few years, steadily increased. He altered Carlton House again, he altered the Pavilion; he altered his cottage in Windsor Great Park; and some said that, for vanity's sake, he even had altered his age. Be that as it may, when Parliament reviewed the monstrous sum of fifty thousand pounds spent on furniture at Brighton in excess of more than half a million granted to the Regent from the Civil List, the scorching speeches of the Whigs, and Mr. Brougham, incited the mob to further aggressive demonstration.

On his return to Carlton House from the opening of Parliament in 1817, a hostile crowd waylaid and pelted his carriage with stones, gravel, potatoes, rotten apples, every sort of rubbish. No serious damage was done other than the mysterious appearance of a neat round hole in one of the windows such as might have been made by a bullet; although no sound of gun-shot had been heard. As a result of this attack upon his person, the Regent ordered prayers of thanksgiving to be read in all the churches for his 'safe deliverance from the barbarous assault of a lawless multitude'.

To his daughter, engrossed with her husband in their new home at Esher, came no echo from that 'lawless multitude', who threatened the life of her father as they stormed through the industrial cities of England bearing on high maledictory placards—'No Regent!' Nor did she know that their leaders who sowed the seeds of discord and agitation looked to her as the harbinger of Spring's promise, when their grievances and discontents would vanish with the blossom of re-birth. From the bow-windows of Whites' to the felons' cells at Newgate, the country stood united in glad anticipation of the coming of her child.

During his campaign abroad, Prince Leopold had become acquainted with and much attached to a shrewd, observant, wise young doctor serving as Staff Surgeon in the 5th Army Corps. A month or so before his marriage Leopold appointed Dr. Stockmar to be his Physician-in-Ordinary.

Charlotte, who at first had held aloof from this German doctor, soon became as much attached to him as was her husband. She begged him to attend her confinement; but Stockmar, perceiving that his English colleagues would resent a foreigner's assistance in the case, refused to have anything to do with it.

Greatly did he regret his decision when he noted the old-fashioned pre-natal methods prescribed by Doctors Baillie, personal Physician to the

Princess, and her accoucheur, Sir Richard Croft. Stockmar had little faith in the prevalent medical belief of purging, bleeding, and lowering the diet of an expectant mother. Gravely apprehensive, he warned Leopold of the danger that might result from thus weakening the patient's resistance during pregnancy. It was useless. The doctors insisted on following their customary drastic treatment, until, on November 3, 1817, after a painfully protracted labour of something over fifty hours, the Princess was delivered of 'a fine, large, dead boy'.

Exhausted from her long ordeal, Charlotte did not appear unduly to grieve for her loss. The bulletins, issued at intervals after the birth, announced her Royal Highness to be 'extremely well'. She was given nourishment; she slept. Leopold, who throughout those three critical days had not left his wife's room for one moment, and was almost as exhausted as herself, retired to rest. At midnight Sir Richard Croft awakened Stockmar to tell him he was not at all satisfied with his patient's condition. Would Dr. Stockmar agree to attend a consultation? After some hesitation he did agree, but so soon as he approached the bed he knew he had been called too late. 'Here comes an old friend of yours to see you,' announced Baillie, with false cheer. Stockmar leaned over her where she lay, feverishly tossing on her pillows. She complained of chill and pains in her chest; he felt her pulse and found it rapid, fluctuating, weak, her breathing difficult. Her cheeks were flushed; her head reeled. They had been plying her incessantly with wine. She seized Stockmar's hand, stared up at him and said: 'They've . . . made me tipsy!'

The Regent was staying at the house of Lady Hertford in Suffolk when he received news from Claremont of that protracted birth. In the afternoon of November 3, unable to endure the suspense, he returned to London in the chaise which had brought him the doctors' reports. All through that fog-bound moonless night he travelled, passing three horsemen hastening with messages along the way. He stopped the first—to hear that the Princess was still in labour; he stopped the second who announced the progress to be slow. . . . But the third galloped by unheeded, unseen, in the grey-shrouded dark of the dawn.

PRINCESS CHARLOTTE AND PRINCE LEOPOLD AT THE OPERA, 1817
Painted and engraved from an original drawing by George Dawe, National Portrait Gallery

CHAPTER NINE

1817—1821

THE death in childbirth of Princess Charlotte was a national calamity that struck at the very heart of Britain. The whole country mourned its blighted hope, not only of a future queen but of that 'fine dead boy', a future king. 'It really was as if every household,' Brougham wrote, 'had lost a daughter.'

The wretched young husband, who, in his agonized despair, had turned to Stockmar with the rending cry, 'I am now quite desolate . . . Promise to stay with me always,' remained in the close-shuttered silence of his empty rooms at Claremont, while the dismal bells tolled the country's grief throughout the land. And men who, a few days before, had spat envenomed hate at the dead girl's father, sank their voices now in sympathy for him who sat bewildered, stricken, bowed beneath the blow of this—his first meeting with sorrow. He wept till he made himself ill. Fearing for his sanity his doctors cupped and bled him; yet still he went on weeping. Brougham, coldly disaffected by this welter of emotion, told Grey: 'The grief is somewhat overdone.' But Leigh Hunt, for once, stayed his caustic abuse of the Regent to write that tenderest of elegies to her:

> . . . . who was a wife
> Leading a blest and flowery life,
> And who had just lain down, and smiled,
> To give her lord and love a child,
> When lo, she felt it must not be,
> And altered; and both child and she
> Slipped from him to eternity.'

Queen Charlotte was at Bath undergoing a cure when she received the fatal news. Her gentlemen attempted to break it to her gently. She forestalled them. Interpreting the look of startled horror on the faces of those who read the message, she covered her eyes and fell to convulsive sobbing —terrible to see in one so old, so frail.

The public, however, had no compassion for her who had shown little of kindness or affection to her granddaughter. Hideous rumours were floated around the name of the aged Queen. She and Sir Richard Croft had been in league to poison the Princess. . . . So fantastic were these tales, so numerous the letters accusing the unfortunate Croft of criminal negligence in the treatment of his patient, that his mind became unhinged, and a few months later he put an end to his misery by blowing out his brains.

Three days after the funeral the Regent, in a state of collapse, went down to the Pavilion. He stayed there for eleven weeks, as much an object of pity to himself as to all loyal Brightonians. In December he wrote to his mother that he was 'still very much and very truly indispos'd. I do not know under what denomination to class the attack . . .' defined with a gleam of his lovable humour as 'a sort of mishmash, Solomongrundy, Olla podrida kind of a business. . . .'

It was during those months of his mourning at Brighton that he decided to examine more closely the reports, brought to him by his agents, of his wife's conduct abroad.

Caroline, left in total ignorance of her daughter's death, had read of it by accident in an English newspaper while staying at the Villa d'Este on Lake Como. Decked in a pathetic travesty of mourning—white gown and black crêpe cap trimmed with lilac ribbons—she received consolation visits from her friends. The poor soul had not many; all, with exception of the Ladies Charlotte Bury and Anne Hamilton, had now deserted her.

Conspicuous among her Italian retinue was one Bartolomeo Bergami. Having substituted for the first letter of his name the more aristocratic P, he prefixed to his acquired appellation of Pergami, the title of Baron. The observant Lady Charlotte summed up this individual at first sight and in one glance as : 'Six foot high, a magnificent head of hair and mustachios that reach from here to London.'

'Here' was Genoa, where Caroline had installed herself in a palace of red and white marble with gilded panels, painted ceilings, and rooms over-filled with faded furniture. Wandering at will when her restless spirit moved her, she had traversed Europe from North to South crossing the Red Sea into Palestine. Her first stop after her exit from England was Brunswick, thence to Geneva where she became acquainted with the ex-Empress of France, Marie-Louise. Between these two royal ladies existed a certain similarity of circumstance. Both were separated from their husbands, and both were accompanied by a young boy; but the one was Napoleon Francis, the ex-King of Rome, the other William Austin, the Deptford docker's son.

To Marie-Louise the impressionable Caroline attached herself with frenzied *schwarmerei*. They danced together, sang together, were always seen together, until the hare-brained Princess reached a peak of imprudence which rapidly froze their warm friendship. The ex-Empress could understand and pardon much but not the appearance, at a ball, of the Princess of Wales dressed as Venus and stripped to the waist. All the ladies were blushing, the gentlemen leering, and the Princess was waltzing late into the night–an exhibition that 'unfeignedly grieved' Lady Charlotte to see. 'It was really as if, in leaving England, she had cast off all commonsense and conduct, and had gone suddenly mad. . . .'

From Geneva she went on to Milan; and there first encountered Bergami. With him and his sister, doubtfully known as the 'Contessa' Oldi, Caroline journeyed south trailed by the Regent's spies. Wherever she went she was fêted–and followed. All Europe stood aghast at the tales noised abroad of her latest indiscretions. Not the least of these were the favours she showered on Bergami. As her major-domo, courier, First Chamberlain, or what you will, he waited on her, sat with her and was admitted at all hours to her chamber. At Athens, at that time under the rule of the Turk, the itinerant Princess and her vagabond companions watched the dancing of the dervishes, the pious ecstasy of which may have infected Caroline, who herself, it seems, could never cease to dance. 'Since de English neither give me de great honour of being a Princess de Galles–I will be Caroline, a happy, merry soul.'

And in her happiness and merriment, she flung to the winds the last shreds of her tattered reputation. When at one of her festivals it was suggested by a well-meaning friend that everything she said or did would be carried to Carlton House, she retorted, 'I know . . . the wasp leaves his sting in the wound. So do I. The Regent will hear of it? I hope he will. I love to mortify him! . . .' But how deeply in return she would be mortified, Caroline, in her wildest adventures, could not know.

Her goal was Jerusalem, and thither she proceeded with a ferocious armed escort, a quantity of mules, donkeys–and Bergami. She made her entrance into the Holy City riding on an ass, and thereby caused much irreverent amusement to her French maid, Louise Dumont, who subsequently, in a court of jurisdiction, blithely damnified the morals of her mistress.

In Jerusalem she was accorded hospitable welcome by the Capucin Friars, but something to their dismay she insisted, as return for their kindness, on founding an Order of Chivalry in her name; and this despite the protestations of the Brotherhood who argued that no Saint Caroline was included in the Calendar. Then she needs must make a Knight of poor scared little 'Willikin', and a Grand Master of Bergami; and after she had pinned upon the broad breast of the gallant Barone the Star of the newly self-canonized St. Caroline, the party remounted their donkeys and mules and went careering on their joyful way to Jericho.

In August the Princess and her rollicking attendants sailed westward, bound for Europe. They embarked in dead calm and awful heat. The sailors knelt and prayed for wind and rain; Caroline, whose high spirits were unquenched by perspiration, ordered a tent to be raised on deck where she could take shelter from the blistering sun; and in this tent she slept at night attended by her chamberlain, Bergami.

In October 1817, she was in Karlsruhe, still diligently watched. Her antics reached a climax when, at a hunt breakfast given by the Grand Duke of Baden, she came attired in a scarlet riding-habit with half a pumpkin on her head–to keep it cool, she explained to her stupefied host. He must have been much diverted to see, when she mounted her horse, how the Princess of Wales lifted high her skirt to offer him and his guests a gratuitous view of her ungainly fat legs in pink tights.

The Regent had heard enough.

*   *   *

The conglomeration of evidence, both factual and fictional, submitted to him during his wife's exile, resulted in that sensational inquiry of 1818, known as the Milan Commission.

While Caroline's conduct throughout her travels had aroused gravest suspicion, none who condemned or condoned her seems to have taken the commonsensical view of her case. Not once did it occur, even to that most staunch of her advocates, Brougham, to seek medical opinion upon her state of mind. No hint of hereditary weakness was brought forward in her cause when she stood disgraced, the victim of false witnesses, to be judged in the House of Lords.

On January 1, 1818, Lord Eldon received a letter from the Regent, more hopeful than coherent, expressing his determination 'to extricate myself from the cruellest, as well as the most unjust predicament that even the lowest individual, much more a Prince, ever was placed in by un-shackling myself from a woman who * * * * *

'Is it then, my dear friend, to be tolerated that * * * * * is to be suffered to continue to bear my name, to belong to me and to the country, and that *that* country, the first in all the world, and myself its Sovereign, are to be expected to submit silently to a degradation, under which no upright and honourable mind can exist? This, then, was my main object for collecting certain of my confidential servants here.'

Although Mr. Twiss, editor of the *Life of Lord Eldon*, has disobliged us by deleting certain passages in the Regent's description of his wife, it is clear that the 'unshackling' process had begun. There were other reasons also why the Regent was now determined to take action. That double tragedy at Claremont which had bereft him of a daughter, had bereft the country also of two potential heirs. He must marry again and beget him a son. If he died childless the Crown would pass to his brother York, whose barren Duchess was dying. The Duke of Clarence, next in succession after York, lived the life of a country squire in retirement at Bushey, surrounded by his misbegotten family. On the death of his niece Charlotte, he had faced, for the first time, the possibility that a child of his born in wedlock, might well become the Sovereign of Britain. And as the doubtful prospect of highest elevation dawned upon the simple mind of William, he completely lost his head. Undeterred by repeated rejection, he pursued Princesses on the Continent and heiresses in England with frantic offers of marriage.

'Clarence has been refused by the Princess of Denmark, and is going, it is thought, to marry Miss Wykham,' wrote Creevey in February, 1818; and in that same month the Regent received from his sister Mary hysterical confirmation of Creevey's report.

The Princess Mary, who, at the age of forty, had been rescued from long spinsterhood by her cousin, 'Silly Billy', Duke of Gloucester, still maintained her lively interest in the Family's affairs.

'. . . The Q. is half *distracted* just having *received William's letter* in which he tells her he has proposed to & been accepted by Miss Wickham . . . I told him it was a thing that never could be & that you never could give your *consent*. He said . . . that he adored *you* & that he felt your kindness & that happen what might it could make no change in his aff[n] for you, but that he had *nerves* to go through with it & so had Miss Wickham. . . .

I told him I was sure it would break the Q's heart. He said I love her very much but a man must judge for himself in this world . . . & in spite of all they say I will marry her & the Prince's consent will be *rung from him at last* so he had better give it *at once*. . . .'

Consent was not 'rung' from the Regent; yet William, all undaunted, and innocently unaware that he and not his child was fated to follow his brother to the Throne, continued in quest of a wife. The Duke of Kent, fourth son of George III, was also in quest of a wife; and to Creevey, while on a visit to Brussels, he imparted his secret hopes, fears, and views of his future.

He could scarcely have chosen a more unreliable confidant than that prince of gossip-mongers, Mr. Creevey. That he was a close friend of all the leading Whigs the Duke of Kent must certainly have known; but he surely had no knowledge that the sympathetic Mr. Creevey would jot down in his journal, for posterity's delight, every word of this private conversation.

The Duke had decided, he said, to bring an end to his long association with Madame St. Laurent. 'God alone knows the sacrifice it will be to me, whenever I shall think it my duty to become a married man. It is now seven and twenty years that Madame St. Laurent and I have lived together ...' The Duke, however, seemed equally perturbed at the thought that he must sacrifice to William his unlikely expectations, for, 'the Duke of Clarence is the elder brother', he admitted, 'and has certainly the right to marry if he chooses, and I would not interfere with him on any account. If he wishes to be King–to be married and have children, poor man–God help him! let him do so. For myself, I am a man of no ambition and wish only to remain as I am. . . .' Then, with delicious inconsistency, he goes on to name two ladies between whom his choice had wavered: the Princess of Baden and the Princess of Saxe-Coburg, widow of Prince Leiningen . . . 'But', the Duke continued, 'before anything is proceeded with in this matter, I shall hope and expect to see justice done to Madame St. Laurent. She is of very good family and has never been an actress, and I am the first and only person who has ever lived with her. . . .' He was at further pains to make it clear to Mr. Creevey that Madame St. Laurent must be left with adequate provision, a certain number of servants and a carriage, and that he expected the Government to provide, besides the perquisites of Madame, the payment of the Duke's own debts. At this juncture the striking of a clock reminded the Duke of an appointment, and Mr. Creevey that the session was closed. He took his leave–and hurried off to tell his tale to the Duke of Wellington, who was much amused; as was also Lord Sefton when he received a letter from Creevey giving an embroidered account of this confidential talk with the ingenuous Duke.

'Nothing could be more *apropos* than its arrival,' wrote Lord Sefton in reply, 'as it was put into my hand while a surgeon was sounding my bladder . . . to ascertain whether I had a stone or not. I never saw a fellow more astonished than he was at seeing me laugh as soon as the operation was over.'

Yet, notwithstanding the Homeric mirth that greeted the matrimonial intentions of these two worthy Princes, they each found the wife of his heart. Both led their brides to the altar the same day. Clarence had chosen, and wisely, the gentle mouse-like Princess Adelaide of Saxe-Meiningen, almost thirty years his junior and with whom, at first sight, the susceptible William fell deeply and truly in love. The Duke of Kent was not in love, but he too chose wisely when he took to wife the stout, buxom, rosy-cheeked widowed Princess of Leiningen, daughter of the Duke of Saxe-Coburg-Saalfeld, and sister of Charlotte's Prince Leopold.

The Regent, who lustily led the cheers at that double wedding in Kew Palace, may have shown a little more enthusiasm than he felt. While his two middle-aged brothers, proud and happy, full of highest hopes, drove away with their respective brides, he returned to London in the dumps. The case against his wife had not progressed according to his plan. The Commissioners appointed to examine the evidence appeared to be reluctant to pursue it. What, the Regent wished to know, was the cause of the delay? . . . Brougham was the cause of the delay. He had suggested that a formal separation be agreed between the parties, and that the Princess of Wales should forgo her future right to be crowned as Queen Consort, in consideration of financial recompense.

The Regent would not hear of it. He wanted the assurance of his freedom by divorce and no half-measures. His Ministers, remembering that earlier Investigation from which the Princess had emerged triumphant, quailed. To institute proceedings on the dubious witness of a pack of foreign servants might, they feared, produce a similar result. The final report of the Commissioners urged the Regent to 'abstain from taking further steps under the present circumstances'.

The 'present circumstances', tactfully unspecified, were the existing facts of the Regent's marriage to Mrs. Fitzherbert and his association with the Ladies Jersey, Hertford—and others, each a trump card for the defence. Such faint-heartedness proved fatal. Although the Regent called himself the 'Sovereign', he was not. The only Sovereign who had the right to Kingship lived his living death, in a lost world of dreams; but around him clung a nimbus, defiant of decay. He was the King, old, blind, mad, yet withal deep-rooted in the hearts of his people, the vast majority of whom had never known life without him. And while that venerable figure with its long silvery beard wandered through his empty rooms, hugged in his purple dressing-gown, singing in his cracked weak voice the hymns he used to love, his son must be the Heir Apparent still. As such, if dragged through the shame of divorce, the dishonour would be his and not the Throne's. With this in his mind he besought his Ministers to reconsider their decision; and he might in the end have had his way, but for the intervention of his mother's death.

That shattered him.

In her declining years he had come to regard her as the mainstay of his existence. His devotion to this ailing old woman, from whom in his youth he had been so long estranged, was a source of wonder to his friends and enemies alike. All remarked how, when the Queen visited the Regent at the Pavilion or Carlton House, he would allow none to serve her at table but himself. Those numerous rambling letters he wrote her reveal his veneration for, and almost childish dependence on her judgment.

She had never recovered from the shock of Charlotte's death. For months she had been suffering from dropsy; and, as summer faded into autumn, it was evident she would not live to see the old year out. She died peacefully on November 17, 1818, at Kew, seated in a low arm-chair with her eldest and most loved son beside her, and her hand holding his to the last.

It was said that the King, in his shadowy life, knew nothing of her who had left him, nor of any event, great or small. Yet, when the voice of his wife, unheard in his deafness ceased brokenly to greet him, and the slow difficult tears of old age, unseen in his darkness, fell for grief of him no more, then he drooped, refused to eat–and as stubbornly refused to die. It was as if he were determined to sit between his first-born and the Crown until the shifting sands of Time ran out.

But while death stood uncertain on the threshold of those silent rooms, new lives were born to the House of his name, and some as swiftly faded.

The first child of the Duke of Clarence lived for three hours; the second did not live at all. The Duke of Kent, who had taken his bride to Amorbach immediately after his wedding, returned with her to England a few months later. They travelled through Germany and France in a hired carriage which the Duke himself insisted on driving. He sat on the box and his wife sat inside, seven months advanced in pregnancy. With her was the Princess Fedora, her daughter by a former marriage, her maids, her two lap-dogs, and a cage full of canaries.

On May 24, 1819, in Kensington Palace, the Duchess of Kent gave birth to a Princess, whom the nation regarded as of the least account; not so her father, the Duke. Buoyed on faith fostered by a fortune-telling gipsy, who had prophesied he was destined to be the father of a Queen, he decided to name his daughter Elizabeth, of glorious precedent. The Regent, however, like an adipose Bad Fairy, arrived at the last minute to attend the christening, and insisted that the child be called Alexandrina for its godfather, the Czar. The Duke tentatively offered a second name: Elizabeth. There was un uncomfortable pause. The Duke then suggested Georgiana. The Regent objected on the grounds that the name Georgiana must be second to none in the country; so if a second name *must* be added let it be her mother's and not a variation of his. The Archbishop, holding the baby, looked pained; her father furious. Yet despite the muttered protests of the offended Duke, the infant was christened Alexandrina Victoria.

Later in the year the Duke of Kent, a firm believer in oracles, consulted another gipsy who warned him of two deaths in the Royal Family; this gave him greatly to hope. The King was a certainty for one, and with any luck the Regent or the Duke of York would follow. Both were dropsical and gouty. He had lived a regular life which they decidedly had not. He would outlive every one of his brothers, and the Crown would come to him and to his children.

In the autumn of 1820, the Duke and Duchess of Kent departed for Sidmouth with their infant daughter, whom her ageing aunts at Windsor and no one else, had rapturously declared to be 'a beautiful fat baby'. At Sidmouth, with his wife and child, the Duke of Kent remained throughout the early winter months; and on a mild January afternoon he went for a walk in the rain. He returned home soaked to the skin, changed his clothes, and forgot to change his stockings. A streaming cold resulted which flew to his lungs, and killed him in a week.

Poor optimistic Edward journeyed back to Windsor in his coffin; but before he arrived there, the long clouded life of his father, the King, had come to its merciful end.

The gypsy's warning was fulfilled.

*   *   *

The accession of George IV brought to him no change of circumstance save that of title. For nine years he had reigned as virtual Sovereign of his father's subjects; and they, resignedly inured to economic distress and prohibitive taxation, saw no hope of relief from their grievances in his legal ascent to the Throne. Since the cessation of War, the Radical movement, accompanied by bursts of spasmodic outrage, had, in this last year of the Regency, flared up again at Manchester. Sixty thousand agitators, led by the notorious Orator Hunt, poured into St. Peter's Fields carrying black flags from which stared out in white sepulchral letters, the words: 'Equal Representation or Death!'

Preceded by bugles, drums, bands, and dense crowds of ragged men and women in the wildest state of enthusiasm, Hunt, wearing a white hat, drove in an open barouche to a platform in the centre of the meeting place. He had scarcely begun to speak before he was interrupted by panic-stricken yells of–'Break! Break! the Red-coats are upon us! . . .' They

217

broke, scattered in all directions by charging yeomanry slashing right and left with their swords. Over a hundred were wounded and two lost their lives in the stampede.

The Radical press made the most of this 'massacre of innocents', as they called it, with lurid prints of a murderous officer shouting orders to his mounted troops to trample under their horses' hooves a mass of shrieking women, children, and men, unarmed, defenceless, weakened from starvation. 'Chop em down! Give them no quarter! . . . Remember the more you kill the less poor-rates you'll have to pay!'

That Peterloo riot – prompt Government suppression notwithstanding – left behind it smoke enough to blaze again three weeks after the death of George III.

A dismal greeting to the new King was the Cato Street Conspiracy. A gang of ruffians, headed by Arthur Thistlewood, had plotted to murder the chiefs of His Majesty's Parliament – not in Parliament's House, but in the house of Lord Harrowby while they were sitting at dinner.

Dorothea Lieven, writing to her lover, Prince Metternich, gives a highly flavoured account of 'the details . . . so revolting that one can scarcely believe human beings like ourselves . . . conceived such an abominable project. I got Wellington to tell me about the whole affair. Thistlewood had chosen Wellington as his victim. . . . There had been a long fight over Castlereagh. Every one wanted the honour of cutting his throat. . . .' And when they had finished off the Duke, his host, and other members of the Cabinet, the conspirators had planned to bundle the heads of the victims into bags, cart them away to the Bank, and exhibit them there to the populace. The soldiers would then be called to arms, and the new rule of 'The People' proclaimed. . . . 'I feel cold from head to foot', concludes Madame de Lieven, 'thinking of those men.'[1]

The King, who had certainly more reason than this most beautiful, most hated and most loved of political intriguers, 'to grow cold at the thought of them', was, at that time, too absorbed in thinking of one woman to think of 'those' – or any men at all.

Lady Hertford's reign had ended with the Regency; and Lady Conyngham, without the smallest effort, and possibly as much to her amaze as to the chagrin of Egeria, had now succeeded her as favourite and unacknowledged Queen of George IV.

It was soon after the death of his mother that he turned to the amiable

[1] The conspirators were trapped by Bow Street runners in a hay-loft in Cato Street off the Edgware Road. Thistlewood escaped after he had stabbed to the heart one of the constables. The next morning he and nine of his accomplices were arrested. Thistlewood, with four others, were executed on May 1.

Marchioness Conyngham to seek in her receptive arms the comfort he had lost.

She was the daughter of a wealthy city merchant, mother of five adult children, and the wife of an accommodating husband. In her youth she had been pretty and at fifty she was fat; but in her worshipful shallow blue eyes the King saw himself englamoured. She was gentle, placid, bovine, and the King at fifty-eight was at her feet. Never since his boyhood had he experienced such poignant, fierce intoxication as this last leaping flame of autumnal fire to re-awaken a spring fever in his blood.

The world looked on in wonder at the unaccountable infatuation of the King for his 'Q' as they called her; yet, against all contrary belief, it is probable that the relationship between these two was guiltless–not from any moral hesitation on his part or hers, but for the more obvious reason suggested by one of the wags of the day:

> 'Still the old hunter loves to *walk*,
> Where he has *run* before,
> A liquorish tooth can make him talk
> When he can act no more.'

Talk with her he did, by the hour, of the smallest trivialities that could neither tax her limited capacity nor provoke him to argument or contradiction.

And therein lay the secret of her overwhelming sway upon her elderly impressionable lover. She offered him the novelty of contrast. She was practical, domesticated, unexacting, as Fitzherbert, for all her outward poise and calm, had never been; as Lady Hertford, in her imperious profundity, could never be. At the Pavilion Lady Conyngham's position was unchallengeable and supreme. Cosily wrapped in her white cashmere shawl she sat with the King at his table, her husband at the foot, and, either side of it, her sons and daughters. They, taking the lead from their father, showed no resentment at this somewhat embarrassing state of affairs, and were amply rewarded by the King for their compliance. Royal appointments were handed to the sons, and wealthy husbands to the daughters. Lord Conyngham, who in 1816 had been created a marquis in the Irish Peerage, was presented four years later with an English barony. On the marchioness were showered jewels of fabulous worth, pearls the size of peas; the Royal Stuart sapphire, wrested from the widower of Princess Charlotte, graced the homely head of Lady Conyngham. Horses, servants, carriages, were hers. The King's palaces were hers; his will was entirely hers. When she wished to alter the lighting in the Saloon at the Pavilion, the King fatuously told her: 'Thank you, my dear, thank you. . . .

You cannot please me so much as by doing everything *you* please to show you are mistress here. . . . ' People were wondering what would be the end of it?

Divorce from his wife looked to be the end of it.

Nothing commensurate with any former monarch's passion for a lady had been known since the love convulsions of Henry Tudor for the ill-fated Anne Boleyn. And the question whispered now on every lip was—would Caroline of Brunswick be called upon to suffer as did Catherine of Aragon?

The nation stood on tenterhooks pending the doctors' bulletins of the King's health. He had been seriously ill. A few days after the death of George III he was attacked by a chill that turned to inflammation of the lungs. The strenuous treatment of Dr. Tierney, called to attend him in the absence of Sir Henry Halford, did not improve his condition by bleeding him of a hundred and fifty ounces. So grave was the prognosis that everyone thought—and some hoped—that he too would be laid in state in Windsor Chapel beside the body of his father. But he had no intention, at this eleventh hour, of renouncing the Crown for which he had waited so long. Several weeks, however, elapsed before he regained his strength. When Prayers of Thanksgiving were apathetically offered up to Heaven in the churches, Brougham's prayers were, somewhat surprisingly, heard to be loudest of any. 'I have never prayed so heartily for a Prince before,' he told Creevey. 'If he had gone, all the troubles of these villains (his Ministers) went with him, and they had Fred. I[1] their own man for his life. . . . Meanwhile, the change of name which Mrs. P. has undergone has had a wondrous effect on publick feelings. She is extremely popular. . . . The cry at the Proclamation was God Save the Queen! . . .'

At which the King's rage knew no bounds. The realization that his 'Infernale' was recognized and accepted in the eyes of his subjects as his Consort, filled him with the liveliest dismay.

His first step at disassociation from his hated wife—after spending a considerable time poring over ancient prayer books—was to strike out her name from the Liturgy. His weakling Ministers were careful to exonerate themselves for their accordance to this omission by alleging that the words 'And all the Royal Family' included the unspecified Queen Caroline. In any case she was past praying for, so let it rest at that. But from the pulpits of Whig clergymen who would not let it rest at that, ascended earnest supplication to 'enrich Her Majesty with Heavenly Grace, to endue her with the Holy Spirit, and to bring her to God's everlasting Kingdom. . . .' Most vexing to the Monarch, who greatly feared she would be brought to his.

[1] The Duke of York.

Caroline, having chosen to travel abroad as Countess of Cornwall, boldly emerged from her incognita as soon as she read in the news-sheets of the death of her uncle, the King. But, far from receiving more respect for her exalted rank, she was treated with contempt, and exposed to petty insults by half the Courts of Europe. Infuriated, mortified, she resolved to return to England and reclaim her rights, of which procedure Brougham strongly disapproved.

Determined to prevent any further complications he went to meet and waylay her at St. Omer. He brought with him the Whig Lord Hutchinson, and a Government proposal that she should renounce her title of Consort and take in compensation a grant of £50,000 on condition she agreed to live abroad.

It would have been better for all parties had Brougham presented his proposition in April when he first discussed it with Lord Liverpool. Had he done so then she might have been persuaded to accept; instead of which, and in view of the removal of her name from the Liturgy, she emphatically rejected the proposal. To England she would go, and to England off she went, pursued by Brougham's urgent pleas.

'ST. OMER, *half-past 5 o'clock, June 4*, 1820.

. . . Mr. Brougham once more implores Your Majesty to refrain from rushing into certain trouble, and possible danger; or at least to delay taking this step until Lord Hutchinson shall have received fresh instructions . . . Your Majesty will put an end to every kind of accommodation by landing in England.'

And an hour later this:

'ST. OMER, *June 4*, 1820–6 *o'clock*.

MADAM,

I entreat Your Majesty once more to reflect calmly and patiently upon the step about to be taken. . . . But if Your Majesty shall be determined to go to England, before any new offer can be made, I earnestly implore Your Majesty to proceed in the most private and even secret manner possible.'

It is doubtful if the Queen, posting all-speed to Calais, received either of these messages; for by the time Brougham's couriers arrived with their despatches on the quayside, she had boarded the passenger-packet and was half-way across the Channel.

Accompanied by her Lady-in-Waiting, Anne Hamilton, young Austin, and Alderman Wood, M.P., who had totally eclipsed Bergami as her counsellor and friend, she landed at Dover on the afternoon of June 6.

As she bustled ashore in her scarlet, ermine-lined pelisse and white leghorn hat, she was met with a tremendous ovation. Guns cracked salutes from the Castle; a mass of people came roaring to the beach to cry their welcome to 'the Queen, God bless her!'—very touching. She had suffered no ill effects from the rough crossing, and with her face freshly painted, wreathed in smiles, she delightedly bobbed and bowed to the exuberant applause. At Canterbury, where she lay the night, a torchlight procession paraded the town in her honour. Even had she wished to follow Brougham's advice 'to proceed in the most private and secret manner possible', she could scarcely have done so, since in every village, every hamlet, and all along the road, rapturous spectators lined up to see her pass.

She came into London from Greenwich over Westminster Bridge, where a hip-hip-huzzahing hysterical mob swarmed about her open landau. Followed by a couple of dirty old carriages in which sat her chattering gesticulating Italians, she drove through the shouting streets, and as she passed Whites' Club she gaily nodded to the men in the window. But she did not know, as she and her cavalcade went rattling along the Mall, that she was watched from another window—in an attic at Carlton House—by her husband and her sister-in-law, Mary. . . . 'And that Beast, Wood,' groaned the King, 'sat beside her!' A fact already noted by Greville, who rode out to Greenwich to meet her and remarked with disgust that Wood, a city alderman, was given precedence in the carriage before Lady Anne, the daughter of a Duke.

No such fine distinction of etiquette, however, troubled Caroline. The voice of the metropolis had claimed her for its own. She was moved by it, charmed by it; exultant. Thus, in pandemonium unprecedented, she arrived at the house of Alderman Wood in South Audley Street, and stood on the balcony curtseying her thanks to her rackety, loud-tongued disciples. Around midnight they dispersed to spend the early hours of the morning smashing the windows of all who refused to acknowledge the Queen.

'So now we are in for it!' said Brougham.

The battle was on, the lampoonists were busy, and the lads of the town bawling their song to tune of that merry old jig:

> 'Oh dear, what can the matter be,
> Oh dear, what can the matter be;
> *Oh dear*, what can the matter be?
> Caroline's come — lack-a-day!'

I hoped she'd have stayed—then I'd get a new spouse and
I mentioned my wish to my friends in the House and
They made her an offer of fifty bright thousand
If she would keep out of the *way*!'

But with the mob at her heels and despite all remonstrance, entreaties and bribes, she refused to keep out of the way. And 'if my head is on Temple Bar it will be Brougham's doing', she ungratefully informed her Solicitor-General, Mr. Denman. Why Brougham should have been held responsible for any such dire *sequela*, only she, poor half-crazed creature, could have told. She was proud, she was happy, she feared nothing—for what had she to fear? 'I have committed misconduct but once in my life', she confessed to her startled ladies—'and that was with the husband of Mrs. Fitzherbert!' And now that she was Queen more than half the country had declared itself ready to fight for her . . . Amazing!

In South Audley Street a deafening din disturbed the night's rest of peaceful citizens. All those who refused to doff their hats as they passed the door of Wood's house where she lodged, were manhandled. The carriages of Cabinet Ministers, driving home from a late session, were held up and pelted with stones by hooting crowds, who let off squibs under the heads of their terrified horses. The houses of all known supporters of the King were attacked, windows broken, doors wrenched from their hinges. Yet, while Lady Conyngham's residence suffered no assault, Lady Hertford's house in Manchester Square sustained much damage, which, as Greville commented, was 'odd enough'—particularly as the once supreme favourite had, since her fall from grace, withdrawn herself from party politics and from the Court.

When asked by some inquisitive and spitefully intentioned person, 'if the King had ever talked to her of Lady Conyngham?' she replied with haughty chill: 'Intimately as I have known the King, and openly as he has always talked to me upon every subject, he has never ventured to speak to me of his mistresses.'

The King's abortive abuse of his own marriage vows added fuel to the fury of the Queen's Yahoos. 'In their sense of justice', observed that prime agitator, Cobbett, 'they compared what they had *heard* of the wife with what they had *seen* of the husband. . . . So far as is related to the question of guilt or innocence they cared not a straw; but they took a large view of the matter . . . determined that she had been wronged and resolved to uphold her'. And in so doing drove the Government to take the narrowest view of 'the matter'. Having abandoned all hope of a peaceable compromise between the King and his wife, the Lords went into Secret Committee. From Italy came messengers carrying the famous Green Bag, crammed with evidence collected during the Queen's exile, some of which had already been examined by the Milan Commission, and the rest of it gathered from the wayside as she passed. Even so, with her guilt in the Bag, the Government had gravest doubts of the issue. If the Queen's adultery were proven she would stand convicted, according to the Civil Law, of High Treason against the Sovereign and State. Well might she have trembled for her head had it not been so inflated by crowd-worship.

It was, then, with the utmost misgivings that, on July 5, Lord Liverpool introduced to a Secret Committee of peers, a dramatically entitled Bill of Pains and Penalties to deprive the Queen of her privileges and rights as Consort, and to claim a dissolution of her marriage.

The motion, unanimously agreed by the Lords, was delivered to the Queen by Sir Thomas Tyrwhitt. She flung it back at him with a reply expressing heated indignation that the Bill should presume her guilty solely on the report of a Committee before whom not one single witness had, so far, been examined. But though she knew it not, there were witnesses – a host of them – brought from Italy, daily disembarking at Westminster Stairs, and all only too willing to denounce her. 'Everybody thinks that the charges will be proved and the King divorced', wrote Greville in his Journal. He and Creevey, who had hurried back from Brussels shortly after the death of the late King, kept up a running commentary on the case.

'I cannot resist the curiosity of seeing a Queen tried', confesses Creevey. Nor it seems could anybody else, although few were so lucky as he, in not only obtaining a pass to the House on the opening day, but a place within two yards of the Queen's chair.

Outside the Houses of Parliament were herded Caroline's slubber-degullions, hallooing and shouting 'God bless her!' flaunting their banners and emblems of loyalty – green bags hoisted on the tops of poles. The King's men and all men who wavered were set upon and booed. The country was split and stood equally divided. The Radicals and half the Army and the Navy believed the Queen to be innocent, the victim of a systematic persecution.

During the five weeks' adjournment while Brougham prepared her defence, she had removed herself from South Audley Street to Branden-burgh House, Hammersmith.[1] There, day after day, she received deputa-tions from her sympathizers. Thousands flocked to stare at her, perched on her balcony overlooking the river. She seemed to live at her window,

[1] Formerly the home of the Margravine of Anspach.

CAROLINE AND THE
W A T E R M E N   A T
BRANDENBURGH HOUSE

From a contemporary
print in the author's
possession

nodding and laughing down at that thronged water-way. In barges and rowboats and wherries they came—from the lowest, filthiest quarters of the town, from dockyards and taverns, from thieves' dens and slum-alleys, swarming and clambering over the banks and into the gardens of Brandenburgh House—her ragged, degraded supporters. But she loved them—blew kisses and, weariless, bobbed in response to their yells for—'the Queen!'

A few days before the trial she returned to London, and to save herself the journey back and forth from Hammersmith, took up residence in the house of Lady Francis in St. James's Square. On the morning of August 17, attended by Lady Anne Hamilton, she drove in state to Westminster led by a frenzied escort who threateningly accosted any silent respectable citizen suspected of adherence to the King.

In Grosvenor Square the Duke of Wellington's carriage was held up by a ruffianly mob armed with pick-axes, and demanding that he declare himself for the Queen. 'Yes! Yes!' muttered the Duke, simmering, red as a turkey-cock, and bade his coachman drive on; but they would not let him drive on. They sprang to the step, thrust their heads through the windows and insisted he raise his hat and cry—'the Queen!'

'Very well then—damn you!' roared Wellington, 'the Queen—and may all your wives be like her!'

Punctually at ten o'clock the Queen arrived at, or as Creevey put it, 'popped into the House, made a *duck* to the Throne and a jump to her chair', where she squatted, gazing unflinchingly around her at the glum-faced silent Lords.

She had taken immense care with her *toilette* but the result would not all have satisfied Lord Malmesbury. Had he been present there that day among his peers, he likely would have raised despairing eyes to Heaven to see her gowned in black figured gauze with enormous white episcopal sleeves, and her head swathed in a white veil whence escaped a few straggling black ringlets, palpably not her own. She had smeared paint on her cheeks and mascara on her eyebrows, and resembled, according to Creevey, nothing so much as a Dutch toy with a round lead-weighted bottom.

The case for the Crown, opened by Sir Richard Gifford, the Attorney-General, continued for more than ten weeks. All the previous charges against the Queen were brought up again, with particular stress laid on the dismissal from her bedchamber of Austin, her adopted son, and the admittance of Bergami to a room adjoining hers. Brougham may have had good reason to feel some uneasiness at the introduction of Austin's name at this point in the proceedings. He had lately received a disturbing letter from his brother James, containing certain information in respect of the boy 'Willikin'.

It was in March, 1818, that the then Princess of Wales had confided to James Brougham a secret known to no other living person—so she said. William was *not* as she had represented him to be, the son of Austin, but the natural son of Prince Louis Ferdinand, of Prussia, killed at Jena. The child had been entrusted to Caroline's care by Prince Louis and brought to England in charge of a German nurse, since dead. The Princess admitted she 'had got a child from Austin who accidentally had a mark on his arm the same as William. . . .' This child she sent away—'God knows where—' and substituted in his place the son of the Prussian Prince. Caroline had made the most of her attachment to Louis who, she claimed, had loved her all his life.

While neither Brougham nor his brother believed one word of this romance, it was almost certain that the Queen must have chattered of her 'secret' to others less trustworthy than James Brougham. If so, the prosecution might well be provided with a powerful weapon to strike down the defence; but the Crown had more damning evidence at its command than the Queen's alleged liaison with the defunct Prince Louis. And when the first witness, one of her servants, Teodore Majocchi, was called, her case looked to be lost with her reproachful shriek—'O! Teodore!' or as some would have it '*Traditore!*' Nor did she leave it at that. Before Brougham could stop her she started up from her seat, and fled the Court as if pursued by Furies.

The loathsome business went on—and it went on, blackening the Queen, so it appeared, past all redemption. The main evidence revolved around the fact that she and Bergami had slept in the same tent on deck during the whole of the voyage to and from Constantinople, and that Bergami had attended her when she went to her bath. Witness after witness, including the maid Dumont, whom Creevey describes as 'that *chienne*', followed Gifford's careful lead through a litter of lies, impressed upon the Court by the Attorney-General as 'this most scandalous, degrading and licentious intercourse.'

'But', declared Creevey, 'it does not signify a damn! . . . The Bishops won't support the divorce part of the Bill, so that the title ought to be —"A Bill to declare the Queen a w—— and to settle her upon the King for life, because from his own conduct, he is not entitled to a divorce"'. And on September 6, he was elatedly reporting. . . . 'Do you know this Bill will never pass! My belief is it will be abandoned on its adjourning.' Brougham, too, admitted that 'he felt secure.' When Majocchi was recalled he poured question after question into the limp Teodore, then flicked him away at his last terrified gasp of '*non mi ricordo*'.

The defence was opened three weeks later with Brougham's historic speech. The House sat galvanized, struck with admiration and astonishment at that inspired appeal to the Lords to 'save the country—save yourselves—save the Crown which is threatened with irreparable injury. Save the altar which is no longer safe when its kindred Throne is shaken'. And with a gesture that would have done credit to Kean, Brougham produced his dramatic finale. 'I pour forth my fervent supplication to the Throne of Mercy, that mercies may descend upon the people of this country richer than their rulers have deserved, and that your hearts may be turned to justice. . . .'

The House was in his upraised hands; indeed there were some who believed he had missed his vocation, and would have been equally successful on the boards as at the Bar. So overcome was one of the Lords that he burst into tears, and left his seat sobbing with his knuckles in his eyes.

Only at one point was the defence dangerously weakened by the corroborative evidence of two English officers of the ship's crew, Lieutenants Howard and Flinn, called by Brougham and cross-examined by the prosecution. Both swore that the Queen and Bergami had occupied the same tent on deck; a damaging admission in that it proved legal assumption of adultery by place and opportunity. But by the time Brougham had done with them, Flinn, who had repeatedly perjured himself, collapsed on the floor in a faint.

The Trial veered again in favour of the Queen when Brougham heard that Restelli, one of the Queen's grooms and an important witness for the Crown, had been hurried out of the country before he could be called for cross-examination. Swift to swoop upon this significant point, Brougham flung it at Gifford in the seemingly innocent question: 'I wish to know of my learned friend whether we can have access to Restelli . . . Is he here?'

The Attorney-General made no reply.

'My Lords', with ineffable calm uttered Brougham, 'I wish Restelli to be recalled.'

'If my learned friend', floundered Gifford, 'wishes to call Restelli, he certainly can.'

It was clear that his learned friend certainly could not. On being further pressed by the Lord Chancellor, the harried Gifford admitted that Restelli had been sent to Milan.

'Here's a breeze of the first order!' exclaimed Creevey—and a breeze that bore away with it all hopes of success for the Crown.

The King, who throughout the whole proceedings had kept his safe distance at Windsor, took less offence at Brougham's speech in its entirety than at his quotation from Milton which His Majesty, not incorrectly, assumed to be an attack on his tenderest parts.

'If shape it might be called that shape had none
Distinguishable in member, joint or limb . . .'

'He might at least have spared me *that*!' complained the King. And to Brougham's injury Denman added insult in his comparison of the Queen to Octavia, wife of Nero, with pornographic allusion—in Greek—to particular Roman excesses; a gross imputation against him that the King never forgave or forgot.

Denman finished his peroration by imploring the peers to bid the Queen, 'Go and sin no more', which, since he had spent several weeks in proving her to be wholly unsinful, caused intense amusement to the Lords.

The Bill gained a majority vote of twenty-eight, and a week later, sank to nine. Thereupon Liverpool, foreseeing that so slight a majority was unlikely to ensure its safe passage through the Commons, announced its immediate withdrawal.

The news of the Queen's acquittal drove her rowdy admirers to the most frantic demonstrations of delight. Drunk with joy and gin, they roared through the streets carrying effigies of the perjured witnesses hung upon gallows. All the ships in the Thames were draped with bunting. Flags flew from every window in the poorer quarters of the town, where at night, for the better part of that week, illuminations blazed sky-high. The Mayor and Corporation of London presented their heroine with the Freedom of the City. A riotous pilgrimage, accompanied by a procession of Brass Founders all dressed in armour and bearing banners inscribed 'The Queen's Guard are Men of Metal', reeled along the road to Hammersmith, singing, shouting, throwing stones after dark at any window that refused to show a light. On the garden wall of Marlborough House, Prince Leopold's residence, a row of flambeaux shed their fiery challenge on the neighbouring gloom of the King's palaces.

On November 30, the Queen went in state to St. Paul's to return thanks for her safe deliverance. Her carriage, decked with laurel and white ribbons, was led by a scallywag mob—'Beautiful, absurd, frightening . . . a strange memory for me, that procession', relates Princess Lieven who saw it. It was an indication also that nothing but Liverpool's dismissal of the Bill had saved the country from revolutionary convulsion. Even so, the Radical papers, subsidized by the Whigs, bandied their scurrilous skits at the King's expense supported by all the young intelligentsia. From Pisa, that fiery knight-errant, Shelley, enlisted himself the Queen's champion in his stinging satirical drama, *Oedipus Tyrannus, or Swellfoot the Tyrant.*

'Gentlemen swine, and gentle lady-pigs,
The tender heart of every boar acquits
Their Queen of any act incongruous
With native piggishness, and she reposing
With confidence upon the grunting nation,
Has thrown herself, her cause, her life, her all,
Her innocence, into their hoggish arms. . . .'

Yet, despite Brougham's masterly defence, there was scarcely one reputable member of society who did believe in her 'innocence'. An alternative ruling, however, might well have resulted in disaster to the Throne. In the sleeve of his gown Brougham held a trump card–the King's marriage to Mrs. Fitzherbert. Had the Bill not been abandoned Brougham could–and most certainly would–have produced witnesses to that marriage, and were the evidence proven, the King would have forfeited his right to the Crown with the inevitable consequence of a disputed Succession, to plunge the country into Civil war.

But the excitation that had centred round the Queen was fast subsiding. The pendulum of popularity swung back towards the King, who had survived those months of measureless shame with quiet dignity and courage. Of all the crowds that had infested the riverbanks at Hammersmith, none but a few scattered remnants were left amid a flotsam and jetsam of orange-peel, paper bags, every sort of rubbish cast up and rotting in Thames mud. The mob, glutted with obscenity, had chewed over the last fly-blown morsel of filth to find in it no flavour. The farce was played out.

Theodore Hook, in the latest Tory news-sheet, *John Bull*, flung a final squib at poor subdued Caroline bobbing on her balcony to her dwindling supporters.

'Would you hear of the triumph of purity?
Would you share in the joy of the Queen?
List to my song, and, in perfect security,
Witness a row where you durst not have been. . . .

Damsels of Mary'bone, decked out in articles
Borrowed of Croker's for shillings and pence;
The eye of vulgarity anything smart tickles;
Drabs love a ride at another's expense.

So swarming like loaches,
In ten hackney coaches,
They make their approaches,
And pull at the bell;
And then they flaunt brave in,
Preceded by Craven,[1]
And clean and new-shaven
Topographical Gell.'[2]

When, on November 8, the King emerged from his retirement to attend the play at Drury Lane Theatre, the warmth of the welcome that met him drove the colour from his cheeks and the tears to his eyes. With the Star on his chest and his hand on his heart he stood in the Royal Box bowing his thanks. Hats were flung in the air, handkerchiefs waved, the cheering kept the curtain down and the King on his feet for several minutes. A few rowdies called for 'the Queen!'–but very few. From the gallery a voice shouted good-humouredly: 'Where's your wife, Georgie?' . . . He saw little of the play, although he loudly applauded every scene and all the actors in it; but in order to be sure that this loyal demonstration was not a transitory whim, he went to Covent Garden Playhouse the next night, and was accorded there an even greater welcome.

That decided him. The voice of the people had spoken, and he could now go full speed ahead with the preliminaries for his Coronation which had been too long delayed by the unhappy events of the last few months. And as the great day approached, his confidence in the nation's inherent respect for monarchy restored his faith in himself. He had, however, little faith in his Government Chief, Lord Liverpool.

During the spring of 1821, Liverpool had caused the King much offence by refusing to confer the vacant canonry of Windsor on a thirty-year old curate, Mr. Sumner, late tutor to the sons of Lady Conyngham. To have his preferment taken from him after it had been bestowed, and at Lady Conyngham's request, was gall to the curate and wormwood to the King. A bitter correspondence between the Monarch and Lord Liverpool resulted in a visit of the Premier to Brighton, where the King informed him that his promise must, in honour bound, be kept. Liverpool stubbornly maintained that the King's Ministers and not the King were, in this instance, responsible for His Majesty's honour. 'Then you want your King to be *dis*honoured?' snapped offended Majesty. 'On the contrary–but if he persists', was Liverpool's adamant reply, 'I can no longer serve him'–'Very well, I give in.' The King stalked to the door. 'You have

[1] The Honourable Keppel Craven: [2] Sir William Gell: Gentlemen-in-Waiting to Queen Caroline, both called as witnesses for her defence.

won'—with an unfair advantage to Liverpool, whose threat of so drastic a change in the Ministry a few weeks before the Coronation would undoubtedly have led to further delay, if not to a definite postponement —as the King was well aware.

Thereafter, this trivial molehill was magnified into a mountain of mortification, 'that influenced' says Greville, 'every action of his life in relation to his Government'. The Tories took fright and the Whigs took heart. Their leaders, wooed by proxy and the charms of Lady Conyngham, were entertained at the Pavilion, when the mistress of the house, on whom the King had bestowed the somewhat ambiguous distinction of Lady Steward, acted hostess . . . 'Perhaps even at this moment we have already been turned out', Wellington dismally remarked to Princess Lieven. And so it might have been had the Lady Steward willed it. Her domination was phenomenal. None to see her placid, plump, wrapped in her white cashmere shawl, playing patience with the King while her contented husband dozed, could have guessed her to be the pivot around which two great political parties revolved. The caricaturists showed her balancing the crown and sceptre on the tip of her tilted nose.

Seated beside her on a ruby covered couch in his satin-draped Saloon, his swollen fingers toying with her hair, stroking her comfortable shoulders, or plaiting the fringes of her shawl, the King unfolded his Coronation plans. He would not drive—he would walk to the Abbey from Westminster Hall along a raised canopied platform. Either side this covered way—only a few hundred yards or so—tiers of seats must be erected for the benefit of privileged spectators. His crowning would be a pageant of glory and splendour surpassing that accorded to any of his Royal predecessors.

Encouraged by the dove-like croons of his lady, he talked himself into the fond belief that his people had never for one moment swerved in their fidelity to him during his recent martyrdom, to which, through no fault of his, he had been so cruelly subjected. This wondrous sight which he would present to the nation—at the nation's expense of a quarter of a million—would be his gift, in gratitude, to his loyal subjects for their undying devotion. Then, so soon as the Coronation was over, he would pay a long deferred visit to Ireland, his spiritual home. He could never forget how the Irish had rallied to his side with their offer to make him their Regent—an offer that had come just one day too late! He had always so intensely loved the Irish. Sheridan, Burke, MacMahon, Lady Jersey, —poor soul was it true she was dying?—all his most cherished friends had been of Irish birth or extraction. . . .

The date, July 19, was fixed; preparations were hurried apace. True, the death of the youngest member of the Royal Family, the infant Princess Elizabeth, daughter of the Duke of Clarence, greatly distressed the King—not so much for the loss of a three-months old baby whom he had never seen, as for the grief of his brother. Poor William! He had set his hopes of Britain's future in this second Queen Elizabeth-to-be, his sole surviving legitimate child.

'For God's sake come down to me to-morrow morning', wrote the King to his physician, Sir William Knighton,[1] in attendance on the baby. 'The melancholy tidings of the sudden death . . . of my poor little niece have just reached me and overset me beyond all I can express. . . .'

A death that overset the country too. All eyes were turned to those nurseries at Kensington Palace that housed another baby, hitherto ignored; the daughter of the late Duke of Kent. The Duchess of Clarence had not been successful in her childbearing—yet; and unless a future heir were born to William, Duke of Clarence, that 'beautiful fat baby' at Kensington would remain where she stood, third in the line of Succession.

As her kneeling ladies watched her toddle from her mother's arms to theirs, 'C'est le roi Georges en jupons!' they declared. She could walk, she could talk, she could lisp her own name—'Drina', the Princess Victoria.

On the morning of July 19, the crowds that all through the night and at daybreak had gathered outside the Abbey, saw the flushed sky unclouded and the sun, red as a holly berry, rising from the opal mist above the river. Not a breath of wind stirred the full-leafed plane trees as that expectant multitude, drawn from towns and cities, villages, from every point of compass in the Kingdom, moved onward to their vantage posts. Behind them marched the soldiers, the measure of their tramping lost in the peal of St. Margaret's bells, the clink and clatter of mounted troops, of carriages, coaches, disgorging the lords and their ladies, velvet-robed, satin-gowned, jewel-studded, mantled in glistening gauze. On they came in their thousands, the scum and the dregs, the rich and the poor, the needy, the starved and the bloated, the thin and the fat of the land.

The boom of guns at half-hourly intervals marked the passing of time to the moment of seven o'clock, when all ticket-holders must be in their places. But the seats set aside for the peers were by no means overfilled; indeed they looked to be half-empty.

The arrival at five-thirty of an open carriage drawn by six bays, caused a sensation; a mingled hooting and cheering, hisses, catcalls and cries of 'The Queen!'

[1] A professional toady who subsequently managed to secure for himself the appointment of private secretary to George IV.

She had come.

Against the better judgment of her counsellors, against the King's denial of her claim to be crowned, she had committed her last abysmal folly; and even her raffish supporters bid her 'go!' . . .

She would not go. Attended by Lord and Lady Hood and the ever faithful Lady Anne, she left her carriage at the barricades and hurried along the blue-carpeted platform to the Abbey. The King, who may have foreseen some such disturbance, had stationed prize-fighters at all the entrances; yet one can hardly believe that the strength of six pugilists would have been required for the forcible ejection of Queen Caroline.

Although since her trial she had been in failing health and had lost much weight, her courage stood high to sustain her when, dressed in her ill-chosen finery, she drove through the cool of the dawn to the Abbey and demanded admittance at three of the doors. At each of those three she was refused. The officers on guard, summoned to deal with her request, asked her to produce her ticket. She replied she had no ticket, and as Queen of England needed none. That argument availed her nothing. In vain did she haggle, insist, and entreat; in vain did the anguished Lord Hood urge her to accept one of his tickets which would have enabled her to pass. She claimed her right of entry as Queen Consort and not as one of the public. But she who had hoped for applause from her followers, satirized by Hook as 'that galanty show', heard only cries of 'Be off with you! –Shame!' . . . And that broke her. With a swing of those once impertinent shoulders she turned and went back to her carriage. Those near enough to see her get in and drive away heard, in pity, her laughter; saw her tears.

When the guns boomed the hour of ten, a stir like a sigh, a rustling silken movement, a waving of plumes, swept through the packed Hall where participants in the procession had assembled.

In order to ensure that his entrance would be punctual to the minute, the King had slept the night at the Speaker's house in Palace Yard. Unfortunately Lord Gwydyr, acting Lord Great Chamberlain, and suffering from nerves, had taken so long to dress himself that the King, in a fever of impatience, was kept waiting twenty-five minutes. At length the over-wrought Gwydyr arrived, offering as feeble excuse for this delay that he had torn his robes getting into them. Then, preceded by the Household band and His Majesty's herb-women and their attendant maids strewing flowers, the King set out upon his walk to the Abbey.

The members of the peerage in their robes of state, led the procession followed by the Privy Councillors, theatrically garbed in Elizabethan fashion of blue and silver doublets and trunk hose; after them, in single file, walked the Royal Dukes, the bearers of the Crown, the Sceptre, the Patina, the Chalice, the Bible, three Bishops and–His Majesty the King.

He came, was seen, he conquered; he hushed every voice in a second's awe-filled pause, before the in-drawn breath of that wonder-struck audience was released in a surge of applause like the beating of waves. He came–in a glory of sunshine, under a canopy of cloth of gold borne aloft by the Barons of the Cinque Ports. His train of crimson velvet, nine yards long, glittered with golden stars; but it was his hat–a Spanish wide-brimmed black sombrero, ornamented with three white ostrich feathers and the gay plumage of a heron's wing,–that held every eye transfixed. A hat! . . . Surely no King in history has gone to his crowning in the hat of a buccaneer. And under that hat, casting its careful shade over those pouchy Guelph eyes, shone the face of the boy Florizel; that young-old face with its 'petit nez retroussé' and its 'very uggly' ears, hidden in the blond curls of a juvenile wig. But while the mesmerized assemblage stared to marvel, his gaze was riveted before him, seeing visions–of himself.

The scene inside the Abbey was one of splendour unforgettable. Tier upon thronged tier rose either side the aisles to the vaulted roof. Tinted sun-shafts, rayed from stained-glass windows, speared the echoing shadows to emblazon with dazzling dye of violet, amber, carmine, the golden tunic of a herald, a breast-plate, a mitred bowing head. And as the organ notes swelled upward, the boys of Westminster sang: 'Hallelujah, Hallelujah'–to the Highest; or as Leigh Hunt, who had waited for this day of days to pay off his last score, would have it:

> 'Rego, Regis,
> Good God, what's this!
> What! only half my Peeries!
> Regas, regat
> Good God, what's that!
> The voice is like my Deary's!
>
> I decline a
> C Regina,
> Rex alone's more handsome:
> O, what luck, sir
> Exit Uxor:
> Rursus ego a man sum
>
> Roar us, Chorus,
> On before us,
> Hairum, flairum, stout O;
> Drag rag, pretty woman, periwig and trumpets,
> Lord! if I had'nt the gout O!

234

O how *bona*
My *corona*
Sitting so how *dulcis*!
My *occulus* grim
And my *sceptrum* slim
And sweet as I hold it, my pulse is!

Toily, oily,
All turmoily,
Hooting, tooting, quaking,
Drag-rag, feather bed, periwig and hat-band
Every inch I'm a——King.'

As all who saw him admitted, where, solitarily enthroned, he sat. The intolerable heat, enhanced by the weight of his cumbrous robes, caused him the excruciating agony as of fifty bee-stings in his gouty toe. At one moment, during that four hours' ceremony, it was feared he would faint; but he speedily recovered, and as if to fortify himself, was seen repeatedly to raise his left hand to his lips and kiss the ring given him by Lady Conyngham. When the Archbishop lowered the Crown on his head, that vast congregated tension broke in trumpet-tongued enthusiasm to drown the silvery chant of the *Te Deum* and the organ's thunderous voice.

The Royal brothers were the first to pay him homage, led by the Duke of York; and as he took this most loved of them all in his arms, the King clung to him weeping in a state of emotion that verged upon hysteria. Yet, for a man nearing sixty, he bore the fatigue of that long ordeal remarkably well.

On the return procession to Westminster Hall, the King wore robes of royal purple and carried the Orb and Sceptre. Then followed the Grand Banquet, over which His Majesty presided at a crescent-shaped table placed at the end of the Hall facing the entrance doors; and while God's newly Anointed and his privileged guests sat at their feast, they watched the traditional ceremony of the Challenge.

The hereditary office of King's Champion had descended to the Reverend John Dymoke, Rector of Scrivelsby in Lincolnshire, who, doubting his equestrian skill, had called upon his twenty-year old son to enact the part for him.

Accompanied by the Duke of Wellington, Lord High Steward, and Lord Howard of Effingham, Deputy Earl Marshal, whose robes of state almost extinguished their gaily caparisoned chargers, the youthful Champion rode into the Hall on a white horse hired from a circus. But his shining armour and plumed helmet could not disguise his too evident stage-fright; nor, as one eye-witness noted, his girlish appearance which was altogether 'too much that of a maiden-knight to be the Challenger of the world on the King's behalf'. However, he managed to get through his performance without mishap, flung down the gauntlet three times, and backed with his attendant horsemen from the Hall. To be sure, the grace of this exit was a trifle marred by the behaviour of Lord Howard's horse, which would persist in walking sideways on two legs and stroking the air with its forefeet. The vigorous language addressed to it by its scarlet-faced rider afforded some comic relief, and caused the King to laugh so much that he all but fell under the table. At the end of the Banquet His Majesty's health was drunk three times three; he returned thanks in a voice that rang to the rafters and retired exhausted, driving home to Carlton House in a closed carriage.

The Carnival was over.

She, who had been denied her share in it, sent a sad little message to Creevey, 'I have never been a Queen', and made her last bow to the public from her box at Drury Lane Theatre the night after the Coronation. That effort was too much for her defiant spirit. She fainted half-way through the second act. They carried her off, put her to bed, gave her drugs to ease her pain, and castor-oil–'to have turned', said Creevey, 'the stomach of a horse'. Then they bled her of sixty-five ounces–and killed her.

For months she had ignored the danger signals of her disease, diagnosed by her doctors as 'inflammation of the bowels'. She had always lived on hope, since the day when she had come to meet her bridegroom 'vastly happy with her future expectations. . . .' And now that hope had left her she was content to live no more.

On August 3, in the presence of Brougham and Denman, she made and signed her Will leaving five hundred pounds to Lord and Lady Hood, her old carriage to her medical adviser, Dr. Lushington, her body to Brunswick, and everything else to William Austin.[1]

Brougham, who was with her at the last, said 'she talked incessantly on every subject for three hours', and never of herself until, to cheer her, he spoke of her recovery . . . 'No,' she told him quietly, 'My dear Mr. Brougham, I shall not recover; and I am much better dead, for I be tired of this life. . . .'

★   ★   ★

On July 31, King George IV embarked in his royal yacht for Ireland, and anchored off Holyhead on August 6. There he received a message that

[1] Austin died in a private mental home in Chelsea in 1849.

the Queen lay critically ill. This placed him in a difficult position. Dublin was eagerly awaiting his arrival. Should he or should he not postpone his journey? His Ministers were reluctant to advise him on so delicate a matter. In the meantime the weather had changed; heavy gales were blowing, and he decided, for his comfort's sake, to put ashore. He landed on the coast of Wales, and stayed at Plas Newydd as the guest of Lord Anglesey until Wednesday, August 8. When he returned to his yacht the winds were too high and the sea too rough for him to have attempted the crossing. On the following day, while the gale still raged, came the news of his wife's death.

At his order the flags of the squadron were lowered. Thereafter he spoke not a word. Those about him said, 'he seemed to be affected—not afflicted'; but all night, above the lash of the waves and the creek of gear and sail, could be heard his heavy tread restlessly pacing the floor of his cabin. . . . None envied him his thoughts.

He stood on deck to watch the dawn break through that haggard sky. The winds had fallen, the day was calm; and the sun rose clear and splendid, to spread a cloth of gold across the sea.

AFTERWORD

I have purposely avoided following the life of George IV to the end of his reign. As Prince Regent he represents an era, unique in its splendour and essentially his own. As King he is scarcely known to us. The colourful highlights of his Regency fade into the shadows of old age. That stout familiar figure, buttoned in his frogged fur-collared overcoat, driving in his yellow tilbury along the Marine Parade at Brighton, was seldom seen after the year 1823. He visited the Pavilion for the last time on January 23, 1827; and Brighton saw him no more.

His prolonged absence was attributed to some affront which he believed had been offered by the townsfolk to Lady Conyngham; but his increasing bulk, of which he was bitterly conscious, was the more likely cause of his retirement from those nostalgic memories of his youth. The three remaining monotonous years of his life, lived in almost complete seclusion, were painfully chequered by illness and gout. A few days before his death on June 26, 1830, he confided to the Duke of Wellington his earnest desire to be buried in his nightgown.

The story goes that when the Duke was left alone with the dead body of his master, curiosity compelled him to discover the reason for this singular request. He approached the bed, unfastened the King's garment, and found lying on the lifeless heart a jewelled miniature of Mrs. Fitzherbert.

COOMBE HILL,
October 1950–October 1951.

BIBLIOGRAPHY

R. ACKERMANN, *The Microcosm of London*, 1800–1810.

J. H. ADOLPHUS, *The Royal Exile, Memoirs of Queen Caroline*, 1821.

ALBEMARLE. *George Thomas, Earl of Albemarle, Fifty Years of my life*, 1870.

H. ANGELO, *Reminiscences of Henry Angelo*, 1830.

JOHN ASHTON, *Social England under the Regency*, 1890.

JOHN ASHTON, *Florizel's Folly*, 1899.

A. ASPINALL, *Letters of George IV*, 1938.

A. ASPINALL, *Letters of the Princess Charlotte*, 1949.

AUCKLAND, *The Journal and Correspondence of William, Lord Auckland*, 1862.

KAROLINE BAUER, *Memoirs of Karoline Bauer*, 1885.

HILAIRE BELLOC, *Napoleon*, 1932.

G. F. BERKELEY, *Anecdotes of the Upper Ten Thousand*, 1867.

MARY BERRY, *Journal & Correspondence*, 1865.

BESSBOROUGH, *Lady Bessborough & her family Circle*, edited by the Earl of Bessborough and A. Aspinall, 1940.

J. G. BISHOP, *The Brighton Pavilion & its Royal Associations*, 1876.

COMTESSE DE BOIGNE, *Memoirs*, 1907.

HENRY BROUGHAM, *Life & Times of Lord Brougham written by himself*, 1871.

LADY BROWNLOW, *Emma Sophia, Countess Brownlow, Reminiscences: The Eve of Victorianism*, with preface by Lieut.-Colonel Baron Porcelli, 1940.

ARTHUR BRYANT, *Years of Endurance*, 1942.

ARTHUR BRYANT, *Years of Victory*, 1944.

ARTHUR BRYANT, *The Age of Elegance*, 1950.

BUCKINGHAM, *Memoirs of the Duke of Buckingham & Chandos*, 1856.

LADY CHARLOTTE BURY, *The diary of a Lady-in-Waiting*, edited by A. Francis Steuart, 1907.

BYRON, *Poetical Works*, edited by E. C. Coleridge, 1905.

E. BERESFORD CHANCELLOR, *Life in Regency & Early Victorian Times*, 1926.

WILLIAM COBBETT, *History of the Regency & Reign of King George IV*, 1830.

COLCHESTER, *Diary & Correspondence of Charles Abbott, Lord Colchester*, 1861.

THOMAS CREEVEY, *The Creevey Papers*, edited by Sir H. Maxwell, 1903–1905.

CREEVEY, *Life & Times*, edited by John Gore, 1934.

DORMER CRESTON, *The Regent and his Daughter*, 1932.

CROKER, *The Croker Papers, edited by L. J. Jennings,* 1884.

GEORGE CROLY, *Personal History of George IV,* 1846.

MRS. DELANY, *Autobiography & Correspondence, edited by Lady Llanover,* 1862.

DR. DORAN, *Lives of the Queens of England of the House of Hanover,* 1855.

LADY DOUGLAS, *A vindication of her Conduct during her intercourse with the Princess of Wales, with remarks on 'The Book',* 1814.

SYLVESTER DOUGLAS, *The Diaries of Sylvester Douglas, Lord Glenbervie, edited by Francis Bickley,* 1928.

JOHN DRINKWATER, *Charles James Fox,* 1928.

DRUID, THE, *Post & Paddock, with recollections of George IV, and Sam Chifney,* 1856.

SIR GILBERT ELLIOT, *First Lord Minto, Life & Letters,* 1874.

FARINGTON, *The Farington Diary, Edited by J. Grieg,* 1922.

SIR JOHN FORTESCUE, *Letters of George III,* 1927.

ROGER FULFORD, *Royal Dukes,* 1933.

ROGER FULFORD, *George the Fourth,* 1935.

PHILIP FRANCIS, *Memoirs of Sir Philip Francis, edited by J. Parkes,* 1867.

GRANVILLE, *Correspondence of Granville Leveson-Gower, Earl Granville, edited by Lady Granville,* 1916.

CHARLES C. F. GREVILLE, *The Greville Memoirs, edited by Henry Reeve,* 1875.

CAPTAIN GRONOW, *Reminiscences & Recollections,* 1810-1860.

J. A. HAMILTON, *George IV (Dictionary of National Biography)*

HANSARD, *Parliamentary Debates.*

B. HAYDON, *Autobiography, edited by E. Blunden,* 1927.

EDWIN HODDER, *Life of a Century,* 1901.

HOLLAND, 3rd Baron, *Memoirs of the Whig Party in my time, edited by his son,* 1852.

ROBERT HUISH, *Memoirs of George IV,* 1831.

ROBERT HUISH, *Memoirs of H.R.H. Princess Charlotte Augusta of Wales,* 1818.

LEIGH HUNT, *Poetical Works, edited by H. S. Milford,* 1923.

JERNINGHAM, *The Jerningham Letters, (1780-1843), edited by Egerton Castle,* 1896.

CAPTAIN JESSE, *Life of George Brummell, Esq., commonly known as Beau Brummell,* 1886.

CORNELIA KNIGHT, *Autobiography,* 1861.

LADY KNIGHTON, *Memoirs of Sir William Knighton, Bart.,* 1838.

CHARLES LANGDALE, *Memoirs of Mrs. Fitzherbert,* 1856.

JACOB LARWOOD, *London Parks,* 1881.

LADY SARAH LENNOX, *Life & Letters*, edited by Countess of Ilchester & Lord Stavordale, 1901.

DORIS LESLIE, *Royal William (Life of William IV)*, 1940.

SHANE LESLIE, *George the Fourth*, 1926.

SHANE LESLIE, *Letters of Mrs. Fitzherbert*, 1944.

SHANE LESLIE, *Mrs. Fitzherbert: A Life*, 1939.

LIEVEN, *Private Letters of Princess Lieven to Prince Metternich*, 1820–1828, edited by Peter Quennell, 1937.

H. E. LLOYD, *George IV, Memoirs of his Life & Reign*, 1830.

JUSTIN MCCARTHY, *History of the Four Georges & William IV*, 1901.

MALMESBURY, *Diary & Correspondence of James Harris, First Earl of Malmesbury*, edited by his Grandson, 1844.

ANDRÉ MAUROIS, *Ariel, a Shelley Romance*, 1924.

ANDRÉ MAUROIS, *Byron*, 1930.

ANDRÉ MAUROIS, *History of France*, 1949.

LEWIS MELVILLE, *First Gentleman of Europe*, 1906.

THOMAS MOORE, *Memoirs of Sheridan*, 1825.

THOMAS MOORE, *Memoirs, Journals & Correspondence*, edited by Lord John Russell.

CARL PHILIP MORITZ, *Travels in England, a reprint of English translation*, 1924.

CLIFFORD MUSGRAVE, *Royal Pavilion, a Study in the Romantic*, 1951.

MRS. PAPENDIEK, *Mrs. Papendiek's Journal*, edited by her grand-daughter, Mrs. Delves-Broughton, 1887.

W. H. PYNE, *Royal Residences*, 1819.

QUEEN CAROLINE, *Sir Edward Parry*, 1930.

W. F. RAE, *Sheridan*, 1896.

THOMAS RAIKES, *Journal*, 1856.

HENRY D. ROBERTS, *Royal Pavilion, Brighton*, 1939.

MRS. MARY ROBINSON, *Memoirs, written by herself*, 1801.

SIR SAMUEL ROMILLY, *Memoirs*, 1840.

HOLLAND ROSE, *William Pitt*, 1911.

SHELLEY, *Complete Works*, edited by R. Ingpen & W. E. Peck, 1926–1930.

LADY HESTER STANHOPE, *Memoirs*, 1845.

LORD STANHOPE, *Life of Pitt*, 1861.

LYTTON STRACHEY, *Queen Victoria*, 1921.

BARON STOCKMAR, *Memoirs by his Son*, edited by F. Max Muller, 1872.

D. M. STUART, *Daughters of George III*.

H. M. THACKERAY, *The Four Georges*.

G. M. TREVELYAN, *British History of the Nineteenth Century*, 1930.

G. M. TREVELYAN, *English Social History*, 1944.

HORACE TWISS, *The Public and Private Life of Lord Chancellor Eldon*, 1844

C. E. VULLIAMY, *Royal George*, 1937.

HORACE WALPOLE, *Letters, edited by Toynbee*, 1903.

HORACE WALPOLE, *Correspondence, Yale Edition*, 1937–1948.

LADY ROSE WEIGALL, *Memoirs of Princess Charlotte*, 1874.

W. H. WILKINS, *Mrs. Fitzherbert and George IV*, 1905.

SIR NATHANIEL WRAXALL, *Historical and Posthumous Memoirs, edited by H. B. Wheatley*, 1884.

Annual Register, The Times, The Morning Chronicle, Gentlemen's Magazine, Lady's Magazine, London Chronicle, Sussex Weekly Advertiser, etc.

INDEX

Geneva, 210

Genoa, 200, 210

George II, King of England, 16–17, 52, 128

George III, King of England, accession to throne, 17–18; marriage, 17–18; declining health, 18, 65–6, 82–6, 87, 132–3, 139, 147–8, 153; autocratic, 20–3; attempts to deal with family troubles, 28–9, 32, 39, 42, 46–7, 54, 55–7, 66, 68–9, 77, 85, 92–3, 96, 104–5, 120–1, 129, 137–8, 140–1, 143–6, 152, 153–4; dislike of Whigs, 31, 41, 43–4, 46; attempts on life, 69, 124, 132; pronounced cured, 89, 91, 133; insanity, 154–5, 156, 162, 169, 206, 215, 216; death, 217; other references to, 15, 16, 19, 25, 52, 60, 71, 81, 88, 109, 110, 111, 117, 118, 123, 126, 128, 158, 163, 181, 213, 218, 221

George Augustus Frederick, Prince of Wales, later Prince Regent, later King George IV ('Florizel') ('Prinny'), early life and education, 15–16, 18–19, 20–5, 29: relations with father, 23, 39, 46, 54–7, 68–9, 77, 84–5, 92, 129, 137–8; affairs with women, 27–8, 37–8, 100, 102, 134, 152, 173; and specifically: with Mary Darby (q.v.), 34–7; with Maria Fitzherbert (q.v.), 47–64; married to, 64–5, 66, 71–80, 81–2, 100–3; separation, 104–6, 129–30; reunited, 131, 133, 149, 151–2, 157; final break with, 161–2, 173, 238; with Lady Jersey (q.v.), 103, 105, 117, 120, 122, 127, 128, 129–30, 131; with Lady Hertford (q.v.), 149–51, 157, 173, 218; with Lady Conyngham (q.v.), 218–20, 231; relations with Fox (q.v.) and Whigs, 30–1, 38–9, 41–2, 43, 44–6, 53, 59–61, 74–5, 95, 96, 148, 163–5, 172, 184, 187, 188, 193, 198, 229; heir apparent, 31; scandals, 32, 46–7, 82, 97–8, 100, 172–3; physique and character, 32–3, 79, 116, 133, 162, 173, 205, 217, 220; and Brighton (q.v.), 40, 58, 78–80,

81–2, 93–5, 98–9, 196–8, 207, 210, 238 (see also Pavilion, The); and Carlton House (q.v.), 42–3, 89, 139, 158–61, 203, 207; debts, 43, 65, 67–9, 70–1, 77, 94, 100, 102, 104, 105, 121, 123, 196; relations with mother, 46, 87, 91–3, 97, 174–5, 198, 215–16; Regency debated, 86–8; becomes Prince Regent, 156–8, 162; break with Frederick, 96–7; marriage to Caroline of Brunswick (q.v.), 105, 116, 117–18, 118–23; separation, 125–6, 141; seeking divorce, 141–6, 149, 167–8, 171–3, 184–6, 187, 196, 200, 210, 212–13, 215, 220, 222–4, 228, 237; and Charlotte Augusta (q.v.), 125, 139, 140–1, 166–71, 173–4, 176–8, 187–90, 191, 192–3, 198–200, 205, 206, 208, 209; and Brummell, 135–6, 173; entertaining foreign Royalty, 158–61, 179–80, 181–4, 185–6, 187; quarrel with Duke of Sussex, 193; stages Grand Jubilee, 194–6; accession to throne, 217; Coronation, 232–6; as King, 238; public opinion of, 68–9, 77, 91, 98, 124, 127, 145, 172–3, 182–3, 184–5, 187, 192, 201, 203–4, 205, 207, 223, 229–31; other references to, 44, 108, 109, 112, 113, 114, 124, 140, 147, 178, 211, 216–17, and passim

Georgiana, Duchess of Devonshire, 45–6, 50–1, 131

Germany, 80, 128, 216

Gifford, Sir Richard (Attorney-General), 225–7

Gillray, Cartoonist, 77, 78

Gordon, Duchess of, 78, 92

Gravesend, 112

Gray's (Jewellers), 36, 102

Green Park, 181, 194

Greenwich, 112, 222

Greenwich Hospital, 113

Grenville, Lord, 145, 147, 150, 156, 157, 163, 164

Greville, Charles, 189 n., 222, 223, 224, 231

Grey, Charles, 74, 75–6,

Grey, Lord, 148, 150, 156, 157, 163, 164, 193, 209

246

248